ALMOST PERFECT

ALSO BY JOE COX

100 Things Wildcats Fans Should Know and Do Before They Die
(with Ryan Clark)
Fightin' Words: Kentucky vs. Louisville (with Ryan Clark)
Voice of the Wildcats: Claude Sullivan and the Rise of Modern Sportscasting
(with Alan Sullivan)
The Kentucky Wildcats Fans' Bucket List (with Ryan Clark)

ALMOST PERFECT

THE HEARTBREAKING PURSUIT OF PITCHING'S HOLY GRAIL

JOE COX
FOREWORD BY JIM BUNNING

GUILFORD, CONNECTICUT

An imprint of Globe Pequot

Distributed by NATIONAL BOOK NETWORK

British Library Cataloguing in Publication Information available

Library of Congress Cataloging-in-Publication Data

Names: Cox, Joe, 1980- author.
Title: Almost perfect : the heartbreaking pursuit of pitching's Holy Grail /
  Joe Cox.
Description: Guilford, Connecticut : Lyons Press, [2017] | "Distributed by
  NATIONAL BOOK NETWORK"—T.p. verso. | Includes bibliographical references
  and index.
Identifiers: LCCN 2016032870 (print) | LCCN 2016035848 (ebook) | ISBN
  9781493019502 (hardback) | ISBN 9781493019519 (e-book)
Subjects: LCSH: No-hitters (Baseball)—History. | Pitching (Baseball)—United
  States—History. | Pitchers (Baseball)—United States.
Classification: LCC GV871 .C69 2017 (print) | LCC GV871 (ebook) | DDC
  796.357/22—dc23
LC record available at https://lccn.loc.gov/2016032870

796.357
C

CONTENTS

FOREWORD

On June 21, 1964, I pitched a perfect game. I didn't know it at the time, but it had been 84 years since somebody had pitched one in the National League. Mine was only the fifth one in either of modern baseball's major leagues, and only the seventh one recorded in the history of big league ball. As of the beginning of 2017, there have been sixteen more.

I used a little bit of superstitious trickery to aid my perfect game. You see, three weeks prior, I had a perfect game going into the 7th inning against the Houston Colt-.45s in Philadelphia. I got to the seventh inning, gave up a hit, and then gave up several runs in the eighth, almost losing the game. While the perfect innings were racking up, everybody had been giving me the traditional silent treatment. So I said to myself, "If I ever get into another game like this, I'm going to talk about it on the bench. I'm going to scream it to the rafters."

When the perfect game happened, I was on the bench saying, "Hey, you guys, I'm pitching a no-hitter, a perfect game. Now start diving for those balls!" People looked at me like I was nuts.

The first couple innings of that perfect game, I didn't have good control. I threw some pitches their batters should have hit, like some hanging sliders right down the middle of the plate to Jim Hickman, who fouled them back. Ronnie Hunt was on that team, too, and he was notorious for getting hit with pitches. Work him outside, I told myself. I didn't want him to stick an elbow out and get him with a pitch and break it up that way.

But those at-bats were mid-game, and this book has stories of pitchers who lost their perfect game on the guy who would have been the 27th out. Talk about being an inch away from immortality!

I was more afraid of the 26th out. The only hitter on the Mets' bench who had hit me fairly well was George Altman. I was hoping he would not be the last hitter, because I would have been a little more nervous with him in the batter's box with two down in the last frame. When the ninth inning started, I called my catcher to the mound and said, "Let's hope Casey Stengel pinch-hits Altman first instead of second." Sure enough, Casey used Altman first. I threw him hard sliders and then threw him an off-speed curveball, and he struck out on it. The last hitter was someone I had faced in the first game I pitched in the National League: John Stephenson. When I faced him all that time ago, my manager, Gene Mauch, ran out to the mound and said, "Can't spell curve." All right, Mauch was saying, let's throw hooks to this guy. So I was glad to see Stephenson. On the fifth curve, he struck out, and I had the perfect game. Yeah, I pitched very well. But there was a lot of luck—in fact, just the right amount.

As for the hard-luck games in this book, I remember Billy Pierce going into the 9th inning, two outs, and somebody getting a hit. I remember the Harvey Haddix game well. Of the more recent games, the only game I remember was Armando Galarraga pitching for the Tigers, with the play at first base where the umpire blew the call by at least a yard. Galarraga took it like it was just another game. He didn't realize, I believe, what that would have meant to his career. I know my perfect game meant a lot to mine. I'm rooting like heck for anybody who is getting close to a perfect game, because you usually only get one shot at that.

My full career, not just one game, landed me in the Baseball Hall of Fame. It's the highest honor baseball gives, so I am humbled by it. When I started baseball as a kid, ending up in Cooperstown never entered my mind. I didn't think I was good enough. Baseball will surprise you sometimes.

So will life, right? After baseball was over, I had no idea I would ever be in politics, but a friend convinced me to run for local office, and I won a seat in the city council of Fort Thomas, Kentucky. When my state senator switched parties to become the chairman of a committee, I ran against him and beat him by just 396 votes. Not exactly swept to victory!

I had a lot of close races, in fact, but I was fortunate enough to be elected to six terms in the House of Representatives and two more terms in the United States Senate.

I think the competitive drive that I developed in baseball helped me a great deal in politics, because it's all competition in politics. It's your idea against somebody else's. It's your "yes" vote against a "no" vote. It's being able to convince people to vote for your plan rather than someone else's.

Baseball's competitive drive carried over to politics, for sure. And something else from baseball carried over, too. Something straight out of this book in your hands. As hard as we try, politics, like baseball, is almost never perfect.

My political career is over now, and I get to focus a great deal on my family. I have 35 grandchildren, and as of this writing I'll be having my 18th great-grandchild very shortly. My wonderful family is probably the biggest legacy I will leave. If I live another five to ten years, I will very probably have more than 100 grandkids and great-grandkids. That is incredibly special to me.

And with family I think we see another part of life where baseball just might teach us some good lessons. In family, just like baseball, there is adversity, times of heartbreak, and the up-and-down nature of it all. I've got nine kids. There have been ups and downs with each and every one of my children. Maybe you can look at it as nine innings in a game because I had to deal with the ups and downs with each child, not unlike what I had to do inning after inning on the pitching mound.

Yes, as this book shows, baseball isn't all ups. For me, the toughest part of baseball was the fact that it took me almost five full years in the minor leagues to make the majors. I pitched at least 1,000 innings in the minor leagues. It took me a long time to get all of those skills honed well enough to get to the Bigs. There was no doubt in my mind, but there were a lot of people who thought I should quit and get a job.

Almost Perfect is a book about arguably the most dramatic shift from up to down that can occur in a baseball game. On the cusp of baseball immortality—but not quite reaching it—is a place where, perhaps, the most valuable and relatable stories of the game are found.

—Jim Bunning, September 2016

Jim Bunning won 224 games in the major leagues, struck out 2,855 batters, was chosen for the All-Star team nine times, and pitched a perfect game. He was inducted into the Baseball Hall of Fame in 1996. In politics, he served for a dozen years in the House of Representatives and in the US Senate before his retirement in 2010. Bunning now lives in northern Kentucky with his wife of 64 years, Mary Catherine.

INTRODUCTION

It breaks your heart. It is designed to break your heart.

> —*Former Major League Baseball commissioner*
> *A. Bartlett Giamatti, on baseball, from his*
> *essay "The Green Fields of the Mind"*

Since the first officially recorded game in 1846, baseball has captured—and broken—hearts. Every single game, by necessity, has a loser. Every pennant race can leave only one winner, and while the World Series delights fans of one team, it often depresses the fans of all the others. As poet/MLB commissioner Giamatti went on to write, the game begins in spring, blossoms in the summer, becomes a daily companion in the life of those who love it, and then slips away suddenly in the early fall.

Heartbreak in baseball often begins with the idea of perfection. This is in spite of the fact that the nature of baseball is anathema to perfection. A batting average of .300 is a great achievement—and that signifies failure on 7 of every 10 at-bats. But what about the pitcher? He stands as the lone figure who controls play, who battles against an uncompromising standard of glory. About once every three years,* a major-league pitcher has found himself in the crosshairs of perfection. Up to that moment, 26 opposing batters have come to the plate, and 26 batters have been set down without reaching base. No hits, no errors, no walks, no hit batters, no catcher's interference, no anything—except perfection. Of those select few men who have stood one step from the summit of single game pitching perfection (and it is noteworthy that no man has approached the feat twice), some are Hall of Famers, while others have been haphazard pitchers who had one great day. Twenty-one fortunate

---

* That is, in the history of what is generally acknowledged to be modern Major League Baseball.

men* retired that 27th batter and completed a perfect game. They are held in a unique place in the history of baseball; their names and stories are passed down, written about, and remembered forever.

But what about the others? What about the men who aimed for perfect, strained to an inch away, and then watched the dream skid past their infielders or drop in front of their outfielders? Those almost perfect pitchers make up their own unique club. Three pitchers qualified for the hard-luck club by actually recording the 27th consecutive out, but due to other circumstances, failing to pitch what the grand classifiers of Major League Baseball have deemed as perfect games. An unlucky 13 hurlers did not get that 27th consecutive out, instead losing out on perfection by one outcome or another. Two pitchers hit batters. One threw ball four. Ten gave up base hits, although one was robbed of perfection under such bizarre circumstances that it cannot be fairly claimed that he allowed a hit.

As with their pitching brethren who joined the Perfect Game club of immortality, some of the 16 pitchers who were almost perfect were staff aces, and some were journeymen who had a great day. In 2015, for the first time, a member of the Almost Perfect club was enshrined in the Baseball Hall of Fame. Five of the 16 were All-Stars, but on the other hand, 3 of the 16 left Major League Baseball with fewer than 50 career victories.

Untold articles and books have been written about a single perfect game or about the entire roster of perfect game pitchers. While studying the days of perfection is an interesting exercise, as a fan of baseball or simply as a human being, it is certainly arguable that the 16 almost perfect pitchers, and their stories of near misses, are more relevant to everyday life. The bad calls and the hard-luck hits are more common to human experience than the glory of immortality. They are certainly more common to baseball experience. Ask a Cubs fan about heartbreak, or someone who remembers the '51 Dodgers, the '64 Phillies, or the '86 Red Sox. The fans who lived through those dark days and who dared

---

* As of Opening Day 2017.

to dream again, dared to face schoolyard taunts and water-cooler put-downs—those are baseball fans.

And likewise, the pitchers who battled perfection down to the wire and lost the battle are those who are somehow more human, more identifiable than their historically blessed counterparts who won the battle. We all know what it is like to fail, which is perhaps why the lessons of life flow more freely from the defeated than from the triumphant. This is certainly the case with the almost perfect pitchers.*

What paths did these almost perfect pitchers take to nearly, but not quite, crafting immortality? And how did they deal with losing their grasp on pitching's ultimate prize? All of them, from stars like Billy Pierce and Mike Mussina to more anonymous pitchers like Ron Robinson and Brian Holman, had a deeper story. The day that they were almost perfect is but a part of their story. What had they experienced before, and how did their lives go after their near-misses? Did they accept their almost perfect game stoically, or continue to wonder "What if?" decades later? Did they blame anyone, or were they thrilled to have come as close to perfection as they did? What did they learn, and what can we learn from them? With 16 men, there are 16 answers, and each is moving on a very human level.

As a history, there is surprising depth in these stories. Each man's almost perfect day has a unique backdrop of time and place in baseball history. Whether it was the racial integration of the game, the battle over labor stoppages, or teams fighting to keep players that they couldn't pay, the periphery of these great games is so important that at times, they're not only stories about baseball but also tales about life and about America.

Yet not at all least, within this volume are stories about 16 great baseball games, through the lens of the men who dominated them. Who

---

* This is especially the case for Harvey Haddix, who endured the insult of losing the game in which he was almost perfect.

did they face? How did they arrive in the crosshairs of history? Were they lucky, brilliant, or both? How did these games impact the teams and the careers of those involved? How did three pitchers manage to throw a perfect 27 consecutive at-bats without being credited for perfect games?

At its core, this book about baseball is a book considerably about heartbreak. In these stories of heart-stopping near-perfection, my suspicion is that readers will encounter not only their own memories of teams, players, and internal changes in baseball, but that the accounting of these almost perfect pitchers' feelings and experiences will leave readers contemplating their own near-misses, and identifying with Dave Stieb or Milt Pappas or Armando Galarraga. In the end, we don't know what it's like to be perfect, but we do know what it's like to be something short of that mark. And we all know what it means to keep going. There is always another batter to face, another task to complete, another day to battle, which is the limit of human potential. Another day to maybe, hopefully, be almost perfect.

CHAPTER 1

"THERE'LL SURE BE RAIN, FOR YOU HEARD THE THUNDER"

July 4, 1908
Philadelphia Phillies at New York Giants
George "Hooks" Wiltse

It is somehow fitting that the initial near-perfect game came to pass on that day long marked for American significance by audacious dreamers chasing what was then believed to be an unreachable goal—July the 4th. On July 4, 1908, in the first game of a doubleheader at New York's

George "Hooks" Wiltse, whose near-perfect game (and 10-inning no-hitter) was part of a bizarre and memorable 1908 season   NATIONAL BASEBALL HALL OF FAME

1

Polo Grounds, George "Hooks" Wiltse was almost perfect. Philadelphia Phillies batters strode to the plate, and one by one, 26 consecutive batters made outs. In many ways, the game Wiltse played looked like a contemporary baseball game. Three strikes yielded an out, four balls brought about a walk, three outs in an inning, nine innings in a game. But at the same time, baseball was a very different game than it is today, and in the course of human events, the living embodiment of the battle for the nature of baseball could be found in the New York Giants dugout beside Wiltse on his historic Independence Day.

Wiltse's Giants were managed by the implacable John Joseph McGraw. Born eight years after the end of the Civil War to an Irish immigrant and his wife, McGraw belonged to the era's old school of baseball. He broke into the major leagues in 1891, a 5'7", 150-pound dynamo who played shortstop and third base for the Baltimore Orioles. Baltimore joined the National League the following year, and McGraw became a mainstay on a squad that won three straight pennants from 1894 to 1896.

McGraw and the Orioles weren't just the best team—they were probably the dirtiest. Major-league games were often arbitrated by a single umpire in this era, and the Orioles not only took advantage of every trick in the book, but they probably wrote most of them. Whether it was hiding extra baseballs in the outfield grass, cutting the basepath short when the umpire's back was turned, or doctoring the foul lines near home plate so their skillful bunts would roll fair instead of foul, the Orioles did it all. Front and center was McGraw. One author notes, "McGraw's favorite trick, when he was playing third and a runner tagged up there, was to gently hook a finger into the runner's belt." The brief moment of confusion would often turn an apparent sacrifice fly into a double play concluded at home plate. Some tricks were even dirtier. The same writer, to use the term loosely, credits McGraw with sharpening his spikes, in the mode often later associated with Ty Cobb.

Dirty baseball was successful baseball ... but was it good for the future of the game? Many believed not. Bill James notes that in the 1890s "ballplayers developed an exaggerated reputation as unsavory characters. Many of the players realized that they were losing respect, as men, because of the way the game was played on the field." Cincinnati Reds owner John Brush, who ironically later owned the Giants—and thus, employed McGraw—led a proposal for a "purification plan" to clean up the dirty play. McGraw admitted that if rules cleaning up the game were enacted, he might have to "abandon my profession entirely."

The game was changed by outside and inside influences. National League president Ban Johnson soon had to deal with competition, as the upstart American League challenged the supremacy of the NL. The new league featured less dirty baseball, fewer fistfights, and a more genteel atmosphere. Accordingly, the National League was forced, despite McGraw's protestations, to clean up its tactics.

But even more important were forces within the game McGraw knew. In New York, McGraw took over as manager of the Giants in 1902. He inherited a pitcher in his second full season who, at first glance, would seem extremely unlikely to ally with McGraw. Christy Mathewson, simply stated, was everything McGraw was not. Matty, as he was known, was tall and handsome. McGraw was short and glowering. Matty graduated from Bucknell University, while McGraw's uneven education came from the school of hard knocks. If McGraw would break or bend any rule for an advantage, Mathewson was unfailingly honest. While such stories sound apocryphal, one modern writer relates, "There are tales that umpires would surreptitiously look to Matty on a close play, to get his opinion—a shake or nod of the head—knowing that he would never call it dishonestly, even to benefit his own team."

McGraw, however, quickly learned to tolerate Mathewson's decency and honesty when he realized that the young pitcher was one of the best of his generation—or of any subsequent generation for that matter. For all that the two men did not have in common, they both loved to win. And together they had.

After McGraw took over in late 1902, Matty was his ace. In 1904, the Giants won 106 games, and easily took the pennant, although McGraw and owner Brush hated American League president Ban Johnson so much that they refused to play a second edition of the newly created

World Series. In 1905, the Giants won the pennant again, and then trounced the AL champion Philadelphia Athletics 4–1 in the Series, courtesy of three Mathewson shutouts. Matty won 64 games between '04 and '05, and posted a miniscule 1.12 ERA in mowing through the National League in the latter campaign.

And so it was that in 1908, Hooks Wiltse—within his own team's dugout—was caught between one of baseball's oddest, but most spectacularly successful, couples. Matty would abide McGraw's shenanigans, and McGraw would live with Matty's all-American earnestness. And stuck between both men and the ideals that they symbolized, baseball gradually moved forward, transforming from a game for roughs into America's game.

It certainly does not appear that the Wiltse family needed any convincing as to the merits of baseball. Born in 1880, George was the youngest of seven brothers, and by the time he made good with the Giants, his brother Lewis had pitched for the Pittsburgh Pirates, the Philadelphia Athletics, and the Baltimore Orioles. After Troy of the New York State league had claimed George away from the family carpet-making business for the princely sum of $275 per month, he promptly won 20 games in 1903, and caught the eye of the New York Giants.

The young southpaw made an immediate impression, winning his first 12 major-league decisions in the 1904 campaign, a record that was unequaled for more than 70 years. Wiltse was a solid if lesser part of the early Giants dynasty. But by 1908, "Iron Man" Joe McGinnity, who had long been New York's second pitching option behind Mathewson, was 37 years old and fading fast. July 4, 1908, found Wiltse at 27 years old, pitching very well as the Giants' #2 starter, and looking very likely to best his previous season high of 16 victories. Wiltse was steady, but not overpowering. He was thin and left-handed, and was a good athlete—*Baseball Magazine* noted him as one of the best-fielding and best-hitting pitchers in the game in an article after the 1908 season. Wiltse employed an almost sidearm delivery, which probably gave extra bite to his curveball. As with most pitchers of the era, he won by keeping hitters just off-balance enough rather than embarrassing them. Accordingly, his fortunes depended largely on the team behind him.

While the Giants had slid to second and fourth place in the two seasons since their back-to-back pennants, the team had high hopes of overtaking the upstart Chicago Cubs (of Tinker-Evers-Chance fame) and reclaiming the top spot in the National League. As July 4th dawned, the Giants were 39-28, three games out of the lead for the league flag. Aside from Mathewson and Wiltse, the Giants had good reason for optimism. Center fielder "Turkey" Mike Donlin had returned from a salary haggle that had turned into a season-long sabbatical in 1907 and was in the midst of a season that would see him hit .334 and drive in 106 runs. Future Hall of Famer Roger Bresnahan anchored the team behind the plate. In keeping with the game of the times, the Giants played small ball—totaling 20 home runs as a team, but featuring a lineup in which each regular stole at least 13 bases. Nearly forgotten on July 4th, but soon to become a name that would resound in baseball infamy, was a 19-year-old utility player with a handful of major-league at-bats named Fred Merkle. But on July 4th, it was Wiltse, and not yet Merkle, who had a rendezvous with history.

The Philadelphia Phillies certainly didn't intend to make Wiltse famous on July 4, 1908. Carrying a four-game losing streak, the Phillies arrived at the Polo Grounds at 27-32, good for fifth in the eight-team National League. Losing streak aside, the Phillies had high hopes for the first game as they handed the ball to their staff ace, George McQuillan, to oppose Wiltse. McQuillan was a rookie, but was in the midst of such an outstanding season that one baseball historian has termed him "the Doc Gooden of the Deadball Era." After going 4-0 with an 0.66 ERA in 41 innings late in 1907, McQuillan picked up where he left off the following year. As was typical for the era, McQuillan did not rely heavily on strikeouts—he fanned just 114 batters in 359⅔ innings in 1908. But he was nearly untouchable in any meaningful context—his 1.53 ERA was third in the league that season, and his 23 wins placed fourth. The modern WAR (Wins Above Replacement) stat rates McQuillan as the third best player in the entire National League in 1908—behind only Pittsburgh's legendary shortstop Honus Wagner and Mathewson. Still, Wiltse, while perhaps not quite as flashy as McQuillan, ended up posting the sixth best WAR score in the league himself. The first game of the scheduled Independence Day doubleheader figured to be a pitchers' duel.

Eight thousand fans journeyed to the Polo Grounds for the morning game. A contemporary sportswriter noted, "[Y]oung women came to the game bareheaded, in summery, fluffy, warm-weather apparel, and the young men without their coats. It was more like a picnic at the seashore than a ballgame in the heart of a sweltering metropolis." It might have been like a picnic in the stands, but at the plate, Giants and Phillies batters alike were having no picnic.

Wiltse was in control from the outset. He opened the game by inducing Eddie Grant to fly out to left, then fanned Otto Knabe, and coaxed a groundout from John Titus. Unfortunately, the Giants wasted a leadoff single by Fred Tenney against McQuillan and did not score in their half of the inning. In the visitors' second inning, the Phillies grounded to second, lined to short, and then ended the inning with Fred Osborn grounding back to Wiltse. Another Giants leadoff single resulted in no further damage as Cy Seymour was picked off second base by the Phillies. Still, no immediate harm was shown by Wiltse, as he survived a line drive to left fielder Spike Shannon to lead off the third, and then allowed a groundout and fanned McQuillan to end the frame and his perfect first trip through the Philadelphia lineup. The game remained scoreless as Wiltse was doubled off first on a line drive after his own failed sacrifice bunt attempt again ruined a third straight leadoff single by the Giants.

Wiltse's bid at perfection was mildly threatened when Eddie Grant led off the Philadelphia fourth with a line drive that center fielder Donlin had to hustle to snag. But after a popup and a routine flyball, four perfect innings were in the book for Hooks. The Giants could not score in the home half of the fourth inning, although there was drama, if not runs. Philadelphia's Mickey Doolin grabbed umpire Cy Rigler after a close call on a stolen base and was promptly ejected from the game. Rigler, while a relatively new ump, cut an imposing figure and was generally well respected. Unfortunately, this incident would not be the last time he would figure in the day's outcome.

Future Hall of Famer Sherry Magee fouled out to first to begin Philadelphia's fifth crack at Wiltse. After a grounder and a popup that Al Bridwell handled at shortstop, the fifth inning was complete. On the other side of the frame, for the fourth time in five innings, the Giants wasted a leadoff single, and the game remained scoreless. Reserve Ernie Courtney, taking the place of the banished Doolin, became Wiltse's third strikeout victim to begin the Philadelphia sixth inning. After grounders to shortstop and first base, Wiltse was two-thirds of the way to a perfect game. In the bottom of the frame, Fred Tenney again led off with a single, but was doubled up on a line drive. McQuillan was yielding baserunners, but not runs, and the game continued scoreless.

While the term "perfect game" has been otherwise indicated not to have been in common circulation at this time, this isn't to say that the crowd in the Polo Grounds didn't attach significance to Wiltse's performance. In *Sporting Life* magazine, one columnist indicated, "As the fans realized what Wiltse was aiming to accomplish they cheered him on inning by inning, the volume growing apace with the progress of the game." A newspaper columnist waxed more poetically, "[F]rom the sixth on Master Wiltse got a hand every time he came in from the box, and it was the kind of hand you can hear over in Greenpoint, and the sort that makes you look up at the sky and say, yes, there'll sure be rain, for you heard the thunder." Even if the fans didn't have an exact term for what they were witnessing, they knew it was mesmerizing, and the deeper that Wiltse pitched into the game, the more animated the hometown rooters grew.

In the seventh inning, Eddie Grant grounded back to Wiltse. Hooks struck out Otto Knabe for the second time in the game (Knabe whiffed only 46 times all season), and then ended the inning via a groundball to short. Wiltse was six outs from perfection—if the Giants could score a run. But in the seventh, McQuillan had his first one-two-three inning of the game, and the deadlock continued.

Sherry Magee began the eighth inning by lining out to center field. After a pair of grounders, one to shortstop and the second back to Wiltse himself, Hooks was three outs from history. Cy Young had pitched a perfect game, but there was little precedent for the spot in history where Wiltse found himself. In the bottom of the frame, despite a one-out bunt single from Al Bridwell, the Giants could not break through off McQuillan, and so the game headed scoreless into the ninth inning.

Thirty-three-year-old Ernie Courtney, in the game for the ejected Mickey Doolin, began the ninth inning by flying out to Mike Donlin in center field. One down. Catcher Red Dooin followed suit by grounding to Al Bridwell at shortstop, whose throw to Fred Tenney beat Dooin to first base for the second out—26 men up, 26 men down. Standing in the way of history for Hooks Wiltse were two opponents—his own team's inability to score a run . . . and George McQuillan.

Unlike Wiltse, McQuillan was not a particularly talented hitter. He went on to hit .117 for his major-league career, and his 1908 batting average of .151 wasn't much better. Wiltse worked the count to one ball and two strikes, and then threw a pitch that would've entered him—perhaps—into baseball immortality. It was a curveball—"sharp breaking . . . which came up toward the plate about six inches on the outside and then broke across the corner waist high." But Rigler, the sole umpire, watched the pitch come in, and called it ball two. One writer diplomatically noted, "Wiltse and Bresnahan thought they had him struck out, but umpire Rigler called it a ball." However, another more direct account simply stated, "Rigler thus robbed the pitcher of a perfect game."

Cy Rigler's missed call, which the umpire himself apparently freely acknowledged thereafter, might have had little impact. But the next offering from Wiltse broke inside and struck McQuillan flush in the shoulder. The perfect game was gone. Still, Eddie Grant grounded back to Wiltse, and the game continued.

After New York could not break through in the ninth inning either, Wiltse returned to the mound for the 10th inning. He induced a grounder to short, struck out John Titus, and got Magee to foul out. Finally, after 10 innings of mastery, the Giants took care of business. Devlin led off with a single, and an attempted sacrifice bunt from Shannon was promptly fielded and thrown into right field. With runners now at second and third and no one out, Al Bridwell grounded to short, and when Ernie Courtney could not come up with the ball, the game was over. Giants 1, Phillies 0. And while Hooks Wiltse had just missed a perfect game, a 10-inning no-hitter was nothing to sneeze at.

The pitching of a no-hit game, as it was then termed, even in the Dead Ball Era, was an accomplishment to be cherished. A contemporary reporter gushed, "Wiltse is the first left-hander who ever pitched a ten inning victory in which his opponents made no hits. It was a wonderful performance and likely to remain as a major league record for a long time to come." Another writer compared the game favorably to Cy Young's recent perfect game.

In an unpublished autobiography, Wiltse himself wrote of his near-miss only briefly, stating, "I missed being the only pitcher of all time to pitch a perfect ten inning game against Philadelphia because Cy Rigler miscalled a strike. He admitted afterward he could have called it one. It was a tough break for the next pitch struck McQuillan on the shoulder and put him on first base. It had been a perfect game for eight and two-thirds innings."

If anyone was particularly bothered over Wiltse's loss of the perfect game, it appears to have been the umpire whose missed call was universally acknowledged. More than a century ahead of Jim Joyce's botched call in the Armando Galarraga game, Cy Rigler stood in Joyce's shoes, as the possible object of scorn for his own role in ruining the perfect game. Of course, unlike Joyce, Rigler's call was second-guessed only by the players, spectators, and writers present in the Polo Grounds on the day of the game. With no radio or television, the story passed through the news cycle quickly and without significant comment.

Much like Joyce after him, Rigler was a genuinely well regarded and professional umpire, who was humble and apologetic for his mistake. Rigler was only 26 years old at the time of his missed call, but he had already made a name for himself in professional baseball. One biographer credits Rigler with introducing, along with major-league umpire Bill Klem, the now uniform gesture of a raised right arm to call a strike, in the Central League in 1905. Rigler weighed 270 pounds in his prime, and was an authoritative, but well-liked umpire. He remained a star of his profession and was part of the crew for the first MLB All-Star Game in 1933.

Well regarded or not, Rigler clearly was embarrassed by the snafu. In 1953, Wiltse told an interviewer, "Every time I saw Charlie Rigler after that he gave me a cigar. He admits [the disputed ball] was one of the pitches he missed." The occasional handful of cigars from Rigler aside, Wiltse moved on after his historic near-miss, and a much more historic heartbreak lay in his future.

⌇

The Giants remained locked in a tight pennant race over the summer, with the Cubs and Pirates as the other two combatants in the fight. On September 23rd, the Giants and Cubs played a game at the Polo Grounds with huge pennant repercussions. The game was tied 1–1 in the bottom of the ninth inning when the Giants loaded the bases with two out. Standing at first base was rookie Fred Merkle, a promising young prospect who was playing only because first baseman Fred Tenney was out of the lineup with lumbago. It was a tight spot in an epic pennant race, and when Al Bridwell lined a base hit up the middle, Moose McCormick trotted home and the Giants had staked a pivotal 2–1 win, putting them into first place.

Except that they hadn't. Merkle, at first base, saw the ball go through the infield, McCormick touch home, and he apparently raced off the field ahead of a throng of Giants fans who rushed the field. The Cubs' Johnny Evers grabbed a ball, caught the umpires' attention, and tagged second base. Umpire Hank O'Day called Merkle out for failing to touch second base. The hour was late, the field was overrun, and the game was called a 1–1 tie.

When the Giants and Cubs finished the regular season tied for the pennant and Mathewson lost a one-game playoff to Chicago, the near-miss of a perfect game for Hooks Wiltse took a backseat to the near-loss of a pennant. And Hooks had a good view of Merkle's error, as he was coaching first base, and failed to prompt the green young prospect to trot down and touch second base. History seems to have forgiven Hooks, though. Rather than any blame being foisted off on the veteran coaching at first base, the infamous play was immortalized as "Merkle's Boner," and the young baserunner would spend the remainder of his days trying to live down the mistake. Indeed, Frank Deford notes that no fewer than three different Giants (Wiltse, Mathewson, and McGinnity) had ultimately claimed to have been coaching first base and to have failed to drag Fred Merkle to second. Perhaps the baseball karma of not dragging poor Cy Rigler over the coals too harshly for his error prompted some unseen baseball deity to absolve Hooks Wiltse of a much more costly missed play on his own part as first-base coach. Wiltse suffered heartbreak, but not the scorn of history.

─────

Obviously, a great deal of time has passed since July 4, 1908. Baseball has grown and expanded, shifted and realigned, but the stories of heartbreak are all set forth under the same basic template. The actors in the plot of near-perfection play their roles and then the game rolls on, passing each by on its way to the next rounds of heroes and villains, of almosts and not-quites.

It was the man behind the mask who stayed in the game the longest. Cy Rigler used his size, his commanding presence, and his consistently excellent work to help clear up the game of baseball, one game at a time over the next three decades. The old days of scuffles and dirty play were like ancient memories by the time Rigler retired after the 1935 season.

So highly respected was Rigler that he was promptly named as National League chief of umpires. Two months later, at age 53, Cy Rigler passed away following brain surgery in Philadelphia.

A year and a half before, John J. McGraw, the voice and face of old-time hardscrabble baseball, had been laid to rest in New Cathedral Cemetery in Baltimore, Maryland. McGraw was 60 years old when he passed away of prostate cancer and uremia in 1934. McGraw had been vociferous in his opposition to the rabbit ball and the home run–heavy style of play it favored, and for a time he had succeeded, stymieing Babe Ruth's Yankees by beating them in the 1921 and 1922 World Series. But, of course, the Babe laughed last. McGraw resigned as a manager in June 1932, and his 2,763 victories are second only to Connie Mack, who said of his contemporary, "There has been only one manager—and his name is McGraw."

The cruelest fate, though, was reserved for the man who was the face of what baseball would become—Christy Mathewson was not only ahead of his time, he was soon out of his time. Mathewson won 373 games, tied for third-best all-time. But the wins were almost secondary to the matinee idol looks, the impeccable manners, and the complete mastery of self that announced to the American public that a great baseball player could be a gentleman. Grantland Rice said of Mathewson, "He gripped the imagination of a country that held 100 million people and held this grip with a firmer hold than any man of his day or time."

Mathewson won his last game in 1916, and was managing the Reds in 1918, when he butted heads with infamous first baseman Hal Chase, a reprobate and gambler who paved the way for the Black Sox scandal with his familiarity with gamblers and contempt for baseball's rules. Mathewson could not testify against Chase in a disciplinary hearing, because by that time, he was serving as a captain in the US Army in World War I.

Matty was believed to have been exposed to mustard gas in France during the Great War, and he was diagnosed with tuberculosis in 1921. While John McGraw talked Boston Braves owner Emil Fuchs into hiring Matty as team president in 1923, the strain on Mathewson's body took its terrible toll. During the 1925 World Series, at just 45 years old, Mathewson passed away, leaving a wife, a son, and an entire sport that still reverberates with respect for the great man.

Hooks Wiltse's name is not as well remembered as that of his rotation mate Mathewson, but his last days were much more numerous and afforded many more years to remember the almost perfect day of his prime.

In 1908 Wiltse had the best year of his major-league career, even if it was a year that just missed out on including a perfect game and an appearance in the World Series. Hooks finished 23-14 with a 2.24 ERA, but would never pitch as much or as well again. He did win 20 games in 1909, and lowered his ERA to 2.00, but his arm simply would not hold up against repeated strain. He won 14 games in 1910, 12 games in 1911, and 9 games in 1912. He totaled only four more wins thereafter before ending his major-league career in the renegade Federal League in 1915. Wiltse posted a career record of 139-90, with a 2.47 ERA in 2,112⅓ innings.

He did have one more career highlight when he was called on to play first base in the 1913 World Series after injuries depleted the roster. He had a huge role in winning Game 2 when he cut down two Philadelphia runners at home plate on groundballs in the ninth inning. The Giants won the game but lost the Series, which was their third straight Series loss. Wiltse parlayed his first base play into a spot on McGraw's world baseball tour in the winter of 1913–1914, touring great historic sites across the globe and playing games in Japan, China, Egypt, France, and England among other locales.

After his big-league days ended in 1915, Wiltse bounced around the minor leagues for another decade, pitching, playing, or coaching. In 1925, he was the pitching coach of the New York Yankees, but after a down year that season and another campaign with Reading in the International League, Wiltse gave up organized baseball.

He returned to his hometown of Syracuse, New York, where he sold real estate and involved himself in local politics, serving as an alderman and then a deputy property assessor. Wiltse lived long enough to see the Giants leave New York and settle across the country in San Francisco. He passed away of emphysema on January 21, 1959, at age 79. By the time of his death, the glory days of deadball were long forgotten by all but a few survivors of the era. The Giants of McGraw and Mathewson had given way to the Giants of Mays and McCovey. And several other pitchers were making their peace with the heartbreak of the days when they were almost perfect.

July 4, 1908 (1st game)
Polo Grounds, New York, NY

	1	2	3	4	5	6	7	8	9	10	R	H	E
PHI	0	0	0	0	0	0	0	0	0	0	0	0	1
NYG	0	0	0	0	0	0	0	0	0	1	1	9	0

W: Wiltse
L: McQuillan

The End of Wiltse's Perfect Game:

Top of the Ninth Inning, Two Outs.
A 2-2 count to pitcher George McQuillan.
Hit by pitch.

CHAPTER 2

IN RELIEF OF THE BABE

June 23, 1917
Washington Senators at Boston Red Sox
Ernie Shore (in relief)

Baseball is a game of strange bed-
fellows. Circumstance, timing, and
perhaps even destiny can take two
men from different backgrounds
and tie them together forever—
either in the close-knit fabric of
being teammates or in the enmity
of rivalry. If heartbreak is a constant companion of baseball, then
the odd synergy of connection is
also deeply rooted. There can be no
other possible explanation for the
many ties between the two men
who share joint ownership of a
near-perfect game. One was urban,
the other rural. One was boisterous and from a troubled background, the other was reserved and

Ernie Shore, who made history by
being almost perfect—in relief
NATIONAL BASEBALL HALL OF FAME

from a solid family. But they arrived in the big leagues together, came to
prominence together, and were reunited on a team that would grow to
become the greatest dynasty in baseball history. For one of the two men,
his moment of near-perfection was at the beginning of a rise to ascen-
dancy as perhaps the greatest player in the evolution of the game. For the
other, it was nearly the end of a brief career. One would be a household
name and a celebrity, and the other would settle back into small-town

civility. One of the two men would make only a negative contribution to the day of near-perfection, while the other mowed through baseball history without struggle or worry.

That said, the star of the second almost perfect major-league performance was not the well-known name of the interlinked duo who share history, George Herman "Babe" Ruth. No, the man who would one day become "The Great Bambino," "The Sultan of Swat," and perhaps the savior of baseball was a mere footnote. June 23, 1917, belonged to Ernie Shore. It was the day when he actually was perfect, and he combined with Ruth to be historically almost perfect.

Ernest Grady Shore was born on April 24, 1891, in rural North Carolina, not far from Winston-Salem. He came from a family of farmers, and lived near his paternal grandfather's farm as well. Shore departed from the family line, relating that setting tobacco "just kills your back. It wasn't for me." While he grew to love baseball, he also loved academia. Shore enrolled at Guilford College, where he not only earned his degree, but began teaching mathematics in the baseball offseason. Indeed, at least one contemporary account of his near-perfect game refers to him throughout as "Prof. Shore."

Even before his graduation from Guilford in 1914, Shore had drawn acclaim as a pitcher. He was a lanky right-hander, and he himself once told an interviewer, "If my fastball was breaking, I could beat anybody." Shore's major-league debut was apparently not such an occasion. Picked up by John McGraw's New York Giants, Shore made his first appearance in relief of fellow almost-perfect hurler Hooks Wiltse. He promptly gave up 10 runs in an inning (mercifully, only three were earned, so his ERA was a mere 27.00), and was subsequently cut loose by the Giants.

Shore ironed out his problems in the North Carolina State League in 1913, pitching for his college coach, Chick Doak. Jack Dunn of the Baltimore Orioles (then a minor-league team) saw Shore and snagged him for the 1914 season. Dunn's Orioles were a very talented squad, as Shore showed himself to be a top prospect, just as Dunn's other rookie pitcher—George Herman Ruth—began to hit his stride. Financial troubles beset the Orioles, and Dunn ultimately sold Shore, Ruth, and Ben Egan to the Boston Red Sox for cash—reported at times to be as little as $8,500 or as much as $30,000. Shore and Ruth—sold together—would soon break into the majors for good together.

Ruth was three years younger than Shore, and his childhood was quite different. As the son of a saloon keeper and an invalid in inner-city Baltimore, Ruth's hobbies at age six included stealing money from his father, finishing off customers' beers, and enjoying chewing tobacco. Indeed, Ruth's family situation was so tenuous that until he obtained a passport at age 39 and requested his birth certificate, he actually did not know his own age. In light of his poor background and behavior, the local courts found George to be incorrigible and his father sent him to St. Mary's Industrial School for Boys, by all accounts a rather grim place, but one in which Ruth met a Xaverian monk named Brother Matthias Boutilier, a giant French-Canadian who taught him to play baseball. Big for his age and talented, Ruth soon began dominating baseball games against older boys at St. Mary's. His lack of social knowledge was countered by a profound need for the approval and adoration of those around him, and a relentless zest to live life to the fullest.

When the Orioles signed Ruth in March 1914, he left St. Mary's and headed for spring training. That was his first train ride and the first time he had left Maryland. When he arrived, he promptly checked into the first hotel he had ever stayed in and ordered food from a menu for the first time in his life. He loved food, he loved women, and what he lacked in self-discipline, Ruth made up for in good-natured enthusiasm. Ernie Shore was Babe Ruth's first roommate, and right away settled into experiences like learning several weeks into the season that Ruth had been sharing his bathroom utensils. One writer notes that Shore "didn't like a roommate who never flushed the toilet, who walked around naked, who never sat down, never slept. A pride for personal flatulence and exaggerated belches also was not an admired quality."

Fortunately for both men, and for the Orioles, the one common trait of Ruth and Shore is that both were very effective pitchers. Ruth was left-handed and Shore was a righty, and the two picked their way through the International League until they were sold to the Red Sox in July 1914. After a few appearances in Boston, Ruth was sent to Providence for further seasoning, posting a 2-1 mark in 1914 for Boston. Shore, on the other hand, was an immediate hit, and went 10-5 with a 2.00 ERA in half a season with the Red Sox.

In 1915, Shore continued to be successful, winning 19 games with a miniscule 1.64 ERA, third best in the American League. In fact, Shore was so successful that skeptical opponents accused him of doctoring the baseball. Unperturbed by such allegations, Shore continued to shine, pitching two excellent games in the World Series, which Boston won. Ruth did not see any pitching time in the Series, but his official rookie season in the big leagues was hardly a failure, as he went 18-8 with a 2.44 ERA. Ruth also was quite a hitter, batting .315 with four home runs in 92 at-bats.

Shore was again a World Series hero in 1916. He posted a 16-10 mark in the regular season, although his ERA rose to 2.63. That said, in the Series, he was 2-0 and allowed just three runs in 17⅔ innings. Shore won the fifth game, ending the series and bringing home Boston's second consecutive title. Little did anyone realize Boston would win only one more championship in the next 87 years.

Ruth, whose career proved pivotal to Boston fortunes, was even better in 1916, outshining Shore with a 23-12 mark and a 1.75 ERA, which led the league. He added a 14-inning complete game victory in the Series. The Babe was on his way up, and no one could even guess how high he would reach.

Ernie Shore, on the other hand, was on his way down. In the spring of 1917, one columnist noted, "Ernie Shore and Carl Mays are good hurlers but they cannot stand a great deal of work and it looks very much as if it will be up to Ruth and [Dutch] Leonard to bear the brunt of the pitching responsibility." Indeed, on June 23, 1917, Ruth was 12-4 when Boston hosted the Washington Senators. Shore was 6-4, although his ERA was just 1.92. Ruth was slated to start the first game of a double-header that day, and Shore had just worked five innings in a game the Sox had lost two days before.

The Red Sox were 34-21 on June 23rd, trailing the White Sox by two games in the race for the American League pennant. The team was led by an electrifying pitching staff, as Ruth was superb, on his way to a career-best 24 victories, and young Carl Mays was in the process of add-ing 22 more wins. Dutch Leonard ended the season 16-17, but in light of his 2.17 ERA, Leonard can hardly be blamed. Herb Pennock, who would go on to star for the Yankees, was a spot starter for Boston. And, of course, there was Ernie Shore. The hurlers led Boston to a team-wide 2.20 ERA, good for second in the league.

Offensively, small ball was still the rule. Boston hit 14 homers as a team for the season. Ruth hit two as a pitcher, placing him behind Harry Hooper's three for the team lead. The team hit .246, just below the league average, and was led by center fielder Duffy Lewis, who hit .302 and knocked in 65 runs.

The opposing Senators, sporting a 21-33 record, were in seventh place, hopelessly out of contention by late June, in a scene that became altogether too familiar to Washington backers. Walter Johnson starred for the Senators, whose particularly impotent offense slugged four home runs all season. Future Hall of Famer Sam Rice was a notable exception to the team's mediocrity, and he hit .302 and drove in 69 runs in 1917, albeit without a home run.

Ruth took the mound to face the Senators in the first game of the day's doubleheader. He was opposed by the Senators' Doc Ayers, a solid though unimposing pitcher, in the midst of a career that would end with a 64-78 record. Ray Morgan led off the game for the Senators, and any spectators who were late likely missed Ruth's entire day.

Ruth threw four pitches to Morgan, and home plate umpire Brick Owens called each a ball. After the first pitch, Ruth griped. After the second, he shouted. After the third, he apparently yelled for Owens to "open your eyes." After ball four, Ruth, in his autobiography, wrote that he shouted, "If you'd go to bed at night, you so-and-so, you could keep your eyes open long enough in the daytime to see when a ball goes over the plate." A slightly more reliable source renders Ruth's comment as, "Why don't you open your goddamned eyes?"

Owens was unimpressed. By all accounts, he told Ruth to desist (either "Get back out there and pitch," per the neutral sportswriter, or "Shut up, you lout," per Ruth) or he would throw him out of the game. Ruth immediately told Owens that if he was ejected, he would punch Owens (either in the nose, per the sportswriter, or in the jaw, per Ruth). Owens promptly ejected Ruth. All hell then broke loose.

Ruth wrote only, "I hauled off and hit him, but good." Another account stated that Ruth rushed Owens, that catcher Chester Thomas got between the two, but that Ruth swung on Owens anyway. One report states, "He missed with a right, but a left caught Owens on the back of the neck." Another report reverses that account, with Ruth missing with a left, but connecting with a right-hand punch. Apparently at that point, Ruth was uncontrollable, and it took Thomas (who was also ejected), Boston manager Jack Barry, and a policeman to remove him from the field.

Once calm was restored, Barry had a decision to make. Mays had pitched the day before, and Leonard was set to go in the second game of the doubleheader. Barry told Shore to take the mound. "Hold them while I get somebody ready," he allegedly told Shore. Years later, Shore told reporters that he was only allowed five warmup pitches by the umpire. Contemporary accounts are varied. One describes "a brief warmup," while another notes that "a delay of nearly ten minutes [occurred], during which Shore was warming up." During the delay, backup catcher Sam Agnew had entered the game for Thomas, and so Washington's Ray Morgan astutely took off for second base on Shore's first pitch. He was thrown out by Agnew, and the blot of Ruth on Shore's day was quickly erased.

Shore then retired Eddie Foster on a grounder to the shortstop and Clyde Milan hit a Texas Leaguer behind second base that "only a sensational play from [manager/second baseman] Barry cut off from being a hit." Shore later recalled that after the inning, "Barry asked me if I wanted to continue and I told him sure. I went down to the bullpen and threw and by the time the second inning began I was loose." Shore was not only loose, he was incredibly effective. He was noted for "a wicked overhand fastball that dipped," one writer recalls. "It was dipping sharply on that afternoon at Fenway Park and as the game wore on, Washington batters kept beating the ball into the ground." For his part, Shore was honest about the game. "[After the first inning], I don't think I could have worked easier if I'd been sitting in a rocking chair," he recalled. "I don't believe I threw 75 pitches that whole game. . . . They just kept hitting it right at somebody."

Shore set down the Senators in order in the second inning, and in the bottom of the frame, singles by Larry Gardner, Duffy Lewis, and Ray Agnew brought home a run for Boston. Staked to a 1–0 lead, Shore had all the offensive help he would need. He would require little more work defensively.

Shore cruised through the third and fourth inning, but with two outs in the fifth, his perfect game had its first great test. Charlie Jamieson lined a Shore offering back through the box, where the pitch hit the hurler on the shin. Shortstop Everett Scott raced in to grab the deflected ball and nip Jamieson at first base, keeping the almost-perfect game intact.

Shore struck out only two Senators, but as he worked his way through the third and ultimate round of the Washington lineup, history was clearly in the making. His Red Sox teammates provided a cushion in the seventh inning, with Ray Agnew (who knocked in only 98 runs in a seven-year major-league career) doubling in his second RBI of the game, and Harry Hooper knocking in two more runs with a single. With a 4–0 lead, the only remaining suspense lay not in the outcome, but in whether Shore could stay perfect.

Shore cruised into his last frame. He struck out Howie Shanks, leaving himself with just two outs to go. With one down, Washington catcher John Henry hit what was universally acknowledged to be the hardest hit ball from a Senator all day. One contemporary account notes, "Henry drove out what looked to be a sure hit, but [left fielder Duffy] Lewis came racing in and smothered the ball." Another sportswriter of the time agreed, stating that Lewis "came in like lightning and speared one that Henry had planted in short left." By the later years of Shore's life, his account had the ball "lined ... on the nose, but right at Duffy Lewis in left field." In any case, Lewis made the play, and Shore was one out from a sort-of perfect game.

Pinch-hitter Mike Menosky, a career .278 hitter, hit for Doc Ayers, and stood between Shore and history. Shore later noted that Washington manager Clark Griffith "was a sore loser, a very sore loser. He didn't want to see me complete that perfect game ... so he had Menosky drag a bunt, just to try to break up the perfect game." Jack Barry fielded the bunt and nipped Menosky at first base for the final out. At least, this was how Shore recalled it, years later. Another contemporary account stated that Barry had made "a grand play on a swinging bunt by pinch hitter Menoskey." Another account indicates that Menoskey "lifted to Barry." So whether the play was a bunt, a swinging bunt, or a popup, Menoskey definitely was retired, and after inheriting Babe Ruth's mess, Ernie Shore had been nothing less than perfect.

Once the celebration had subsided, the secondary question was—exactly what had Shore done? He and Ruth had not allowed any hits, so clearly the game was a no-hitter. Was it a perfect game? The only clarification came from American League secretary William Harridge, who tersely answered a newspaper with a statement that "Ernie Shore is credited with a no-hit game in the official scores of June 23." Somehow, the official confirmation of Shore pitching a no-hitter (which seems more or less indisputable) transformed into recognition of him for pitching a perfect game. In 1962, *Sports Illustrated* admitted that there was a dispute still as to whether or not the game was considered perfect. But by that time, other matters had occupied Shore, and he had dealt with much more serious problems than how a handful of statisticians classified his entry into baseball history.

Only a few months after making baseball history, Ernie Shore enlisted in the US Naval Reserves. With World War I expanding and the government's "Work or fight" order pending, Shore came to the aid of his country. It is worth noting that a multitude of other talented players avoided military service altogether. Shore finished out the season, ending up at 13-10 with a 2.22 ERA. Boston finished a handful of games behind Chicago, in second place in the AL pennant race.

Shore missed the 1918 campaign due to his naval duty. He was assigned to officers' school, and became an ensign, apparently the only MLB player to reach such rank, before he left the Navy following the conclusion of the war, and ahead of the 1919 season. He turned 28 years old just before the 1919 season began, and had been traded by the cash-strapped Red Sox to the Yankees, along with Dutch Leonard and outfielder Duffy Lewis, for essentially some warm bodies and $15,000. One writer termed the trade to be "the first of the blockbuster deals that would dismantle the heart of the Red Sox team and reassemble it in New York."

While that assessment is true, Shore did little to help the Yankees. He contracted mumps during spring training in 1919, but surely that cannot be the only reason that the remainder of his career included just seven big-league wins scattered in 1919 and 1920. Shore himself was at a loss to explain the situation, but after two poor seasons of pitching irregularly, the Yankees sent him back to the minor leagues, where he spent an even more ineffective 1921 season. With a career 65-47 major-league record and a 2.47 ERA, Ernie Shore's baseball career was over.

While Shore's career had floundered, so had Major League Baseball. The Red Sox had won the AL pennant without Shore in 1918 (and their last World Series for 86 years), before the White Sox overtook them in 1919. The history of gambling in baseball was one of accumulated small instances until the issue exploded with the Chicago Black Sox throwing the 1919 World Series, which was revealed in the fall of 1920, scuttling another pennant race. Baseball was low scoring, lacked excitement, and its credibility was completely undermined by the revelation that even the World Series was crooked. The game was reeling.

The financial impact of baseball's struggle was certainly felt in Boston, where Harry Frazee struggled to keep his Red Sox squad afloat. The trade of Shore, Leonard, and Lewis in early 1919 was a bad omen for Sox fans, but a worse one came on the day after Christmas 1919, when Frazee sold Babe Ruth to the Yankees. As Ruth reunited with Shore one last time, the Red Sox, the Yankees, and organized baseball would never be the same.

In 1919, as Shore's career had floundered, Ruth had made a transition. He was 9-5 with a 2.97 ERA as a pitcher, but threw only 133⅓ innings, meanwhile playing in 130 games, with the majority of those coming in the outfield. Ruth hit .322, with an unheard of 29 home runs and 113 RBI. Twenty-nine home runs not only led the league, it set a single-season major-league record, and nearly tripled the second-most prolific power hitter's total in the American League. Ruth would have ranked fourth in the American League's *team* home run standings.

Things changed, and suddenly. Some credited a new "rabbit" ball, and apparently the yarn wrapped around the core of the ball was changed before the 1920 season. Others noted that baseball outlawed spitballs and other pitches that defaced the baseball before 1921. Also, after Cleveland shortstop Ray Chapman was killed with a beanball in late 1920, umpires started keeping newer, cleaner baseballs in play, which were easier for hitters to see.

Whatever the cause, Ruth changed the game of baseball, and suddenly added color and panache—and ticket sales—back to the national pastime. He hit 54 home runs in 1920, 59 more in 1921, and reached 60 home runs in 1927—only failing to hit more than 40 in a season twice between 1920 and 1931. The Red Sox foundered near the bottom of the AL standings, and the Yankees won four World Series titles with Ruth. Perhaps more importantly, baseball not only survived, but it thrived.

Babe Ruth became a star, perhaps the biggest the game has ever produced. His 60 home runs in a season was an MLB record for more than three decades, and his 714 career home runs stood as the mark to beat for more than four decades. His accomplishments, like the man himself, were larger than life.

⌒

While life was good for baseball by the mid-1920s, it wasn't very good for the rest of America. The Great Depression hit the nation hard, taking down the majority of America's major financial institutions, and causing enormous rates of unemployment, homelessness, and even suicide. One man who was not exempt from those hard times was Ernie Shore.

The heartbreak of a quick end to a promising career and a drop-off to obscurity was nothing compared to the scratching to survive that went on across much of America. Ernie Shore had returned to Winston-Salem in 1921 and thereafter, as one local writer noted, "tried selling cars and insurance with little success." Shore himself admitted later in life that while he had sold automobiles, after 1930 "they came back faster than they went out." Financial ruin cast a much larger shadow of heart-break than hard luck in baseball. By 1936, Shore owed $20,000, a pre-carious position for a husband and father of three children.

Fortunately, that year, a group of Shore's friends, headlined by a couple of movers and shakers within R. J. Reynolds Tobacco Company, talked the 45-year-old former pitcher into running for sheriff of Forsyth County, North Carolina. While he had no experience, Shore was enticed by the $4,000 annual salary. He took to campaigning with the same com-petitive drive that had helped him in baseball—rising at 4:00 a.m. to meet local farmers before they began their day of work. Shore defeated the incumbent sheriff in a primary, and then won the election in November. A quarter century later, he told an interviewer of the rough days of uncer-tainty before his election, "I don't mind telling you that I needed the job."

Ernie Shore had found his second calling. He served as sheriff of Forsyth County for 34 years before retiring. During that time, Shore presided over a series of changes within his staff and organization. His department increased from 6 deputies up to 70 by the time of his retire-ment, and he was the first North Carolina sheriff who equipped staff vehicles with two-way radios. One writer notes, "He was widely known as a kind and fair sheriff who loved nothing more in the world than a good possum dinner." Shore lived out his days in an atmosphere of quiet respect and dignity. His wife of 54 years passed away in 1980, and later that year, Shore died at the age of 89.

The years after his playing career (following a rough start) ended up being kind to Shore, but not so much to Babe Ruth. Ruth had long dreamed of a career as a major-league manager, a goal that eluded him, much to his disappointment. Baseball loved the happy-go-lucky Ruth as long as he kept hitting home runs, but when that ended, he was suddenly too undisciplined or irreverent for the game he had saved. Ruth contracted throat cancer and passed away in 1948.

Baseball thrived long after Ruth had given way to Gehrig and then DiMaggio as the star of the New York Yankees. The Yankee dynasty continued over the ages, just as Red Sox futility became an equal tradition. While occasional gambling scandals have arisen over the intervening years, never again has gambling seriously threatened the survival of baseball, which entered a half-century of virtual hegemony as the king of American sports.

As it did in the careers of Shore and Ruth, money continues to drive the game. In Winston-Salem in 1956, Sheriff Shore had led a fundraising effort for a new minor-league baseball field that was named for him. The local team used the field for years, but in 2009, they moved to a new stadium downtown. That stadium was named not for a local hero but for the business that financed it. "That's just the way it goes in corporate America," said John Shore, one of Ernie's children.

In 1991, 74 years after Ernie Shore's great afternoon, baseball's Committee of Statistical Accuracy changed the official definitions of no-hitter and perfect game, and in so doing, issued a ruling that Ernie Shore had *not* thrown a perfect game, but that he would be credited only with a combined no-hitter with Babe Ruth. There they reside in the baseball history books—an odd couple, a star and a sheriff, the immature but talented rube and the relatively polished college man who found his best years after baseball. They will forever remain almost perfect.

June 23, 1917 (1st game)
Fenway Park, Boston, MA

	1	2	3	4	5	6	7	8	9	R	H	E
WAS	0	0	0	0	0	0	0	0	0	0	0	3
BOS	0	1	0	0	0	0	3	0	X	4	9	0

W: Shore (7-4)
L: Ayers (1-6)

Ernie Shore's Perfect Game:

Top of First Inning,First Batter.
Babe Ruth walked Ray Morgan on four pitches and was ejected. Shore relieved, Morgan was caught trying to steal, and Shore retired the next 26 batters.
The game was arguably classified as a perfect game until 1991, when the MLB Committee on Statistical Accuracy indicated that it was a no-hitter but not a perfect game.

CHAPTER 3

"150 POUNDS OF SHEER GUTS"

August 5, 1932
Washington Senators at Detroit Tigers
Tommy Bridges

For most baseball players, the talent squeeze arrives early. Even those select few who are the best players in Little League rarely star in high school. The high school stars have to advance to the minors or to college, which further narrows the group. And the lucky few who star at those levels still face an arduous path into and through the farm system to even reach the major leagues. Tommy Bridges, on the other hand, had a relatively easy path to baseball success, but suffered his ultimate heartbreak off of the diamond.

Tommy Bridges during a happy moment, of which there were many during his playing days, but unfortunately fewer thereafter PHOTO PROVIDED BY THE DETROIT TIGERS

Armed with an unimposing physique but an incredible competitive will (and a superb curveball), Bridges made himself a very good, sometimes great baseball player. Pitcher of a near-perfect game, World Series hero, winner of 194 big-league games—that was Tommy Bridges. He was the man of whom Hall of Famer Mickey Cochrane, then his manager, said, "[J]ust look at him and feel proud you were ever on the same team with him. I can say it only one way, he's 150 pounds of sheer guts!"

But there was another side of Tommy Bridges. Elden Auker, a former teammate, wrote of an encounter in Bridges's later years, "I'll never forget the knock on our front door in Birmingham, Mich., early one evening. . . . I turned the porch light on, but still barely recognized the disheveled man standing in front of me: rumpled clothes, dirty white shirt, badly in need of a shave, hair pointing in every direction, smelled like a damn brewery. Looked like hell. Looked like a tramp. I stared at Tommy Bridges and the face of shame stared back."

Auker went on to say, "Every time I see one of those T-shirts you see nowadays, the ones that say, 'Baseball is Life,' I think of Tommy Bridges. Baseball was everything to him. I guess once he could smell the end of his playing career on the horizon, the scent of liquor was the only thing that could kill that frightening odor."

That was also Tommy Bridges. His hardest days were not those spent rising to the top, coping with an almost-perfect game. Those experiences didn't break his heart. That fate was reserved for the days when baseball finished with Tommy Bridges. Bridges's granddaughter, Vicki Lowe, told a reporter, "It's kind of sad, because I don't think he ever got it together."

His great-grandson, Duane Lowe, commented, "I kind of like to think of him being remembered as a person of the way he was when he played."

Gutty curveball ace? Alcoholic struggling to function? Both were Tommy Bridges. If only all of his life had gone as smoothly as it did on one afternoon when he set down 26 batters in a row.

Three days after Christmas of 1906, Thomas Jefferson Davis Bridges was born in New Middleton, Tennessee, about 50 miles east of Nashville. Bridges's father and grandfather were each country doctors, but Tommy's passion was always baseball. He later recalled "throwing baseballs ever since I can remember, ever since I could walk."

His father fed the passion by moving the family into the nearby town of Gordonsville when Bridges was 14. Bridges then played his high school years for Gordonsville High. One account has him telling

Gordonsville High baseball coach Jim Moore, "I would rather pitch than play any other position but will play any place I am needed." Coach Moore had the sense to realize that he had a pitcher on his hands.

Bridges matriculated to the University of Tennessee, where he pitched from 1927 to 1929. While there are no statistics from Bridges's collegiate career, he was sufficiently well remembered that he was named to UT's All-Century team in 2009. Accounts differ on whether he completed a business degree in Knoxville, but for Bridges, the path to further baseball success was wide open.

After a year and a half in the minor leagues, Bridges was summoned to Detroit by the Tigers. His first major-league appearance, on August 13, 1930, came against the fabled Yankees. Before bringing the rookie into the game, manager Bucky Harris is alleged to have asked Bridges if he was ready to face Ruth, Gehrig, and Lazzeri. If the story can be believed, Bridges answered, "I'll be ready."

At 5'10" and a listed playing weight of 155 pounds that may or may not have been inflated, Bridges did not exactly intimidate the Yankee dynasty on first sight. But he retired Ruth on a popup, gave up a single to Lazzeri, fanned Gehrig, and then set down another Yankee to end his first major-league inning. Bridges made eight total appearances in 1930, posting a 3-2 record and a 4.06 ERA.

In his early days as a pitcher, Bridges was remarkable not for the hard-breaking curveball that would become his calling card, but rather for a jumping fastball. In May 1931, Detroit sportswriter H. G. Salsinger wrote, "Tommy Bridges should become one of the best right-handers in the American League. None of the younger pitchers gives more promise. He has a curve ball that is fair, a change of pace that is not deceptive and one of the best fast balls in the major leagues." Salsinger's praise aside, Bridges was 8-16 in 1931, with a 4.99 ERA. The problem, as Salsinger went on to write, was control. Bridges walked 108 batters in 173 innings in 1931. The sportswriter opined, "If Bridges tried to put the ball over and paid no heed to working the corners he probably would have better success than he does now." Salsinger would soon be proven very accurate in that prediction.

Part of the control issue was caused by Bridges's extraordinary curveball. It rapidly became the pitch for which Tommy became famous, if not infamous. Major-league umpire Bill Summers recalled, "Tommy had an overhand curve that dropped off the table. It could be caught in the dirt and yet be a strike." Such a pitch presented an obvious challenge to control. Detroit manager Harris at one point advised Bridges to avoid throwing the curveball until he was ahead in the count. This advice would become pivotal in Bridges's development. While he never stopped walking hitters, he did learn to avoid games like his first major-league start in 1930, when he won 7–5 despite walking 12 hitters.

By August 5, 1932, Bridges had posted a 7-7 mark and lowered his ERA to a respectable 3.46. However, he had been hit hard in his last start by the Yankees, surrendering five runs in just four innings and taking the loss. As he prepared to face the Washington Senators, baseball history awaited.

The 1930s are generally remembered as one of baseball's golden eras. Led by Babe Ruth and the Yankee dynasty, big-scoring offense had become a staple of the game. Unfortunately, inflated scores and the Yankee dynasty cast a false shadow over a fairly difficult era for baseball.

The country still lay under the shadow of the Great Depression, and especially in markets with bad teams, ticket sales were down. Over 75 home games in 1932, the St. Louis Browns drew fewer than 113,000 fans to Sportsman's Park, and the Red Sox posted fewer than 200,000 in home attendance. Radio—some particularly vociferous owners believed—was the latest great threat to baseball, and would kill the game if its growth was not carefully regulated. Also, competitive balance—particularly in the American League—was almost nonexistent. The Yankees won 5 of the 10 AL pennants of the 1930s, and finished in first or second place during the last nine seasons of the decade. The Browns, on the other hand, never surpassed fifth in the eight-team league in the entire decade.

While the Detroit Tigers were not at the low level of the Browns, the team had spent much of its recent history as of 1932 in the bottom of the American League. From 1907 to 1909, led by Ty Cobb, the Tigers had won three straight AL pennants, but lost the World Series each year. They had not returned to the Series since. Cobb retired in 1926, and the team was in the midst of a youth movement in August 1932. At age 29, future Hall of Fame second baseman Charlie Gehringer was the second-oldest starting position player. Gehringer, who hit .298 with 19 homers and 104 RBI in 1932, was the team's biggest attraction. Outfielder John Stone, who was traded after the 1933 season for Hall of Famer Goose Goslin, led the Tigers with 109 RBI in 1932. The pitching staff was still thin in 1932, with Bridges as the fourth starter in a rotation anchored by the forgettable Earl Whitehill (16-12, 4.54 ERA in 1932).

Still, the Tigers were 52-47 on August 5th. And while this placed the team comfortably behind the Yankees, it did mean that the first winning season and upper-half league finish since 1927 was still in play. The Tigers were in the midst of a four-game homestand at Navin Field (to be rechristened six years later as Briggs Stadium) against the Washington Senators, having split the first two games of the series.

The Senators were in fourth place in the American League, entering play with a 58-46 mark. Washington had won the 1924 World Series and 1925 American League pennant. The team had initially struggled after the retirement of ace pitcher Walter Johnson in 1927, but Johnson was now the Washington manager, and the squad had finished second in 1930 and third in 1931. The team was led by outfielder Heinie Manush, who hit .342 and knocked in 116 runs in 1932. Future Hall of Fame shortstop Joe Cronin, then 25, hit .318 and tied Manush for the team lead in RBIs. Forty-two-year-old veteran outfielder Sam Rice, who was bound for the Hall of Fame, hit .323 in part-time duty. While Washington hit just 61 home runs, barely outdistancing just the total of Babe Ruth, the team batted .284, and was fourth in the league in runs scored. Starting pitchers General Crowder and Monte Weaver each won over 20 games, with Crowder totaling 26 victories in 1932. The Senators would send Lloyd Brown to the mound to start on August 5th. Brown was nearing the end of his third consecutive season with at least 15 victories, and was very much a journeyman pitcher. Detroit countered with Tommy Bridges.

Perhaps nothing emphasizes the lack of interest in middle-of-the-pack August 1932 baseball like the fact that Tommy Bridges's near-perfect game is the worst-documented effort of its kind on record. Navin Field seated 30,000 fans, but the listed attendance for the Friday afternoon game was a mere 8,000. The abundance of newspapers only filing reports from the Associated Press's story indicates that the press box at Navin Field was probably about as empty as the stands.

Even without fan interest or media attention, Bridges was outstanding from the first pitch. His trademark control problems were not in evidence on this day, as not only did Bridges avoid walking any batters, but he went to a three-ball count only twice in the entire game. The accounts of the game are also clear that Bridges did not make life difficult for his defense. There were only one or two plays that apparently rose above the routine, and Washington hit the ball out of the infield on only approximately half a dozen occasions.

For three innings, Lloyd Brown matched Bridges, and with the game one-third complete, neither the Senators nor the Tigers had managed even a base hit. But while Bridges dispatched the Senators in the visiting side of the fourth inning, Detroit broke through off of Brown. Harry Davis, Charlie Gehringer, John Stone, and Earl Webb managed consecutive singles to lead off the home half of the fourth inning. Davis's run would prove to be all the help that Bridges needed, but Detroit knocked Brown out of the game, totaling seven runs off the beleaguered Washington starter and his reliever, Bobby Burke.

Staked to a 7–0 lead after four innings, the question was no longer whether Bridges would win, but whether he could make history. His stuff was sharp, with one contemporary account noting, "His curve was breaking so well and his fast one hopped across the plate in such tantalizing fashion that no more than three balls were hit solidly by the Senators." Bridges struck out seven Senators on the day, including fanning Joe Cronin twice. For perspective's sake, Cronin struck out only 45 times in 629 plate appearances in 1932.

As Detroit continued to tack on further runs, finishing the game with 13, Bridges methodically mowed down the Washington lineup. He soon reached the ninth inning, and Washington third baseman Ossie Bluege led off. A .258 hitter, Bluege was easily retired by Bridges. With two outs between Bridges and history, reserve catcher Howard Maple came to bat. Maple had only four major-league hits to his credit, and would manage only six more in his brief career. He could not break up the perfect game, as Bridges struck him out. With two out in the Washington ninth inning and a 13–0 deficit, Senators manager Walter Johnson was faced with a decision.

Few would have batted an eye had Johnson allowed pitcher Bobby Burke to bat. With a 13–0 deficit in a relatively meaningless late-season game, Johnson could have implicitly handed Bridges the perfect game. Not that it would have been that easy—Burke was a career .194 hitter, and he hit .200 with a pair of doubles in 1932. But Johnson instead vetoed the passive gift, and called for pinch-hitter Dave Harris, referenced by one writer as a "pinch-hitter extraordinary."

Harris was in the back end of a seven-year big-league career, a month past his 32nd birthday. He never eclipsed the 325 at-bats he compiled as a rookie for the Boston Braves in 1925, but Harris hit .281 for his career. He had gone 2-for-5 the previous day, and was hitting a career best .346 for the 1932 season.

Only Harris stood between Bridges and immortality. Throughout the game, Bridges had featured his fastball heavily in order to get ahead in the count. Harris was noted as a fastball hitter, but Bridges stuck with the heater.

Harris lined the first pitch into left-center field . . . between short-stop Heinie Schuble and left fielder Gerald Walker, about a dozen feet in front of Walker.

It was a clean base hit, and an end to the perfect game.

One account of the game noted that the crowd of 8,000 "sat in tense silence, wondering at Johnson's action when his team had no chance to win." Harris was referenced in another article as "probably the most unpopular man in Detroit." Tigers fans scarcely felt better after Bridges induced Sam Rice to ground out to first baseman Harry Davis to end his 13–0 one-hitter. The game was then over, but the postgame dialogue was just beginning.

The majority of the postgame discussion centered not around Bridges's tough luck, but rather around whether Walter Johnson had breached baseball etiquette in sending up a pinch-hitter, particularly given the score. In large part, history has concurred with Johnson, as several of the players credited with breaking up near-perfect games were also pinch-hitters, with a couple delivering the blows at the end of lopsided losses. But in the unwritten rules of the time, it was perhaps the equivalent of a modern bunt to break up a perfecto.

The Sporting News pointedly asked, "Was It Sportsmanship?" The article notes, "There was much criticism, even among the Washington players, of Harris and Johnson for calling for a pinch-hitter with his team 13 runs in the rear. It was felt that with Bridges on the verge of baseball immortality, nothing should have been done to wreck his chance; that Johnson should have let Burke bat for himself or that Harris, having been chosen, should have waved wildly at three strikes and passed on to the clubhouse."

The entire controversy seems ridiculous, now. Hitters try to hit, managers try to win. But lest *TSN* be accused of embellishment, the controversy was very real. Senator Joe Judge later said of Harris's hit, "I could have murdered him when he hit that ball." Tiger Earl Webb concurred, stating, "It's no use taking a record like that away from a guy just for a base hit." For his part, Harris expressed genuine regret, saying, "I tried hard to hit all right because that is what I was being paid to do. . . . But I was sure as hell wishing I'd hit that ball right at somebody." And even the great Walter Johnson, while he did not exactly apologize, did go to the Tigers locker room to seek out Bridges and compliment him on his great game.

For his part, Bridges denied any resentment. "I would have done the same thing if I were in Johnson's place," he said. "It was the thing to do. Besides, any pitcher would prefer a bona-fide one-hitter to a gift no-hitter." The good sportsmanship of all parties set the standard moving forward for how to handle a near-perfect miss. Bridges's words show the confidence of a young star, on his way up. There would be another game, another chance. And indeed there would, until suddenly the day arrived when there wouldn't.

Bridges *was* on his way up. He posted a 14-12 mark for the 1932 season and duplicated it in 1933. Twice in '33, he again just missed history. In April, he had a no-hitter going for seven and two-thirds innings, before the Browns broke it up. And in May, he was perfect again against the Senators for seven and one-third innings, before Joe Kuhel homered for Washington's only hit of the game.

But while Bridges failed to claim a no-hitter or perfect game, he rarely failed elsewhere. From 1934 to 1936, he won 22, 21, and 23 games, respectively. He was widely regarded as throwing one of the best curveballs ever seen in baseball. He earned spots in the second, third, fourth, fifth, seventh, and eighth ever MLB All-Star Games. The Tigers peaked just as Bridges did, and won back-to-back American League pennants in 1934 and 1935. They lost the '34 Series, despite solid pitching from Bridges, but in 1935, he was the winning pitcher in the sixth game, which ended the Series. Called in for relief in a 3–3 tie, he surrendered a leadoff triple, but he induced the Cubs to strike out, tap back to the mound, and fly out harmlessly to left field. When Goose Goslin singled in the winning run (player-manager Mickey Cochrane) in the bottom of the inning, Bridges was in the tunnel to the locker room, smoking a cigarette. He told Mickey Cochrane, "I heard the roar of the crowd when you got a hit and I decided to stay put for the rest of the inning just for luck." In 1935, luck was certainly with Tommy Bridges.

While Bridges never returned to the form of 1934–1936, he remained a solid pitcher into the 1940s. He was used less and less (pitching generally once a week), but he continued to be effective. For instance, he was 12-7 with a 2.39 ERA in 1943—but he pitched only 191 innings, far short of his prime years, when he worked 275, 274, and 294 innings. After that 1943 season—weeks before his 37th birthday—Bridges was inducted into the US Army. He did not see any combat action, but spent the majority of the war at Camp Crowder in Missouri playing baseball. While this seems in hindsight to have been a lucky break, others believe that Bridges's downfall began here. His granddaughter, Vicki Lowe, says that Bridges wanted to fight in the war, but because of his age was not allowed, and that his depression began soon thereafter.

After his discharge in August 1945, Bridges won just two more major-league games, and pitched only briefly in Detroit's 1945 World Series victory. He continued to pitch in AAA until 1950, when he was 43 years old. He had excellent minor-league seasons in 1947 and 1948, and Yankee catcher Charlie Silvera maintains that Bridges was given the option to return to the big leagues with the New York Yankees, but that he declined. In 1947, Bridges finally completed a no-hitter, albeit a minor-league no-hitter, at AAA Portland. Bridges won 33 more minor-league games, and finished his big-league career with a 194-138 record.

The Detroit Tigers, who won four AL pennants during Bridges's run with the team, slumped after his career, spending most of the 1950s in the league basement, and not returning to a World Series until 1968. By then, Navin Field had become Briggs Stadium and then Tigers Stadium, and Detroit played in the same location through 1999. The stadium was demolished in 2009, but loyal Tigers fans are leading an effort to keep up the area and hope to convert it into a youth baseball facility.

As for the Senators, they returned to the World Series in 1933, but promptly fell into the basement of baseball for the rest of the franchise's existence. Washington had already cut Walter Johnson loose after the 1932 season. "The Big Train" moved on to Cleveland, where he managed through 1935. The following year, he was among the five initial inductees to the Baseball Hall of Fame. Johnson passed away in the nation's capital in 1946.

Dave Harris's final big-league season was 1934 in Washington. Harris became a policeman after baseball, and died in Atlanta in 1973.

⌇

Life after baseball seems to have been as spectacularly unsuccessful for Tommy Bridges as his life in baseball was successful. He had married his college sweetheart, Carolyn Jellicorse, in 1930 in Nashville. They had a daughter, Evelyn, who was born in 1935. But by 1948, Bridges had become involved not only with alcohol, but with another woman. He and Carolyn divorced, and Bridges married Iona Kidwell and moved to Detroit. While Bridges was noted to have worked as a tire salesman and served as a coach/scout for Cincinnati, Detroit, and eventually the New York Mets, there is reason to question how regular any of these vocations proved to be.

Aside from Elden Auker's comments noted at the beginning of this chapter, others recalled the changes in Bridges. Former Tiger teammate Billy Rogell remembered, "One day, as I was crossing Michigan Avenue, I noticed this guy lying by this [sporting goods] store. I drove about two stores down and I thought, 'Goddamn, that looked like Bridges.' So I backed the car up and got out and sure enough, it's Tommy Bridges. Jesus Christ, he looked horrible." Rogell got Bridges cleaned up and for his trouble, Bridges told him of marrying a waitress he had met, with her husband now hunting down Bridges with apparent malice intended. Rogell got Bridges a job selling beer, but recalled, "He never showed up. He went way down. It was terrible to see that."

Auker shared further similar stories. He loaned Bridges $125 to clean up and try to get a job, only to find Bridges passed out drunk on his front lawn the next morning, with the funds washed away in a torrent of alcohol. His family attributes his erratic behavior to depression, and that seems a reasonable diagnosis.

Bridges spent little time with Evelyn after his divorce. His granddaughter, Vicki Lowe, has few memories of him. She recalled him coming to visit when she was in the fifth grade. Her memory is of running in the backyard, and Bridges seeing her and telling her, "I remember your mama used to run fast just like you." Lowe recalled seeing him again a few years later.

By that time, which was late 1967 or early 1968, Bridges had received bad news—he was dying of liver cancer. Diagnosed in Florida, Bridges and his second wife returned to Nashville. He refused treatment, in his granddaughter's words, "just to have time to come home and die and get it over with." He passed away on April 19, 1968.

His great-grandson, Duane Lowe, when questioned about Bridges's legacy, stated, "It seems that a lot of people thought a lot of him, of [his] high character and integrity. He played the game the way it's supposed to be played—all out—and might even have been a little bit of an over-achiever to be as small as he was and to be able to, at times it seemed like, dominate a ball game."

Never was Bridges's brilliance on the diamond more evident than on August 5, 1932, the day that he was almost perfect, that one of the best pitchers in the history of the game came to the opposing locker room to congratulate him. Bridges is, perhaps, best defined by what happened on the field—the great game he pitched, the fact that he expected no quarter from his opponents, and did not flinch when his perfect game had the *almost* tag appended to it. But life, as Elden Auker noted, is not baseball, and if Tommy Bridges used up so many of the best parts of himself on the diamond, it is a sad reality that he could not have saved more for the years after the cheers died, when baseball was just a memory.

August 5, 1932
Navin Field, Detroit, MI

	1	2	3	4	5	6	7	8	9	R	H	E
WAS	0	0	0	0	0	0	0	0	0	0	1	1
DET	0	1	0	7	0	1	1	4	X	13	15	0

W: Bridges (8-7)
L: Brown (13-8)

The End of Bridges's Perfect Game:

Top of Ninth Inning, Two Outs.
First pitch to pinch-hitter Dave Harris.
Harris singled to left-center field.

CHAPTER 4

BILLY THE KID . . . "WHAT MORE DO YOU WANT?"

June 27, 1958
Washington Senators at Chicago White Sox
Billy Pierce

He was an unimposing old man who lived in a place called Evergreen Park. Nicknamed "Billy the Kid" decades before, he was relatively short and slight, even in his youth. His voice tended a bit toward higher pitch, but was warm and intelligent. In his later years, he had taken to wearing large eyeglasses. He looked like anybody else, and always had.

Early in his baseball career, he was so nondescript that he waited on a teammate as a clerk in his father's pharmacy without the teammate even recognizing him. If he looked like anyone else, he pitched like few others. Billy Pierce was signed by his hometown team and traded to another city and team, where he made his home for decades. There, he pitched his way to starting three consecutive All-Star Games, playing in a World Series, and becoming a local legend. He was traded again, pitched in another World Series, but never moved away from his previously adopted hometown of Chicago.

Billy Pierce, warming up during spring training. Pierce's sunny optimism allowed him to see past just missing a perfect game. His fans still hope for a posthumous Hall of Fame induction.
NATIONAL BASEBALL HALL OF FAME

The unassuming little left-handed pitcher won 211 major-league games, played in seven total All-Star Games, and on one day in 1958, he was almost perfect. It was quite a career. However, for those who loved Billy the Kid, particularly in his adopted hometown of Chicago, it all wasn't quite enough. Not that Pierce minded.

In 2014, the year before he passed away, he commented, "I've experienced a lot of good things in my life. I've got a wonderful wife, great kids and grandkids, and I've been honored by the White Sox and their fans. What more do you want?"

For those who remembered him best, they wanted to see Billy the Kid inducted into the Baseball Hall of Fame.

The pitching career of Billy Pierce had a beginning nearly as inauspicious as the man himself. Growing up in Highland Park, Michigan, a suburb of Detroit, Pierce planned to be a doctor, not a baseball player. His love of baseball actually sprang from a medical cause.

Pierce later told an interviewer, "When I was 10, I refused to have my tonsils removed. My folks offered me a major league baseball, and a good glove, if I'd have the operation. I took the bribe. It really was a thrill to throw around that 'league' ball, and I've been throwing ever since." Pierce began as a first baseman, but recalled that his earliest baseball hero was Tigers pitcher Tommy Bridges, who had a similar physical build to Pierce.

With the attrition of baseball stars who served in World War II, things changed in a hurry for Pierce. At the ripe age of 17, the Tigers signed Pierce, who decided to put his medical school plans on hold "for two or three years." After a few unimpressive months with the Tigers' Buffalo affiliate, Pierce reached the major leagues not quite two months after his 18th birthday. He barely played, making only five appearances and pitching a total of 10 innings with no decisions. Still, Pierce was a major leaguer—and as an added bonus, his aforementioned boyhood hero Tommy Bridges was finishing up his last big-league days on the same team that year of 1945. Bridges pitched 11 innings in four games, so presumably the two men had plenty of idle hours to get acquainted.

That Tigers squad won the 1945 World Series. Pierce did not appear in the Series. Still, as a teenager, he was already a big leaguer with a World Series title. He was demoted to the minors in 1946 with more of the Tigers regulars back and ready to play. Pierce suffered a back injury that caused him to miss most of the season, and then spent the 1947 season in the minors. He fared well enough that he spent all of 1948 with the Tigers, but he pitched only 55 innings over the course of the season. Pierce was stuck on the bench for the pitching-rich Tigers. His career was at a crossroads. Then, help arrived.

On November 10, 1948, Pierce was dealt, along with $10,000, to the Chicago White Sox for outfielder Aaron Robinson. Robinson was a left-handed-hitting catcher, who had three seasons and fewer than 800 big-league at-bats left in his career. Pierce, on the other hand, was just getting started—not that his initial outlook on his new team was terribly favorable.

Pierce was at his fiancée Gloria's house listening to the radio when he learned of the trade. "[I]t was a jolt," he later recalled. More candidly, he told another interviewer, "I was disappointed when I came over here [to Chicago]. . . . I had been around the league in '48, and I'd say the two teams I didn't want to go to the most were Philadelphia and Chicago, because both ballparks at that time were kind of dismal grey. Not too many people were going out there. In '48, Chicago lost [101] games. And there were stockyards here at that time, and with night games, there was quite an aroma."

In time, Pierce would come to regard the smell of Chicago as that of sweet success. Once he got past his initial despondency over the trade, he realized, as he later noted, "Coming over here, to a team that didn't have much, gave me a tremendous opportunity to pitch."

Pierce seized the opportunity and immediately saw a huge increase in his pitching workload. In 1949 and 1950, Pierce won 7 and then 12 games. His pitching was generally better than his record, as his ERA was under 4.00 each season. Pierce was noted for having a great fastball, one supposedly complimented by Joe DiMaggio early in the career of Billy the Kid. What he lacked was control—he walked 112 batters in 1949 and 137 in 1950.

In 1951, Pierce's fortunes improved when Paul Richards—the former catcher who had once overlooked the druggist's clerk who happened to be Pierce—became the manager of the White Sox. Richards subsequently noted, "I worked a little with him on his windup to help his delivery and convinced him that he had to throw a slider and an occasional change of pace, and that was all he needed."

Richards's modesty perhaps denies him the credit he deserves. According to Pierce, Richards taught him the slider. It took Pierce about two seasons to learn to throw the pitch well, but he later stated, "Developing the slider helped me tremendously because it gave me a third 'out' pitch. I threw it almost as hard as my fastball, but I could throw it for strikes better than the fastball or the good curve."

Pierce won 15 games in 1951 and 1952. In 1953, his pitching really took off. He was 18-12 that season, led the league in strikeouts, and started the All-Star Game for the American League. After a disappointing 9-10 season in 1954, Pierce led the American League in ERA (1.97) in 1955, and won 20 games in 1956 and 1957. He started the All-Star Game three times in four years for the American League.

The improvement in Pierce's career wasn't just his doing. As a team, the White Sox slowly rose from last place to sixth to the middle of the division. In 1957, they finished second to the Yankees, and the following season, they had high expectations. The ChiSox were based around pitching, speed, and defense. In the field, the stars were future Hall of Famers Nellie Fox at second base and Luis Aparicio at shortstop. The duo were superb defensively, but combined for only two homers in 1958. Catcher Sherm Lollar ended the season with 20 home runs and 84 RBI, each figure leading the team by a healthy margin.

Dick Donovan and veteran Early Wynn joined Pierce in the pitching rotation. The team was managed by Al Lopez, who had won a pennant with the Cleveland Indians in 1954. The Yankees were the class of baseball in the late 50s, but Chicago's pesky style made them a likely challenger to the pinstriped dynasty.

~

The game of baseball was much different in 1958 than it had been 26 years before when a pitcher had last flirted unsuccessfully with perfection. In 1932, radio coverage of baseball was common only in certain markets. By 1958, it was not only accepted, but it was perhaps the most ordinary way to follow the game. Only 11,300 would journey out to Comiskey Park on June 27, 1958, but many thousands more tuned into Bob Elson, the voice of the White Sox, on WCFL. Television was the newfangled means of covering baseball, but was reserved for All-Star Games, World Series, and other such special occasions.

Furthermore, the major leagues looked much different in 1958 than it had in 1932. Between 1903 and 1953, no major-league squad relocated. The locations of the teams seemed set in stone. But within a five-year window leading up to Pierce's flawed masterpiece, the Boston Braves had moved to Milwaukee, the St. Louis Browns had become the Baltimore Orioles, the Philadelphia Athletics had journeyed westward to a new home in Kansas City, and most recent and shocking of all, the Brooklyn Dodgers and New York Giants had become the Los Angeles Dodgers and the San Francisco Giants before the 1958 season.

Between 1932 and 1958, baseball had also integrated racially. From the late 19th century until 1947, an unwritten agreement had kept all but the lightest skinned players off of major-league fields. Jackie Robinson broke the color barrier in 1947, and a decade later, most (but amazingly, not all) teams had integrated. Integration opened the door of baseball to many more players than simply those who were African-American, and that diversity would change the game forever.

Finally, baseball was no longer solely a pastime of the daytime hours. Beginning in 1939, when President Roosevelt flipped on the lights at Crosley Field via connection at the White House, the national pastime was increasingly played in the evening hours. In the buoyant Eisenhower economy, workers could attend far more games in the evening than in the day, and so it was that night baseball became a fixture everywhere except Chicago's Wrigley Field, where the Cubs stuck to day games for another three decades.

But for all of the changes in baseball, it was still essentially the same game on June 27, 1958. More people listened on radio than in the ballpark, the players were no longer all white, and the game began in a comfortable summer evening instead of a blazing afternoon. When the ballgame started, however, pitcher and batter faced off in their unvaried war, and Billy Pierce faced down history.

On June 27, 1958, the White Sox were a disappointing 30-34 and were in fifth place in the eight-team American League. Like the Sox, Pierce had started the season slowly, and on May 21st was 1-4 with a 5.17 ERA. That said, Billy the Kid had rounded into form and had pitched shutouts in his last two starts over the Red Sox and the Orioles. He was 6-5 with a 3.21 ERA on the season and looked well on his way back to the All-Star Game.

The White Sox were opening a series hosting the Washington Senators. Washington had finished last in 1957 and was on pace to do so again in 1958. Manager Cookie Lavagetto was best known for breaking up Bill Bevens's no-hit bid as a player back in the 1947 World Series. Suffice it to say that Cookie did little as a manager to eclipse that career highlight. The Senators were a bad team and were not well supported. Their season home attendance of 475,288 was last in the league. The White Sox, who were sixth in the eight-team league in attendance, nearly doubled that mark.

Washington's star was outfielder Roy Sievers, who posted a .295 batting average, 39 home runs, and 108 RBI in 1958. Without Sievers, Washington might have finished in the International League. The most notable player on the team was bonus baby third baseman Harmon

Killebrew. Handicapped by the bonus rules* of the time of his signing, Killebrew was in the fifth of five seasons marinating on the Washington bench. Instead of learning the game in the minor leagues, Killebrew batted 31 times in 1958, which marked a total of 254 big-league at-bats over five seasons. In 1959, he would blast 42 home runs, but the season before, he remained an afterthought.

Washington's pitching staff was perhaps even more nondescript than their hitters. Twenty-four-year-old Camilo Pascual showed promise, but much of the staff was made of has-beens or never-would-bes. Twenty-seven-year-old lefty Russ Kemmerer would face Pierce in the first game of the series on June 27th. Kemmerer won 43 major-league games over nine seasons, and was in the middle of his career at the time. He was 4-5 with a 4.04 ERA for the season.

The game in question was a midseason night game between two teams in the bottom half of their league, played in a two-thirds-empty stadium. But as is always the case with baseball, there is no indication of when the commonplace can become exceptional, or perhaps even perfect.

On June 27th, Pierce was efficient from the outset. Leadoff batter Albie Pearson grounded out to first baseman Ray Boone. Rocky Bridges flied to right, and the dangerous Roy Sievers grounded out to third baseman Billy Goodman. After a scoreless home half of the frame, Pierce began the second inning by striking out cleanup hitter Jim Lemon. Eddie Yost then popped up to shortstop Aparicio, and Norm Zauchin grounded out to Luis.

Chicago did not score in the bottom of the second, and so in the Washington half of the third inning, Pierce completed his first jaunt

---

* The bonus rules were instituted in 1947, and required that players signed to a bonus of greater than $4,000 had to spend two full seasons on the major-league roster, or they were exposed on the MLB waiver wire. While the specifics of the rule changed, and it was twice rescinded and then readopted, some version thereof came and went until 1965, when the MLB Draft began.

through the Senator batting order. Ken Aspromonte flied out to Jim Rivera in left field, catcher Steve Korcheck grounded to third, and Russ Kemmerer looked at a third strike to end the inning.

Not content merely to pitch perfect baseball, Pierce led off the third inning by going the opposite way and lining a double to left field. When the next batter, Jim Landis, singled to Sievers in left, Pierce took off, and scored from second. That run would prove to be all of the insurance Pierce needed. One oft-repeated anecdote from the late 50s White Sox involved second baseman Nellie Fox approaching Pierce after the team scored a run for him and stating, "Here's your run, better hold it!" Indeed, on the day he was almost perfect, Pierce had to lean on a single run for eight innings.

The fourth inning was nearly the undoing of Pierce's pitching gem. After Pearson worked a full count before he flied to right, Rocky Bridges lined a pitch down the first base line that landed just barely in foul territory. Bridges then hit a solid groundball up the middle, on which Aparicio, turning in what one contemporary account noted to be "spectacular defense," hurried to his left, fielded the ball, and gunned out Bridges at first base. Roy Sievers then grounded out to second baseman Fox, and four perfect innings were complete.

In the fifth, Jim Lemon led off by flying out to Landis in center field. From that point on, Pierce turned up his intensity another notch. Over the rest of the game, only twice would Washington batters hit the ball out of the infield. But even a harmless grounder was a fate better than that which befell Eddie Yost and Norm Zauchin, as each struck out to end the Washington fifth.

As Pierce completed his second trip through the Washington lineup, Ken Aspromonte led off the sixth inning with a hard-hit grounder toward the left field hole, but third baseman Billy Goodman fielded it cleanly and threw him out. Steve Korcheck helplessly watched a third strike, and Russ Kemmerer harmlessly tapped back to Pierce. Two-thirds of a perfect game was complete.

In their third look at Pierce, the top of the Senator lineup fared no better than before. Albie Pearson grounded out to Ray Boone, who handled the play himself. Rocky Bridges whiffed and Roy Sievers grounded to Goodman at third. His throw threatened to pull Ray Boone off the first base bag, but with a wide stretch, Boone completed the play.

Still working with a 1–0 lead, Pierce cruised into the eighth inning. His control wavered briefly, as he went to a 3-1 count before Jim Lemon flied out to right. Eddie Yost grounded out to Goodman at third, and Norm Zauchin watched a third strike sail past him. Pierce was three outs from baseball perfection.

In the bottom of the frame, a typical White Sox rally broke out. Jim Landis singled, for his third hit of the game. He was bunted over on a sacrifice from Nellie Fox. After a walk and a double steal, Sherm Lollar singled in the two runners, enhancing Pierce's advantage to 3–0.

The game then moved to the ninth inning. Ken Aspromonte was the first batter between Pierce and history, and as he had in the sixth inning, he made good contact, but the assembled fans "were given further reason why Luis Aparicio was voted the league's All-Star shortstop" as he sped to his left, fielded the ball, and threw out the runner. One out, two to go.

Steve Korcheck, who hit .159 in 145 major-league at-bats, would never bat in such a tight situation again. He missed a third strike, and left the elated Chicago fan base waiting for one more out.

While Kemmerer had pitched a fine game, Cookie Lavagetto did not intend to waste his final out on a pitcher who was 6-for-71 at the plate entering the 1958 season. He called for pinch-hitter Ed Fitz Gerald. Fitz Gerald was a 34-year-old backup catcher. He had caught a no-hitter with Pittsburgh in 1951, and in the latter days of his career was a crafty veteran who was used to pinch-hitting. He had started only three games in the season, but was hitting .313 when Lavagetto called for him to hit. Unlike onlookers' opinions surrounding Tommy Bridges's near-miss a quarter century before, no one expected anything from Lavagetto except his best pinch-hitter—which he dutifully delivered.

Pierce later recalled, "The book on Fitz Gerald was that he was a fastball hitter on the first ball and liked it inside where he could pull it. So I threw him a curve away." The curve, Pierce told reporters after the game, "was a good one that had a sharp break." One account termed it a "knee high curve ball." Fitz Gerald waited on the ball and took a late cut, going with the pitch, and poking it down the right field line, beyond the reach of first baseman Boone. It landed fair by about a foot, and Fitz Gerald hustled to second with a double.

Nellie Fox approached the mound as if to commiserate with Pierce, who immediately took the ball and settled back in. He fanned Albie Pearson on three pitches, for his ninth strikeout of the day, and a 3–0 one-hit shutout victory—his third shutout in a row.

Pierce, whose career was eulogized on his retirement as that of a winner and a gentleman, was his typically affable self after the game. "I'll never get any closer than that," he said with a laugh. "It was a good pitch he hit."

He took time to remember his teammates. "Give Luis [Aparicio] plenty of credit," he said. "And Sherm [Lollar] really mixed 'em up beautifully."

Al Lopez was more direct in his assessment. Pierce "couldn't have been any more perfect if he'd struck out the first 26 men," he noted.

Even a quarter century later, Pierce's assessment was essentially unchanged.

"I didn't feel that badly about it—really not that badly," he said. "We were in a little slump and I was just happy to win the ballgame. It didn't mean that much—at the moment. In later years, I wished probably that it had happened. It would've been nice if it had happened.

"But if you're in the game for 17 years like I was, you have a lot of things to look back on. You don't need that one thing. I can live without it."

Indeed, Billy Pierce did produce many other moments to remember in his baseball career. He finished 1958 with a 17-11 mark, as the White Sox rallied to again finish second in the American League. The following season, the "Go Go Sox" broke through and won the American League pennant. Then 32, Pierce battled some injuries and posted a 14-15 mark for the season. Lopez chose not to start him in the World Series, which the White Sox lost in five games—not due to Pierce, who provided four scoreless innings from the Chicago bullpen.

Pierce's innings pitched dropped for each successive season from 1958 onward. After the 1961 season, he was traded (with perfect game hurler Don Larsen) by the White Sox to the San Francisco Giants. Unlike in modern baseball, when players are eternally ready to deliver a carefully crafted sound bite, the first journalists who reached Pierce after the trade found him, for once, positively irritated. "I am not surprised," Pierce said. "But it's a rotten trick and I will make Al Lopez sorry he did it."

In 1962, Pierce summoned up one last great season. He pitched terribly in spring training, but settled in to post a 16-6 mark with a 3.49 ERA. More important than the numbers was how well Pierce pitched down the stretch of the NL pennant race. The Giants finished the season tied with the Dodgers, which under the rules of the time necessitated a best-of-three playoff. With the Giants rotation a complete mess, they turned to Pierce in Game 1. On paper, this looked like a mismatch, as Pierce faced Sandy Koufax of the Dodgers. On the field, it did indeed seem a mismatch. But it was Pierce who got the best of it, throwing a three-hit shutout in an 8–0 route, which gave him a 12-0 mark in San Francisco in that magical season.

The Dodgers took Game 2, but in the decisive Game 3, when San Francisco rallied to take a late 6–4 lead, manager Alvin Dark gave the ball to Pierce on two days' rest to pitch the ninth inning. Three outs later, the Giants were headed to the World Series. Pierce pitched well in the Series against the Yankees, suffering a hard-luck loss in Game 3, but winning Game 6. Pierce called that victory his biggest thrill in baseball. In Game 7, he was warming up in the bullpen when Willie McCovey lined out to Bobby Richardson to end the Series.

Unfortunately, that Indian summer of 1962 was Pierce's last great season. He went just 3-11 in 1963 and returned for a final solid campaign in 1964, posting a 3-0 mark and a 2.20 ERA in just 49 innings, mostly out of the bullpen. A few days later, Pierce announced his retirement.

Pierce won 211 major-league games against 169 losses. His 3.27 career ERA reflects perhaps a better body of work than even his won-lost record reflects. His 1,999 career strikeouts suggest a pitcher who played the game on his terms, rather than merely accumulating statistics.

"I've gotten more out of baseball than most men ever get because of the cards sometimes turning up the wrong way for them," Pierce said. "For me, they've invariably been in my favor."

The White Sox remained in Comiskey Park, which as the years passed went from a stinky junkyard on the South Side of Chicago to one of baseball's hallowed fields. The park closed in 1991, when a new park, soon renamed U.S. Cellular Field, opened. Pierce's likeness and number 19 are featured on the wall of the new park.

In 2005, the White Sox won a surprising World Series, after Pierce, by then 78 years old, threw out the first pitch at U.S. Cellular Field before Game 1 of the AL Division Series.

The Washington Senators suffered a less kind fate. After being victimized in three of the first four near-perfect misses, the poorly supported Senators were eventually moved west by owner Calvin Griffith. In 1961, the Senators became the Minnesota Twins. The franchise remained profoundly affected by the financial imbalance behind big-money baseball, but unlike the Senators, the Twins have survived and occasionally thrived.

An expansion team became the new Washington Senators in 1961, but it was more of the same. The team posted just one winning season in 11 years, and soon became the Texas Rangers. Not until the Montreal Expos would become the Washington Nationals more than two decades later would Major League Baseball return to the nation's capital.

Unlike Washington baseball, Ed Fitz Gerald has remained strong. At the time of writing, the 92-year-old former catcher still survives. This is, unfortunately, more than most of his contemporaries, including Billy Pierce.

After baseball, Pierce entered into business with an Oldsmobile and Cadillac dealership for a couple of years. He was a stockbroker for a few years, as well as a part-time scout for the White Sox. He spent 23 years as a salesman and public relations agent of the Continental Envelope Company.

Pierce invested a large amount of his free time working with the Chicago Baseball Cancer Charity. He initially became involved with the organization after Nellie Fox passed away of skin cancer in 1975. He was president of the organization for years and was passionate about raising money to research the fight against the disease. Ironically, it was gallbladder cancer that claimed Pierce's life on July 31, 2015, at the age of 88.

Pierce had also been active in supporting Fox for induction into the Baseball Hall of Fame. The little second baseman was long considered a borderline case. Indeed, in 1985, his last season on the Baseball Writers of America ballot, Fox received 295 of the 395 votes for Hall membership. He needed 297. Twelve years later, the Veterans Committee inducted Fox posthumously into Cooperstown. As Rob Neyer notes, "[In 1997], the Nellie Fox Society . . . saw its raison d'être inducted into the Hall of Fame . . . and promptly renamed itself the Billy Pierce Society."

Pierce had drawn scant support from the BBWAA voters during his eligibility on their ballot. But as the number of top-line starting pitchers has grown smaller and smaller, those who make noise about such things have made increasingly more noise in support of "Billy the Kid."

Pierce's statistical profile compares relatively well to contemporaries like Don Drysdale (Pierce has more wins), Jim Bunning (Pierce has a better winning percentage), and Whitey Ford (Pierce bested him in head-to-head matchups)—all three of whom have been inducted into the Hall of Fame. In 2014, Pierce was added to the Hall of Fame's Golden Era Committee Ballot, as one of 10 people whose candidacy would be voted on. In the group's lone vote before his death, Pierce was not voted into the Hall of Fame.

In 2005, an interviewer asked Pierce what being elected into the Hall of Fame would mean to him. Pierce admitted, "It would be a tremendous thrill, the culmination of my life, no question about it. My family and I would appreciate it very much. You have no way of knowing how the people vote, I'm sure all of them have their favorites, so we'll just have to see."

When Pierce passed away, the cry to admit him to the Hall of Fame again intensified. The testimony from those who remembered him was unvaried. Pierce was a great pitcher, as good as any, worthy of Hall of Fame induction. And the praise for Billy Pierce the man was even more pronounced than for Billy Pierce the pitcher.

Now his wife of 64 years and his sons await a hoped-for call from Cooperstown. That call, if it comes, will arrive too late for Billy Pierce to be honored in his lifetime. Sometimes, the heartbreak of baseball is that the right decision is a little too long in coming.

June 27, 1958
Comiskey Park, Chicago, IL

	1	2	3	4	5	6	7	8	9	R	H	E
WAS	0	0	0	0	0	0	0	0	0	0	1	0
CHI	0	0	1	0	0	0	0	2	X	3	8	0

W: Pierce (7-5)
L: Kemmerer (4-6)

The End of Pierce's Perfect Game:

Top of Ninth Inning, Two Outs.
First pitch to pinch-hitter Ed Fitz Gerald.
Fitz Gerald blooped a double to shallow right field.

CHAPTER 5

THE GREATEST PITCHING MASTERPIECE IN BASEBALL HISTORY

May 26, 1959

Pittsburgh Pirates at Milwaukee Braves

Harvey Haddix

There are 13 men who set down 26 consecutive major-league batters during a single game, and then could not retire the 27th. There is one pitcher who not only retired 27 batters in a row, but retired 36 in a row, all in a single game—and still carried on, mowing through a pennant-contending team as if they were Little Leaguers. Box-score perfection eluded him, but his performance has to be considered the greatest pitching masterpiece in baseball history, even though he lost the game. If any pitcher ever earned the moniker "Hard Luck" it was "Hard Luck" Harvey Haddix on May 26, 1959.

Harvey Haddix, captured here in perhaps the greatest pitching performance of all time, his near-perfect loss

NATIONAL BASEBALL HALL OF FAME

In 1959, people still liked Ike, although they were about to fall in love with a Massachusetts senator named John F. Kennedy. In a February plane crash, musicians Buddy Holly, Ritchie Valens, and J. P. "The Big Bopper" Richardson had perished. The Barbie doll was introduced, and Fidel Castro was rising to power in Cuba. And baseball was stronger than ever.

In the aftermath of World War II, the 1947 Brooklyn Dodgers had integrated Major League Baseball. After decades of systematic exclusion of virtually any nonwhite players, the game had been thrown wide open. New stars had quickly joined the Dodgers' Jackie Robinson, and players who would not have been allowed to play in the major leagues before flourished—as did the game itself. Baseball was rewarded twice—once with the essential societal change of integration, but again with stars like Robinson, Don Newcombe, Larry Doby, Satchel Paige, Willie Mays, Ernie Banks, and many others.

⌐

In Milwaukee, one such trailblazer was Henry Aaron. Signed in 1952 by the (then Boston) Braves as a skinny 18-year-old shortstop from the Indianapolis Clowns of the Negro Leagues, Aaron was a significant piece in the Braves renaissance. He was not the Braves' first African-American player; outfielder Sam Jethro had debuted with the team in late 1950. But while Jethro was essentially a part-time player, Aaron became a constant presence in the formidable Braves lineup, and the face of the franchise.

The Braves had moved to Milwaukee in 1953, and doubtlessly hoped that a change of scenery would improve the franchise's fortunes. The team had compiled a nearly four-decade run of futility, appearing in only one World Series (and losing it) since their lone 1914 title. But with Aaron in tow in 1954, things were changing. By that point, Aaron had become an outfielder, and he was a solid player as a rookie, hitting .280 with 13 home runs, sufficient to place him fourth in the National League's Rookie of the Year voting. He improved to .314, 27 homers, and 106 RBI in 1955, as he was selected to the All-Star team for the first of 21 consecutive seasons. Two seasons later, led by Aaron's power hitting and Lew Burdette's timely pitching, the Braves won the 1957 World Series, and they returned to the Fall Classic in 1958, before losing to the Yankees in seven games.

With the Braves threatening to dethrone the New York Yankees as baseball's newest dynasty, Milwaukeeans packed County Stadium, where as the 1959 season dawned, Aaron and fellow slugger Joe Adcock gave Milwaukee a potent lineup, and right-handed Lew Burdette teamed with lefty Warren Spahn to form a legendary pitching tandem. May 26, 1959, found the Braves at 23-14, three full games on top of their nearest competitor in the NL standings as they hosted a series with the Pittsburgh Pirates.

The Steel City franchise was working toward the end of a historic run of mediocrity. The Pirates had been active in the National League since 1887, but had last won a pennant in 1927, when as a reward, they were swept by Babe Ruth's Murderers' Row squad of Yankees. From 1949 to 1957, Pittsburgh failed to finish within 25 games of first place in any season.

However, in 1958, Pittsburgh had begun its own renaissance. With Puerto Rican outfielder Roberto Clemente, who had joined the team in 1955, becoming a fledgling star, Pittsburgh also featured steady second baseman Bill Mazeroski and hometown favorite first baseman Dick Stuart. Vern Law and bullpen ace Elroy Face led the Pirate pitching staff.

Given changes that would have been unimaginable a generation before, on May 26, 1959, as the Braves and Pirates prepared to face off, baseball had come into its own. The game of baseball looked much different than it had before, and with exciting new talent, moribund franchises were returning to life. But all backstories were more or less forgotten that night. One thing had remained the same—regardless of who was playing behind or against a pitcher, perfection was still a story worth following. And on May 26, 1959, a 33-year-old left-handed pitcher named Harvey Haddix reached unequaled heights of perfection.

Harvey Haddix was a country boy from small-town Ohio, and in many ways was a very unlikely candidate for a rendezvous with baseball immortality. Luck seemed to blow both ways in the life of Harvey Haddix. When he was five years old, he was riddled with buckshot in a freak hunting accident. No fewer than five bullet fragments were embedded in his skull. But Haddix survived without any long-term consequences. His youth was happy, if not exceptionally prosperous. He later recalled crafting his first pair of baseball spikes by affixing homemade cleats to his dress shoes.

Haddix signed with the St. Louis Cardinals in 1947 at the age of 22. He was small, not so much for a baseball player as for a human being in general. He was officially listed in his prime at 170 pounds on a 5'9" frame, but photographs indicate that the weight estimate might have been generous. Haddix, between being a lefty and built very slightly, reminded some in the Cardinals organization of St. Louis left-hander Harry Brecheen. Brecheen was known as "The Cat," and accordingly Haddix was forever dubbed "The Kitten."

After a year in the Carolina League, three years with AAA Columbus, and a year in the military, Haddix made his major-league debut in August 1952. He pitched well, going 2-2 with a 2.79 ERA in a 42-inning trial. The following year, he was even better. As a 27-year-old rookie (barely sliding under the innings pitched limit for such status), Haddix won 20 games, pitched six shutouts, was an All-Star, and finished second in the Rookie of the Year balloting, behind the Dodgers' Jim Gilliam.

In 1954, Haddix continued where he had left off. He was 12-4 with a 3.25 ERA when the Cardinals went to Milwaukee for a July 1st game with the Braves. In the fourth inning, with a 6–1 lead, Haddix faced the ever-dangerous Joe Adcock. Adcock lined Haddix's pitch back through the box and off the hurler's knee. Haddix left the game and, many believe, was never quite the same pitcher again. Haddix himself noted years later, "I had no spring to push off and I never, ever threw the same after." Indeed, he was 12-4 with a 3.24 ERA before the injury. For the remainder of the season, pitching through pain, he finished 6-9 with a 3.95 ERA.

Haddix had been named an All-Star again in 1954, and he made that squad one final time in 1955, but he finished the season 12-16 with a 4.46 ERA. He never won more than 13 games in a campaign again. In 1956, the Cardinals traded him to the Phillies, who in turn traded him to the Reds after the 1957 season. After a season in Cincinnati, Haddix was dealt to Pittsburgh in January 1959. He was a middle-of-the-pack starting pitcher, a guy who would eat up innings and pitch .500 baseball, more or less. There was no reason to suspect that this was the man who was about to pitch the best game in the history of baseball.

May 26th found Haddix in good form, holding a 4-2 record and a 2.67 ERA leading into his showdown with the Braves. Milwaukee countered Haddix with Lew Burdette, the 1957 World Series hero and 1958 AL Cy Young Award winner. Burdette had not been sharp early in 1959, as he held a 3.82 ERA going into this game, but he was 7-2, and remained one of the top pitchers in baseball.

Haddix was under the weather, fighting a cold, but still interjected some levity into the pregame meeting by forecasting impossibly pin-point pitch locations for each Milwaukee batter whom he would face. "I figured I'd have some fun," he told a reporter in 1984, "so I got into the high-and-tight and low-and-away stuff. Don Hoak broke up the meeting with, 'If you do that, you'll throw a no-hitter.'"

When the lineups were announced at County Stadium, Milwaukee had its terrifying trio of Eddie Mathews, Hank Aaron, and Joe Adcock batting second, third, and fourth. Aaron was off to an astounding start, hitting .453 coming into the game. Mathews was about to be named to his sixth All-Star team, and Adcock had history on his side with Haddix. Haddix sought to counter the Braves essentially with two pitches. While he did throw a curveball and a changeup, on this night Haddix later recalled that he had mainly deployed a fastball, which was probably coming in at under 90 miles per hour, and a slider. One weapon Pittsburgh lacked in its arsenal was star outfielder Clemente, who was held out of the lineup due to an injured shoulder. Many teammates later wondered if Clemente might have changed the nature of the game had he been in the lineup. Haddix himself gave voice to the same thought years later.

After Lew Burdette promptly dispatched the Clemente-less Pirates in order in the top of the first inning, Haddix began his night with some immediate trouble. On Haddix's first pitch, leadoff batter Johnny O'Brien smacked a hard groundball toward left field, but Pirate short-stop Dick Schofield played it cleanly and threw him out at first. Haddix's control briefly faltered on Mathews, but on a full-count pitch, the Braves third baseman lined to first. That was the last time that Haddix would go to three balls on a hitter for the next 12 innings. Aaron then flied out to center and the inning was over.

In the Pirates' half of the second inning, Rocky Nelson led off with a single, but Burdette induced a double play and escaped unscathed. In the bottom of the frame, Haddix whiffed Joe Adcock on a 2-2 pitch, and then needed only five more pitches to draw a pair of harmless ground-outs. It soon became apparent that "The Kitten" was on his game. "I could have put a cup of coffee on either corner of the plate and hit it," Haddix proudly recalled later.

If Haddix was perfect on this night, Burdette was resourceful, and this skill was pivotal in the third inning. After Pittsburgh's Don Hoak led off with an infield single, and was forced out at second, Haddix helped his own cause with a hard line drive through the box that Burdette deflected but could not catch. Outfielder Roman Mejias was thrown out trying to take third on the hit, and even after another hit from Dick Schofield, Burdette ended the inning in a scoreless tie.

Haddix needed only seven pitches to cruise through the third inning, striking out Burdette on three pitches to end his first perfect jaunt through the Milwaukee lineup. He did have something of a close call, surrendering a line drive to Johnny Logan that one contemporary reporter called "perhaps the hardest hit" of the entire game. Schofield flagged down that line drive, and after three innings, not only was Haddix's pitching line spotless, but he had used just 30 pitches to dispatch the first nine Braves batters. On the other side, Burdette had scattered four Pirate hits, but no runs had been scored.

Burdette allowed a fifth hit in the top of the fourth inning, but still no runs. Haddix countered with a strikeout of O'Brien, his third of the game, and allowed two flyouts to center off the bats of Mathews and Aaron. Another double play got Burdette through the fifth inning, and then Haddix needed just four pitches to dispatch the Braves. The two hurlers traded one-two-three turns in the sixth inning, with Haddix throwing only eight more pitches to work through the Braves, including another sharp play by Schofield, who fielded a drive by Johnny Logan deep in the third base hole, and a three-pitch strikeout of Burdette.

The tension mounted in Milwaukee. Not only weren't the Braves hitting Haddix, they weren't even making solid contact. As one reporter noted, "The remarkable feature of this most remarkable performance by Haddix was that few balls were hit hard enough to be labeled 'possible base-hit.'" If Pittsburgh could score a run, the game looked to be over. But in the seventh and eighth, Burdette matched Haddix in setting down the side in order. In the top of the ninth inning, the Pirates threatened, placing runners at first and third with two down, before Bob Skinner tapped out back to Burdette, ending the threat.

The bottom of the ninth inning was as quick and painless as the rest of Haddix's mound surgery had been. With the awareness of his achievement rippling through the stadium, Haddix himself later admitted that he shifted focus—but only for one inning. "It was the only inning I tried for the no-hitter. I wanted to strike everyone out," he later said. He was two-thirds successful. He struck out Andy Pafko, got Johnny Logan to fly to left, and for his 27th out in a row, fanned Burdette for the third time on the day. Harvey Haddix had pitched a perfect nine innings. Unfortunately, the Pirates had failed to score, and so Haddix had to see how much further he could stretch his run of perfection.

Going through a major-league batting order three times perfectly is a feat to be celebrated. Running through the same batch of hitters for a fourth time was unheard of then, and hasn't been accomplished since. Haddix plowed along unfazed, sneaking a cigarette in the dugout after each inning. Teammate Dick Groat would light his smoke, but then disappear, leaving Haddix alone with his thoughts.

The Braves saw only six pitches in the 10th inning, as Del Rice and Eddie Mathews flied to center, and Hank Aaron grounded out to Schofield at shortstop. The 11th inning saw little change. Again, Haddix dispatched three Milwaukee batters in a span of six pitches, with a groundout to Schofield and a lineout and flyout to center. In the 12th frame, Pafko grounded back to Haddix, Johnny Logan flied to center, and Lew Burdette grounded out to third. Haddix had set down 36 consecutive batters—a perfect game plus a third of another one.

However, while the Pirates managed a hit in each of the 10th, 11th, 12th, and 13th innings, they never seriously threatened to break up Lew Burdette's shutout. When Bill Virdon grounded to second to end the 13th, Haddix was due to begin a fifth trip through the Milwaukee order.

Leadoff batter Felix Mantilla grounded a 1-2 offering to Don Hoak at third. Hoak's throw pulled Dick Stuart off the bag at first base. The error allowed the first baserunner for Milwaukee all night, ending Haddix's perfect streak at 12 innings.

After Eddie Mathews bunted Mantilla to second, Haddix walked Hank Aaron intentionally and tried to continue his no-hitter by facing Joe Adcock. On a 1-0 count, Haddix offered a slider. He later described the pitch as neither a good nor a bad pitch—"just good enough to hit."

Adcock, as he had three years prior against Haddix, ripped a colossal shot. That bomb had hit Haddix in the knee. This one hit the heart. Despite a desperate leap from Pirate outfielder Bill Virdon, the blast just cleared the right-center field fence. Haddix had lost the perfect game, the no-hitter, the shutout, and the game. When Adcock passed Aaron, who had left the field for the dugout after he saw the ball clear the fence and Felix Mantilla score the winning run, the confusing end result was that Adcock's shot was ruled a double, and the game's final score was 1–0.

After 12 innings of perfection from Haddix, the Pirates were beaten in the 13th inning. Harvey Haddix had pitched the best game in baseball history—and lost. There was nothing to do but stroll dejectedly toward the dugout. Photographs capture a group of Milwaukee fans behind the Pirate dugout, clearly standing and applauding, not for Adcock, but for the crestfallen left-hander who had just treated them to the greatest pitching performance in major-league history.

After the game, teammate Bill Virdon sat next to Haddix's locker in the Pirates clubhouse, shaking his head. "A pitcher does this once in a lifetime—once in baseball history," remarked Virdon, "and we can't win the game for him."

Harvey Haddix sometimes told the story of one of the many letters he received after his defeat. While there were many congratulatory or sympathetic notes, the one that captured the hardscrabble spirit of baseball best came from a fraternity at Texas A&M University. "Dear Harvey," the letter read, "Tough shit." Haddix did not attempt to cash in on his newfound celebrity, as he turned down offers from multiple television shows. Roommate Bob Smith reflected to *Sports Illustrated*, "The way he saw it then, he pitched a pretty good game, but the team lost. So what was the big deal?"

Baseball is a fickle game, and if Haddix suffered a difficult defeat after pitching his best, the controllers of karma had a pleasant surprise for him a year later. The Pirates went on to finish fourth in 1959, nine games behind the Dodgers, who edged out the Braves in a playoff for the pennant. But in 1960, the Pirates broke through and claimed the National League title by a full seven games over the second-place Braves.

Harvey Haddix at 34 was the oldest pitcher on the Pittsburgh staff. He was 11-10 in 1960, with a 3.97 ERA. In the World Series, he would have to try to slow the New York Yankees. It was an odd series. Pittsburgh won the first game 6–4, before being bombed by the Yanks 16–3 and 10–0 in the next two. The Pirates edged the Yankees 3–2 in Game 4 and won Game 5 by a 5–2 count as Haddix made his World Series debut, working six and a third gutsy innings in Yankee Stadium for the victory. New York retaliated with a 12–0 thumping of the Pirates in Game 6, sending the series to a decisive Game 7.

Vern Law started for the Pirates and held a 4–1 lead in the sixth inning when the Yankees chased him with a four-run frame. New York stretched its lead to 7–4 in the top of the eighth inning, but Pittsburgh answered with a five-run rally keyed by a homer by backup catcher Hal Smith. The Pirates led 9–7. Bob Friend took the mound to close out the Series for Pittsburgh, but allowed consecutive singles. With Maris, Mantle, Berra, and Skowron to follow, Pittsburgh manager Danny Murtaugh had seen enough and called for Harvey Haddix from the bullpen.

Haddix had pitched in relief only once all season. Nearly three decades later, he admitted, "That was the only time in my life I was really nervous." In marked contrast to his (almost) perfect evening, Haddix was not breathtaking on this day. He did get Maris to pop out, but Mantle singled in one run, and a Berra groundout scored the tying run. Still, Haddix retired Skowron without further incident, and the game was 9–9 into the bottom of the ninth.

Pittsburgh second baseman Bill Mazeroski led off and promptly ended the series with a walk-off home run, making the Pirates the shocking world champions of baseball. A quarter century later, Haddix told an interviewer, "With the crack of the bat I knew it was a home run." He had an extra reason to celebrate. The winning pitcher in the grueling 10–9 slugfest—with one relatively mediocre inning to his credit—was "Hard Luck" Harvey Haddix.

~

Haddix bounced around the major leagues until 1965. He won 10 games in 1961, but never reached that mark again. He never returned to the postseason, finishing his career with a 2-0 mark in World Series play. Before the 1964 season, Haddix was traded to Baltimore. "The Kitten" was reunited with "The Cat" again, as Harry Brecheen was the pitching coach for the Orioles. Haddix was 8-7 in his two years with Baltimore, and on the strength of those wins, he finished his career with 136 major-league victories. Brecheen had won 133 games.

Haddix's last season, 1965, coincided with the Braves' last year in Milwaukee. The team failed to post a losing season in its entire run in Wisconsin, but owner Lou Perini sold the team to a group from Atlanta. Heartbroken Milwaukee fans had a short run in exile, however, as Bud Selig purchased the bankrupt expansion Seattle Pilots after the 1969 season and moved the team to Milwaukee, renaming them the Brewers. The Brewers began as an American League squad, but in 1998, they returned to the National League. The 1957 World Series title remains the last for Milwaukee, although the Braves have won a Series in Atlanta.

Joe Adcock finished his career with 336 home runs, not including the shot hit off of Haddix, as it was not officially a homer. Adcock managed briefly with the Indians, but retired to race horses before he died of Alzheimer's disease in 1999. Lew Burdette won 203 games, including the win he picked up over Haddix on May 26, 1959. Burdette pitched a no-hitter himself in 1960, dashing his chance at a perfect game when he hit a batter in the fifth inning. He lived in Florida until 2007, when he passed away due to lung cancer.

The most famous of the former Milwaukee Braves was Hank Aaron, who as an Atlanta Brave on April 8, 1974, set the major-league home run mark, which stood until Barry Bonds broke it more than three decades later. Aaron finished his career with the Milwaukee Brewers in 1976, hitting his 755th and last home run in Milwaukee's County Stadium, which was the home of the Brewers until 2001.

The Pittsburgh Pirates have remained a mainstay in the National League. The years immediately following the 1960 title were up and down, but from 1970 to 1975, the Pirates won the National League East five times in six seasons, including 1971, when they won another World Series. The Pirates added another title in 1979, and posted three straight division titles from 1990 to 1992. That team, led by players like Barry Bonds and Bobby Bonilla, was essentially wrecked due to the Pirates' inability to compensate their free agents. As a perennial small-market team, the Pirates went on to 20 consecutive losing seasons before ending that streak with a playoff appearance in 2013.

Bill Mazeroski, whose home run in 1960 gave Haddix his greatest triumph, was enshrined in the Baseball Hall of Fame. Maz still works as a special assistant coach for the Pirates, and while Joe Carter joined Maz as the only players to end a World Series with a walk-off home run, Maz's moment of fame remains secure.

Roberto Clemente, a beloved figure throughout baseball, was a consistent All-Star and ripped his 3,000th hit in his final game in 1972. Sadly, it was his last game. He died in a plane crash as he tried to carry supplies for earthquake relief to Nicaragua after the season. His heroism and elegant play have stood as a landmark for thousands of Latino players in professional baseball, and he is also a member of the Baseball Hall of Fame.

Harvey Haddix bounced around baseball a good deal as a pitching coach after his playing days were over. He worked for five teams, including the Pirates, where he arrived in time to be part of the 1979 World Series winners, before his ultimate retirement from baseball after the 1984 season.

Harvey Haddix's gem was considered a perfect game until 1991, when Major League Baseball changed the definition of a no-hitter to require the pitcher to complete the game without allowing a hit. Like Ernie Shore, Haddix was subject to a retroactive change in his record for no apparent reason—and unlike Shore, Harvey was alive to see it happen. Officially, Haddix's perfect game wasn't a perfect game—32 years after he pitched it. His wife, Marcia, told *Sports Illustrated* that she was furious when she heard the news, but that Harvey was not. "It's OK," he told her. "I know what I did."

Indeed, with each passing year, the fact that baseball will probably never see another game to equal Haddix's defeat becomes clearer. By exercising superb control and pitching to contact, Haddix somehow used just 115 pitches to work the entire game. In a modern era of a tight strike zone and a high strikeout rate, many pitchers would reach such a pitch count by the seventh or eighth inning—if they were even allowed to do so. As arthroscopic arm surgeries have become increasingly common, modern managers generally resist allowing starters to throw even 115 pitches. Near the beginning of the 2016 season, for instance, Dodgers manager Dave Roberts removed rookie Ross Stripling from a start after precisely 100 pitches—even though Stripling had one out in the eighth inning of a no-hit bid. In the entire 2015 season, Pittsburgh Pirate ace Gerrit Cole, a strapping 6'4", 230-pound hurler, was only allowed by manager Clint Hurdle to reach 115 pitches on one occasion—when he threw 116 pitches on June 7th in seven innings of work. To consider Haddix's performance another way, the last pitcher to work 13 innings in a game was Tommy John in 1983. Despite the increasing likelihood that his defeated masterpiece would remain unequaled, "Hard Luck" Harvey didn't dwell on the matter. "That game probably gets more attention than if I had won it," Haddix said in 1990. "But to me, my most important game was the seventh game of the World Series the next year."

Haddix died on January 8, 1994, of emphysema. While his obituary in the *New York Times* spoke mostly of his near-perfect night, it ended by noting that Haddix was a three-time All-Star who won Game 7 of the 1960 World Series. The obituary then listed Marcia and their three children as his survivors. The ultimate measure of Harvey Haddix lay within those lines—he pitched the greatest game ever and lost, and he won one of the uglier games of his career, and he and Marcia made a family, living their lives as we all do, in the mixed glow of success and disappointment.

In 2010, Marcia Haddix showed up in the news once more. She had decided to sell the set of a dozen silver goblets National League president Warren Giles had given Haddix to commemorate the game. "I polished that silverware for 51 years," she told a reporter. "It's time to stop." The goblets may tarnish, but let's not allow some official designation of the game itself to dull the luster of Harvey Haddix's masterpiece.

May 26, 1959
County Stadium, Milwaukee, WI

	1	2	3	4	5	6	7	8	9	10	11	12	13	R	H	E
PIT	0	0	0	0	0	0	0	0	0	0	0	0	0	0	12	1
MIL	0	0	0	0	0	0	0	0	0	0	0	0	1	1	1	0

W: Burdette (8-2)
L: Haddix (4-3)

The End of Haddix's Perfect Game:

Bottom of 13th Inning, No Outs.
1-2 pitch to second baseman Felix Mantilla.
Mantilla grounded to third baseman Don Hoak, whose errant throw to first ended the perfect game. After a sacrifice bunt and a walk, Joe Adcock ended the no-hitter and game with a blast over the fence that was officially scored as an RBI double when Adcock passed Hank Aaron on the basepaths—after Mantilla scored the game-winning run.

CHAPTER 6

"YOU'VE GOT TO BE KIDDING ME"

September 2, 1972
San Diego Padres at Chicago Cubs
Milt Pappas

Some men amble blandly into history, surprised by brief moments in the spotlight and seemingly out of place. Then there are people like Milt Pappas, who seemed destined to be at the center of a controversy. Pappas didn't need to have a game of near-perfection to be a noteworthy personality. Yet the circumstances and details of his near-perfect game are so intriguing that more than four decades later, Pappas found himself still recounting them.

Born in 1939, the baby given the imposing name of Miltiades Stergios Papastergios (he was born to Greek immigrants) stood apart. He loved baseball by age six or seven, and at around age

Milt Pappas, throwing in spring training as a Cincinnati Red. It was as a Chicago Cub that Pappas would just miss a perfect game, and perhaps be best remembered. NATIONAL BASEBALL HALL OF FAME

nine, he got to serve as the batboy for a local semi-pro team. Pappas recalled, "Here I was, in my Little League uniform and hat, like the greatest kid in the world . . . like I was going to go out to play." The following year, Pappas was on the team. From there, baseball was Pappas's destiny.

In his senior season of high school baseball at Detroit's Cooley High, Pappas went 7-0 with an 0.50 ERA. In the pre-draft era, the battle to sign Pappas was a war. Detroit talent scout Lou D'Annunzio had helped to shape lots of young local talent, including Billy Pierce. But after years of steering such talent to the Tigers, D'Annunzio had become a full-time scout with the Baltimore Orioles. He led the courtship of young Milt Pappas. "He followed me when I was 12 or 13 years old," Pappas recalled.

Accounts indicate that D'Annunzio "practically lived with the Pappas family as Milt approached graduation day" and that "[h]e paid particular attention to Pappas' grandmother." D'Annunzio later recalled that the two "got along fine talking half-Greek and half-Italian." He signed Pappas for a $4,000 bonus (not a coincidental figure, as that was the maximum amount to still avoid the "bonus rules" of the time), and recalled that the grandmother hugged him and said, "We got him."

That said, the Orioles wasted no time in placing the 18-year-old Pappas on the major-league roster. Milt explained, "I figured when it's time, [manager] Paul Richards will let me pitch. I assume he's going to pitch me against the lowly Washington Senators or Kansas City Athletics. . . . Then one night, we're playing the Yankees in Baltimore and Mickey Mantle hit the base of the scoreboard . . . and I said, 'Oh my God, what in the world am I doing here?'

"[Harry] Brecheen says, 'You and George Zuverink, go down and warm up.' And I said, 'That's all for show, George. We're only down five runs . . . hang in there. You'll do fine.' So I'm patting him on the back and bugging people in the stands, and Harry Brecheen comes down and says, 'OK, Milt, you're in there.'

"I finished warming up and went down to the dugout and tripped on the dugout stairs. . . . The first four batters that I faced in organized baseball were Enos Slaughter, Mickey Mantle, Yogi Berra, and Bill Skowron. That was my introduction to the major leagues."

In two innings, Pappas surrendered only two harmless singles and held the Yankees scoreless. "Everything was downhill after that," he joked in 2015. Pappas never had a chance at being inconspicuous.

Pappas threw nine innings of one-run ball for the 1957 Orioles, and briefly went to Knoxville in the Southern League, where he pitched another 11 innings. Those were the only minor-league innings that Pappas ever threw.

In 1958, Pappas began the season still 18 years old, but as a regular member of the Orioles rotation. One author notes, "With a lively fastball and better-than-average slider, Pappas had great things predicted for him."

Pappas posted a solid 10-10 mark in 1958, and in 1959 and 1960, he won 15 games each season. He won his 27th major-league game on his 21st birthday, a pace that few could match. Pappas was remarkably consistent—he didn't fail to win 10 or more games in a season until 1969. That said, he only once eclipsed 222 innings in a season, and he never won more than 17 games.

Pappas's failure to go from the very good to the transcendent is a mystery. He had the kind of stuff that led to annual predictions of 20 wins. Some derided him as a "six inning pitcher," who asked to be removed from games at the first sign of trouble. But Pappas finished 129 of his 465 career major-league starts. For comparison's sake, his 27.8 percent completion mark is quite similar to the 29.1 percent mark of his contemporary and Hall of Famer Jim Bunning.

Pappas consistently won 12–17 games, almost never posted a losing season, and usually posted an ERA around 3.50. He played on a series of mediocre Orioles teams and generally anchored their squads. Twice, he was chosen as an All-Star, saving the second 1962 All-Star Game, and starting the 1965 game.

Still, Pappas wasn't always a popular player. He was a longtime player representative in an era when player reps were starting to do serious battle with baseball ownership. Pappas defended himself against charges of being a "clubhouse lawyer," noting, "Any player rep who does a half decent job gets that reputation."

For whatever reason, after the 1965 season, Baltimore packaged Pappas, pitcher Jack Baldschun, and journeyman outfielder Harry Simpson to the Cincinnati Reds in exchange for outfielder Frank Robinson. The

Reds believed that Robinson was nearing the end of his career, but in fact, he won a Triple Crown and became the centerpiece of some incredible Orioles squads.

The deal has become infamous, ridiculed even in the film *Bull Durham* as one of baseball's most lopsided trades. That said, Cincinnati's logic is hardly difficult to follow. Twenty-six-year-old pitchers with 110 career wins don't exactly grow on trees. Unfortunately, Baldschun and Simpson gave the Reds virtually nothing, and Pappas was not at his sharpest, compiling a 30-29 mark in Cincinnati before the Reds dealt him to the Atlanta Braves in 1968.

Two years and 18 wins later, the Braves tired of Pappas, but Milt's career got a third wind when the Chicago Cubs came calling. The Cubs had suffered a heartbreaking season in 1969, and the following year wanted another solid pitcher to contribute to the team. They apparently paid $75,000 to the Braves for Pappas.

Chicago suited Pappas. The Cubs did not win their division in 1970, although Pappas certainly couldn't be blamed. Milt was only 10-8 in Chicago, but his 2.68 ERA bespoke solid pitching. In 1971, Pappas won 17 more games. He was still just 32 when the 1972 season began, and had amassed 185 big-league victories.

However, by 1972, Pappas's health was crumbling. He broke a finger in spring training and then battled a sore elbow all season long. He began getting almost routine cortisone injections—he estimated 30 by early September. Pappas would later admit that he considered retirement.

Pappas's outlook was also worsened because of a family situation. Pappas's father was ill, and by midseason, it was apparent that he would not recover. Milt recalled, "My dad was dying. When I went to see him at the All-Star Break . . . I was [6-6]. And I said, 'Dad, I love you and I know that I'm probably not going to see you again when I leave here. But I guarantee you that I'm going to have the best year that I've had. And that's because of you, and I love you.' And I left."

Indeed, Pappas lost his first start after the break, but pitched well. He then won his next five, and reached the beginning of September with his record having moved from 6-6 to 11-7 and his ERA dropping from

3.54 to 3.18. His next start, on September 2nd, was at home in Wrigley Field against the San Diego Padres. It would be the greatest game of the best year that Milt Pappas ever had.

Baseball and its American backdrop had changed greatly in the 13 years since Harvey Haddix was almost perfect. Vietnam had escalated and was finally ending, two Kennedys and Dr. King had been assassinated, and the Watergate burglary had taken place, although America would not know that for some time to come. It was an era of distrust, particularly distrust of the establishment.

In baseball, more players were African-American or Latin-American, and fewer and fewer of the players were clean-shaven or wore buzzcuts. Players grew their hair long, and the Oakland A's would soon take facial hair to a level unseen since the 19th-century origins of baseball. Teams had been added in new cities, as the major leagues had swelled to 24 teams. Divisions had been added to the leagues in 1969, and postseason play had expanded to playoffs leading to the World Series.

One of the most recent additions to the major leagues was the San Diego Padres, initially bought and owned by Ray Kroc, who had made his fortune with the McDonald's hamburger franchise. The Padres, unlike McDonald's, were hardly an instant success. In their first three seasons, the team had lost 110, 99, and 100 games. They were rooted in last place of the NL West Division.

And it was the Padres who limped into Wrigley Field on September 2, 1972, unaware of their impending date with history. The Padres were 46-79, on a six-game losing streak and well into the NL West basement. The Padres batted .227 as a team and were last in the NL in runs scored in 1972. In the first game of the series, the Cubs had pelted San Diego by a 14–3 count.

Most of the players on the Padres roster were destined for brief and undistinguished careers. Outfielder Cito Gaston was a mediocre player, but went on to win two World Series as a manager in the 1990s.

Outfielder Leron Lee hit .300 that season, but it was by far the best year of his career. The only noteworthy regular on the Padres was first baseman Nate Colbert, a legitimately feared slugger who bashed 38 home runs and accumulated 111 RBI in 1972. Lee was second on the team in RBI with 47.

The Padres' pitching staff was 11th in the NL in ERA. "Ace" Steve Arlin lost 21 games, and the entire staff was similarly undistinguished. On September 2nd, Mike Caldwell would start for San Diego. Caldwell went on to win 137 games, including 22 in 1978, but in 1972, he was a relatively anonymous rookie with a career 7-7 record.

The Cubs, at 68-58, were in second place, likely too far behind the Pittsburgh Pirates for any September drama, but salvaging a solid season nevertheless. Manager Leo Durocher had been fired midseason, as expectations for a postseason spot were coming up short. But a veteran team still provided plenty of highlights. Future Hall of Famers Ron Santo and Billy Williams were potent offensive threats, and Fergie Jenkins was in the midst of a 20-win season on the mound.

Only 11,144 spectators paid their way into Wrigley Field that day. There had been some rain early on the morning of September 2nd. The Cubs, while not mathematically eliminated, were for all intents and purposes doomed to another season without a playoff appearance, and the Padres were about as awful as their garish mustard yellow and dark brown uniforms.

Milt Pappas was in the middle of a hot streak, in his greatest season ever. But warming up in the bullpen, he wasn't particularly convinced of his stuff. Pappas recalled, "When I felt strong as a bull, I was a thrower. When I didn't feel real good, I was a pitcher. That day, I was a pitcher. . . . So I concentrated on throwing strikes."

In the top of the first inning, Enzo Hernandez flied out to center. Dave Roberts lined back to Pappas, and then Leron Lee grounded out to second baseman Carmen Fanzone. In the bottom of the inning, the Cubs struck Caldwell quickly. Jose Cardenal singled home a run and Fanzone knocked in another. The 2–0 first inning advantage proved to be all the support that Pappas needed.

In the Padres' second at-bat, Colbert flied to left. Cito Gaston then struck out, and Derrel Thomas ended the inning by lining to shortstop Don Kessinger. The Cubs did not score, and Pappas quickly returned to the mound. He completed his first round through the Padre batting order. Johnny Jeter grounded to Santo, catcher Fred Kendall lined out to Kessinger, and then Caldwell fanned helplessly.

In the bottom of the third, the Cubs plated two more runs, with first baseman Jim Hickman punching an RBI single. Staked to a 4–0 lead, Pappas cruised through the fourth inning. Hernandez struck out, Roberts grounded to second, and Lee grounded out to Hickman, who made the play himself to finish the frame.

In the fifth inning, Pappas's luck was tested. Colbert led off with a one-hop groundball into the third base hole. Don Kessinger fielded the ball, although one reporter noted that he "was at least five feet onto the [left field] grass, which was slick because of the morning rains." Kessinger, who later admitted that he worried that he might slip, planted and threw Colbert out cleanly "by a half step." Pappas then got Gaston to ground out to Kessinger and Thomas to foul out to left.

The sixth frame presented no new difficulty for Pappas. Jeter tapped back to Pappas, Fred Kendall grounded to Santo, and Caldwell again struck out. His second run through the order was complete, and Pappas knew he was approaching perfection.

In the seventh inning, the Padres again went easily. Hernandez popped out to Hickman, Roberts looked at a called third strike, and Lee grounded to first base. Pappas cruised along, with only six outs between him and a perfect game.

In the eighth inning, the Padres again tested Pappas. He had lost a previous no-hit bid with two out in the eighth, and after Colbert grounded out and Gaston struck out, Derrel Thomas nearly ended the perfect game. Thomas slashed a hard grounder back through the box. Pappas deflected it, and with the speedy Thomas hustling down the baseline, knew history was on the line.

Pappas recalled, "A little tapper went over my head and I knew nobody had a chance of getting to it except me. I ran back . . . and got the ball . . . and threw a strike to first base. Hell, I could've thrown that ball into the stands. I'm turning and throwing." Thomas was out by a step and perfection continued.

Pappas recalled that by the seventh inning, his teammates were avoiding him. "You could hear a pin drop in the dugout," he stated. "When I finished the eighth inning . . . I walked down the dugout stairs and said, 'Hey, guys, by the way, I'm pitching a no-hitter.' That just opened up Pandora's box. Everybody just started talking and laughing.

"There was a place behind the dugout . . . I would usually go down there and sit down. . . . All of a sudden, the police came down and the ushers came down, and they were yapping and talking and things were going off. So I turned around and said, 'Please, could you put an end to all that noise you're making so I can concentrate on the game?'"

Chicago scored four more runs in the bottom of the eighth inning, and with the game now completely blown open, the only question left was whether Milt Pappas would make history. Leading off the ninth inning, John Jeter hit a flyball to left-center. A reporter noted, "Rookie center fielder Bill North came in for the ball and seemingly had it when he fell on the wet turf."

Pappas wrote in his autobiography, "I could only think one thing. *Shit!* Then seemingly out of nowhere, but actually out of left field came Billy Williams. . . . I didn't have time to pray, but something spiritual passed through my mind. . . . Billy stretched; Billy leaned forward; Billy caught the ball. . . . Outwardly, I showed little emotion, but inwardly, I thought I'd been brought back from the brink of death."

After Billy Williams saved the day, Pappas survived another close call when Fred Kendall lined his first pitch near third base, but just foul. On the next pitch, Kendall hit a routine grounder to Kessinger. "My heart was really pounding now," wrote Pappas.

San Diego manager Don Zimmer sent pinch-hitter Larry Stahl to the plate. Stahl was a 31-year-old outfielder on his third major-league team. He never eclipsed 312 at-bats in a season and was a career .232 hitter. He happened to be hitting .232 for the season that day, too. He often pinch-hit, and in fact, had pinch-hit in the ninth inning of the previous day's game and made an out.

Stahl swung and missed at the first pitch. He took a ball, then again swung and missed. Pappas was poised one strike away from history. Pappas then threw three straight sliders. All hung around the outer edge of the plate. But to Pappas's eternal consternation, second-year NL umpire Bruce Froemming saw it thusly: ball two, ball three, ball four.

Forty-three years later, Pappas remembered, "Bruce Froemming, in his infinite wisdom, called them all balls. The clown! 'Ball four!' And I said, 'You've got to be kidding.' I was enraged and yelling and screaming and swearing at him. I knew he didn't have the guts to throw me out of the game."

Pappas brought up Don Larsen's 1956 perfect game in the World Series, which was ended, as Pappas noted, by a pitch that "almost hit him in the chin. The umpire knew what was going on." Froemming, in Pappas's judgment, did not.

"I said to him," Pappas continued, 'you're just a fatass umpire. You . . . blew a perfect game. Wherever you're at, in a bar, at a party, at home in your bed, you can no longer say 'I called a perfect game.'"

On the mound, Pappas eventually regained his composure and induced Hernandez to pop up to Carmen Fanzone. When the ball was caught, catcher Randy Hundley and the rest of the Cubs mobbed Pappas on the mound. Froemming had taken away the perfect game, but it was still a no-hitter, and that was cause enough for celebration.

Immediately after the game, Pappas was too elated over the no-hitter to haggle. "The pitches were balls," he said. "They were borderline but balls." Pappas went on to say, "I was just hoping Froemming might sympathize since it was a perfect game, but he couldn't be expected to do that."

For his part, Froemming was unapologetic. He said that the perfect game "never entered my mind. They are what they are. It's a ball or a strike. Those three pitches weren't there. They weren't even borderline at all."

End of controversy?

Hardly. In his autobiography, Pappas explained, "I said a lot of things that were meant strictly for public consumption at the time and to keep me from being fined." In the ensuing years, Pappas and Froemming have made clear that they have to agree to disagree on their mutual roles in baseball history.

⁓

Time (and video) did little to dull Pappas's anger. Pappas had been given footage of the ninth inning, and when he viewed it, he noted that after calling ball four to Stahl, Froemming "has a smirk on his face. If I had known that then, I probably would have punched him out."

In 2006, Pappas admitted, "I saw [Froemming] a couple of times after that at functions. He said, 'You still mad at me?' I said, 'Yeah, I'm still mad.'"

Near the end of his 36-year career as an umpire, Froemming spoke to ESPN. "Pappas goes around telling everybody he took it in the shorts, and that's not what was the case," he commented.

Froemming further explained his approach, "As an umpire, you're not thinking on the pitch, 'Geez, this is a perfect game.' You're not into that; you're an official, not a fan. I can't give him something that he doesn't have coming, either. It's either a ball or a strike, and that's the way I've umpired all my life."

Randy Hundley said after the game that the pitches were just off the plate, likely for the same reasons that Pappas did so, but changed his version of events over the years. In 2007, he said that the 3-2 pitch was "a hair low," but that the two previous pitches were "excellent."

Pappas's autobiography reflects some ultimate measure of gratitude for the no-hitter, although he could not shake his conviction that "Bruce Froemming robbed me of a perfect game . . . and he did it deliberately." In 2007, he said of Froemming, "I have to admire the guy for lasting as long as he did. . . . I wish him nothing but the best. I just wish he had retired 37 years ago."

In fact, it was Pappas who was soon to retire after the no-hitter. He completed 1972 by winning his last 11 starts, finishing the year 17-7, perhaps the best single season of his career. Included in that streak was his 200th career win.

In 1973, Pappas struggled to a 7-12 mark, and then hung up his spikes at only 34 years old. Pappas regarded his career positively, noting that aside from Bruce Froemming's tight pitch-calling, "The only other thing that bothered me about my career was not getting into a World Series."

In many ways, Milt Pappas stood as a man ahead of his time. His interest in baseball's labor situation only just predated the mega-paydays of free agency that his generation brought about. When asked if he took pride in being part of the change in the game, he unequivocally admitted, "Oh God, yeah. . . . I had to fight like hell after I won 17 games to get a $10,000 raise."

Pappas also had to fight to draw consideration for the Baseball Hall of Fame. He drew only a handful of votes in 1979 before falling off the ballot. Pappas was not shy in his conviction that his record justifies consideration for the Hall of Fame. When directly asked if he held out hope for induction in the Hall, Pappas was succinct. "No, not anymore," he said. "It is such a political bunch of crap."

He quickly recalled Don Drysdale, whose career record was 209-166. Pappas's record was 209-164. Drysdale, of course, is in the Hall of Fame. Drysdale seems to draw extra credit for his best years, while Pappas's pattern of winning 15, 16, or 17 games in a season is one which would draw Cooperstown consideration today, but does not seem to do so in the era in which Pappas pitched. Again, in many ways, Pappas seems oddly unappreciated because he didn't fit the prototype of his generation.

The Cubs faded back into the lower echelon of their division after Pappas's retirement. Pappas's teammates Billy Williams and Ron Santo entered Cooperstown (posthumously in Santo's case), but just as Pappas never played in a World Series, the Cubs' drought (as of this writing) has now passed 70 years.

The Padres climbed out of baseball's cellar just in time to dethrone the Cubs in the 1984 NLCS. San Diego has notched a pair of World

Series appearances but has yet to win a title. Larry Stahl was purchased by the Reds after the 1972 season, but like Pappas, 1973 was his last year in baseball. He drew 142 career walks, none more famous than the one on September 2, 1972.

Bruce Froemming, as noted before, umpired for 37 years in MLB before becoming a special assistant to the vice president on umpiring. He has still not changed his tune on his pitch calls on September 2, 1972. In a 1987 survey of MLB players, Froemming was chosen as the best home plate umpire in the National League. Future Hall of Famer Tony Gwynn said of Froemming, "[W]hen he makes a call, that's it—he knows what he's doing." Froemming umpired 11 no-hitters, including a perfect game thrown by Dennis Martinez in 1991. He was, however, working first base that afternoon.

Once Milt Pappas finished fighting baseball ownership or the prejudices of sportswriters, he tried his hand at a couple of other ventures. He owned a restaurant, selling gyro meat for a few years. After that, he worked 26 years for a building supply company before he retired.

While Pappas's life after baseball was mostly calm, there was one very unfortunate variance from that trend. On September 11, 1982, his wife, Carole, rose and went on some routine errands before a family dinner with their son, Steve, and Steve's new wife. Carole never came home.

The Pappas family took the matter public, but to no immediate avail. Milt undertook a polygraph exam to clear himself of any possible suspicion. Five years later, Pappas returned home from purchasing a pack of cigarettes and drove past a crowd at a nearby pond. Once he was in his house, police advised him that they believed they had found Carole's body. "It's the first time in my life that I'm totally speechless," Milt told reporters. "I'm totally dumbfounded by the situation that the car and body are three blocks away." Carole Pappas's death by drowning was ruled accidental.

While Milt subsequently remarried, it was clear that the difficult situation was still haunting. "So many questions, no answers," he said in 2015 in reference to the ordeal.

Once the publicity of his wife's disappearance faded, Pappas went back to being known primarily as the guy who was almost perfect but for a stingy home plate umpire. As he discussed that place in history, frustration gave way to a sense of wonder.

Pappas admitted in 2015, "To this day, it astounds me how many people come up to me and say, 'You got robbed.' It's mind-boggling that 40 years later, people still recognize me and talk about that game. I wonder if I had gotten the perfect game, if all this adulation would still be there."

The adulation is still very much present in Chicago, where Pappas was twice invited to Wrigley Field in 2015 to lead the singing of "Take Me Out to the Ballgame" during the seventh-inning stretch.

When asked if it meant something special to be remembered and celebrated, Pappas was emphatic. "Oh God, yeah. I had a long talk with the Rickettses [the new Cubs' owners] and told them, 'You've got former players living in the area. Utilize them!' . . . I love going down there and going up in the suites and signing autographs. . . . I really enjoy it a lot."

It is an odd image. Milt Pappas, the alleged "clubhouse lawyer," the almost-perfect pitcher who had the hardest time letting go of an umpire's judgment call, really did seem to be enjoying himself—perhaps never more so than in 2015. With the Cubs playing their way into the postseason, delighting the fans with an improbable young team, Milt Pappas found himself again genuinely loving baseball. Perhaps the image isn't odd at all—perhaps Pappas was just a genuinely misunderstood man.

On September 2, 2015, on the 43rd anniversary of the day he was almost perfect, Pappas found himself back in Wrigley Field, again called upon to sing with the crowd during the seventh-inning stretch. But he had something on his mind before he sang. He took the microphone and told the assembled masses:

"Hey everybody, greatest fans in baseball, right here. And what a great team that Mr. Epstein and Jed and my buddy Joe Maddon have put together. God bless 'em. This team is going to be around for a long time!"

There he was—Milt Pappas—optimist, excited fan, friend of management, still believing in a possible World Series run. The youthful enthusiasm suggested an almost perfect full circle. Unfortunately, the circle ended abruptly on April 19, 2016, when Pappas, age 76, passed away at his home near Chicago. Cubs CEO Tom Ricketts issued a statement that recalled Milt's "no-hitter that neared perfection" and noted that the organization "will always consider him a part of the Chicago Cubs family."

September 2, 1972
Wrigley Field, Chicago, IL

	1	2	3	4	5	6	7	8	9	R	H	E
SD	0	0	0	0	0	0	0	0	0	0	0	1
CHI	2	0	2	0	0	0	0	4	X	8	13	0

W: Pappas (12-7)
L: Caldwell (6-8)

The End of Pappas's Perfect Game:

Top of Ninth Inning, Two Outs.
3-2 pitch to pinch-hitter Larry Stahl.
Stahl took a slider near the outside corner for ball four. Pappas retired the next batter to complete a no-hitter.

CHAPTER 7

FROM THE TIGERS TO THE DOGS

April 15, 1983
Detroit Tigers at Chicago White Sox
Milt Wilcox

Three decades after his glory days with the Detroit Tigers, Milt Wilcox found himself again aiming for perfection. Just like an early spring day in 1983 when he battled for baseball immortality, Wilcox paused with the ball in his right hand. The crowd leaned in, awaiting his next delivery. With a championship and a shot at the record book on the line, Wilcox gathered himself and carefully made his pitch. But instead of trying to fire pitches past major-league hitters, Wilcox was lobbing tennis balls or other toys in the air, to be grabbed by leaping dogs. Instead of baseball,

Milt Wilcox, who battled injuries to nearly throw a perfect game in 1983, and win a World Series in 1984

PHOTO PROVIDED BY THE DETROIT TIGERS

Milt Wilcox's game became dog jumping, and he was not only the Cy Young of the game, he was the Abner Doubleday of his own sport.

What does one do when athletic glory, even days of near-perfection, yield to pain and surgery and retirement? For Milt Wilcox, it was just a question of finding a new outlet, a way to combine something he enjoyed with the chance to experience the competitive jolt again. "I've been in front of 50,000 people with 50 million watching on television," he said.

"The thrill I get from dog jumping is the same as when I was playing ball."

~

Before his career literally went to the dogs, Wilcox was a gritty, tough pitcher who got the most that he could out of his skills. Years after retirement, he told a reporter, "I didn't throw the hardest. I didn't have the best curveball. But I was a competitor." An early press release recounts a teenaged Wilcox being struck on the forehead by a line drive in a minor-league appearance and bouncing back to angrily strike out the next hitter. "Wilcox's ability to throw a baseball is matched only by his competitive spirit," the release boasts.

Raised in Oklahoma, Wilcox was a second-round draft pick by the Cincinnati Reds in 1968. He advanced through the Cincinnati system, arriving in late 1970, where he impressed the Cincinnati brass enough that he was given an NLCS start and pitched twice in the World Series despite having just 22⅓ major-league innings under his belt. The Reds were stacked on the mound though, and Milt worked just 43⅓ innings in Cincinnati in 1971 before he was traded to Cleveland.

The battle between Milt Wilcox and his body began in earnest in Cleveland. He began the 1972 season looking like perhaps the best pitcher in baseball—in his first six starts, he was 4-2 with an 0.92 ERA. But after a poor start on May 12th, he was diagnosed with strep throat. From there, it was all downhill. "I tried to pitch too soon and hurt my shoulder," Wilcox recalled. "I didn't say anything about it, thinking it would go away. But it didn't. It bothered me the rest of the season." Wilcox then began throwing sidearm because of his shoulder difficulties. This in turn caused him to develop tendinitis, and Wilcox has speculated that it resulted in him tearing his rotator cuff. The 4-2 start ended up in a 7-14 season.

Wilcox quickly went from prospect to suspect. He won eight games for Cleveland in 1973, but amassed a 5.83 ERA. He pitched out of the bullpen with mediocre effectiveness in 1974 before being traded to the

Chicago Cubs in the spring of 1975. Chicago had little use for him, as Wilcox pitched uncertainly in AAA and for the Cubs. In mid-1976, Wilcox was toiling again in AAA Wichita and was losing hope for his career. "I told my wife I felt like it might be my last year," he later stated.

Fortunately for Wilcox, a tough pitcher, like a good dog, can't be kept down. The Detroit Tigers purchased him from Wichita in mid-1976. In AAA Evansville, Wilcox slowly built his arm back. "I couldn't throw real hard, but I had a good sinker," he recalled. "I think that was when I really became a pitcher."

This was a timely development, as a rash of injuries left Detroit very short on pitchers. Tigers manager Ralph Houk called Wilcox back to the big leagues, and Milt was 6-2 with a 3.64 ERA in 106⅓ successful innings. The modesty of failure kept an imprint on Wilcox—he told *The Sporting News* after the 1977 season that he hoped to reach 30 career wins. He was 28-32 when he set this goal. But at the same time, Wilcox felt reason for optimism. "I feel stronger, and I'm throwing harder now than ever before," he said. "I didn't give up because I believed in myself. I always felt I could be a consistently good pitcher in the big leagues."

Wilcox's feeling was right. Over the next seven seasons, he became a mainstay in Detroit, never winning fewer than 11 games in a year and consistently throwing around 200 innings, save for the strike-shortened 1981 campaign. Along the way, he was reunited with the manager who had tabbed him to pitch in the postseason when he was a rookie, Sparky Anderson. The two National League retreads had some things to prove in the American League.

Detroit had become competitive. Their losing record in 1977, when they picked up Wilcox, would be their last until 1989. Heading into the 1983 season, there was reason to think that Detroit could compete for a championship. The outstanding middle infield team of Lou Whitaker and Alan Trammell were joined in the everyday lineup by slugging catcher Lance Parrish, five-tool outfielder Chet Lemon, and the gritty Kirk Gibson. Wilcox was joined in the starting rotation by ace Jack Morris, who accrued the most major-league victories in the 1980s, and solid second wheel Dan Petry. Wilcox began the season as Detroit's fourth starter.

Wilcox's enemy, more than control, command, or opposing hitters, was trying to keep his arm in something approaching decent shape. With his 1972 shoulder and rotator cuff issues, Wilcox had experienced his first significant arm problems at the edge of a new medical era in baseball. Two years later, Dodgers starter Tommy John underwent the ligament replacement surgery that would later bear his name. John's left medial collateral ligament was so destroyed that the surgeon, Dr. Frank Jobe, harvested another ligament from John's right wrist to replace it. In 1976, John won 10 games and was named NL Comeback Player of the Year. Almost immediately, surgical fixes became a solution to the endless pitcher's nightmare of a dead arm. Soon Dr. James Andrews and Dr. Frank Jobe, among others, became as renowned as Tom Seaver or Nolan Ryan, and the impact of modern arm surgery on baseball would be hard to overstate.

John was a young star at the time of his breakthrough surgery, though. Wilcox, particularly before his late 70s-mid-80s run of success, was just a journeyman pitcher. More often than not, he gritted his teeth and found a way to pitch through the pain, usually with the aid of pain-killing injections. Ironically, at the same time that Wilcox relied increasingly on drug injections to pitch, other players around baseball were also relying increasingly on illegal drugs to maintain an on-field edge.

Baseball's ongoing drug problems had not yet become public, but they soon would. The messy 1985 Pittsburgh drug trials would demonstrate that cocaine had become nearly as popular as chewing tobacco in some clubhouses. Before baseball's jaunt through the mud was complete, among the many stars who were disciplined for their contribution to the massive illegal substance problems in the game were Dave Parker and Keith Hernandez. Wilcox was not drawn to recreational cocaine, but instead to injections of Xylocaine for his aching shoulder. He had a reputation as a workhorse, and even if his shoulder was killing him, he would work to keep that reputation alive.

On April 15, 1983, Wilcox prepared to take the mound as the 4-4 Tigers were about to begin a series with Chicago at Comiskey Park. Barely a week into the season, the Tigers were a half-game behind the Cleveland Indians in the AL East. The White Sox were 3-4 and had won twice at

Detroit the week before. The Sox were led by future Hall of Fame catcher Carlton Fisk and featured a trio of other sluggers—youngsters Ron Kittle and Harold Baines and veteran Greg Luzinski. Those three combined for 87 home runs and 294 RBI in 1983. Young pitchers LaMarr Hoyt, Rich Dotson, and Floyd Bannister were formidable starters who went on to combine for 62 victories among them in the 1983 season. Hoyt, who had won against Jack Morris in Detroit four days prior, would draw the starting assignment on the night of April 15th—against Milt Wilcox.

Wilcox would make his second appearance of the season. He had started against Chicago at home on April 8th and taken the loss—allowing six runs in six and two-thirds innings. He had been slated to next pitch against the Yankees, but he had tweaked his knee slightly, so Sparky Anderson moved his start to the 15th to give him an extra day of rest. But on a cold Friday night in Chicago, Wilcox's second shot at the Sox would prove different.

The gametime temperature was 43 degrees, and 19,483 brave souls fought the elements to try to enjoy April baseball in the windy city. It was the kind of night when good contact stings a hitter's hands. Wilcox would rarely allow Chicago hitters to make anything resembling solid contact at the plate.

The Tiger hitters began the game by going down in order against LaMarr Hoyt, with a groundball, a flyball, and a strikeout. Shortly after the 7:36 p.m. start time, Wilcox took to the mound for the first time. His repertoire included an average fastball, a slow curve, and a split-fingered fastball, which he had learned from Tigers pitching coach Roger Craig, who spent the early to mid-1980s resurrecting careers by teaching the pitch. On this night, Wilcox relied heavily on the fastball and curve, especially in the early innings, and mixed in the splitter (also called a forkball) as he grew more comfortable on the mound.

Wilcox kept the ball down, and White Sox hitters began the game by slapping it harmlessly into the ground. Outfielder Rudy Law grounded to Whitaker at second base. Second baseman Tony Bernazard tapped a grounder to shortstop Trammell, who had to hurry, but threw Bernazard out cleanly at first. Harold Baines finished the inning by grounding to Tiger first baseman Rick Leach, who fielded the ball and tossed it to Wilcox at first to end the easy first inning.

The Tiger bats did not wait long to provide Wilcox with run support. Lance Parrish led off the second with a double, and after a groundout, Parrish scored when outfielder Glenn Wilson lined a triple to right-center field. Wilson then came home to score on Chet Lemon's base hit, and Detroit had a 2–0 lead that would be secure all night.

Wilcox got right back to work in the second, inducing the powerful Greg Luzinski to pop up a foul that Parrish tracked down. Ron Kittle, who had homered in the last three games, and went on to win the 1983 AL Rookie of the Year Award, followed Luzinski to the plate. While Wilcox had struggled against the Sox on April 8th, he had fared well with Kittle in their first encounter, retiring him three times, with two strikeouts in the mix. Kittle was no luckier on April 15th, as he became Milt's first strikeout victim. Greg Walker then grounded out to third baseman Howard Johnson, and the inning was finished.

The Tigers went down in order in the third, but it was just that much quicker for Wilcox to return to the hill. Sox catcher Carlton Fisk became the first Chicago hitter to get the ball out of the infield, but his routine fly to left fielder Larry Herndon was as useless as a soft grounder. Third baseman Vance Law grounded to Johnson, and Jerry Dybzinski, a light-hitting utility infielder, tapped back to Wilcox to end the first circuit through the Chicago batting order.

The Tigers failed to add to their lead in the visitors' half of the fourth frame, and Wilcox began his second trip through the Chicago lineup. Rudy Law fouled out to catcher Parrish to lead off the inning. Parrish, who had been an All-Star in two of the past three seasons, and would make the team again in 1983, told reporters after the game that Wilcox "pitched the best ballgame I've ever caught or seen." Wilcox continued his masterpiece by getting Tony Bernazard to ground to Whitaker, and Harold Baines to ground to Rick Leach. He was perfect through four innings.

Detroit failed to add to their lead, and in the fifth inning, Chicago hitters looked not only cold, but absolutely frozen. First, Luzinski watched a third strike. Then Kittle did the same—making his fourth strikeout in five career at-bats against Wilcox. With two out, first baseman Greg Walker lined a hard shot to the right side of the infield, in perhaps the cleanest contact all night off of Wilcox. As quickly as the threat materialized off Walker's bat, it was gone, as first baseman Leach snagged the line drive easily to end the fifth inning.

Detroit added to Wilcox's cushion in the top of the sixth inning. Howard Johnson singled, and after a strikeout, Parrish doubled in Johnson to extend the Tiger lead to three runs. Later in the inning, Chet Lemon singled home another run, and the score was 4–0 when the top of the inning ended.

Not that Wilcox relied on the extra offense. As one contemporary writer noted, "[A]s the night grew chillier, Wilcox grew hotter." In the bottom of the sixth inning, Wilcox struck out the side. He flirted with danger with Carlton Fisk, falling behind by a 3-0 count before coming back to whiff Fisk. Journeyman Vance Law and utility player Jerry Dybzinski also made the walk of shame back to the Chicago dugout after missing third strikes. Wilcox had fanned five of the last six batters he faced, and was in control of the game as he completed his second round of the White Sox lineup.

Wilcox denied paying attention to the usual no-hitter superstitions, although he did admit to reporters after the game that he was nervous. "You know you have a no-hitter," he advised. "I could hear it on the radio and people were talking about it." People would continue to talk about it as the night wore on and history became closer and more tangible.

The Tigers did not extend their lead off of Hoyt and reliever Jerry Koosman. Meanwhile, manager Anderson made his only substitution of the night, bringing in third baseman Tom Brookens to hit against lefty Koosman, and keeping him in the game for defense at third base. As the bottom of the seventh inning arrived, Wilcox got leadoff batter Law to ground out to first baseman Leach, who made the play unassisted. Leach again was involved when Tony Bernazard popped a foul fly into his glove.

With two out, Wilcox had another relatively close call as Harold Baines hit a low liner into left field, but left fielder Larry Herndon made the play cleanly, and completed the seventh perfect inning of the game.

Glenn Wilson and Chet Lemon knocked in additional runs in the top of the eighth inning, staking Wilcox to a 6–0 advantage with only six outs to go to baseball perfection. For his part, Wilcox responded to the growing enthusiasm of the Chicago crowd with another strong frame. Luzinski watched a third strike, and Ron Kittle hit a routine fly to Chet Lemon. When Wilcox snuck a third strike past Greg Walker, for his eighth strikeout of the game, Comiskey Park had determined that the chance to view epic baseball greatness was more significant than rooting for the home team.

After a scoreless top of the ninth inning, Comiskey Park rose and gave Wilcox a standing ovation as he returned to the mound for one last battle with the White Sox. The eternally dangerous Fisk led off the ninth inning. He took no chances with Wilcox, swinging at the 98th pitch of the night, but lofting a soft flyball to left field, only the fourth ball hit out of the infield, but an easy catch for Larry Herndon for out number one. Lefty pinch-hitter Mike Squires batted for Vance Law. He was 0-for-6 on the season, but set his sights on breaking up Wilcox's perfecto. Milt missed with a first pitch fastball, falling behind in the count to a chorus of boos from the Sox crowd. Squires fouled away the next pitch, evening the count. He fouled the next pitch back, going behind by a second strike. The next pitch edged outside and Squires took it for a ball, drawing a louder chorus of boos from his own fans. Squires then took a breaking ball outside, drawing to a full count—only the fourth time all night that Wilcox went to three balls on a hitter. Milt split the plate with his next offering and Squires grounded it gently to first, where Rick Leach fielded it, raced to the bag, and recorded the second out.

Wilcox was doing his best to stay cool. "In the ninth, all I wanted to do was go right at the hitters. I'm not a trick pitcher," he said after the game. But not everyone was as cool. Sparky Anderson admitted that he had never seen a perfect game, and told the media that pitching coach Roger Craig was so nervous that he was shaking in the dugout in the ninth inning.

One man who did not indicate any particular nervousness was Chicago pinch-hitter Jerry Hairston, who was sent up by Sox manager Tony La Russa. Hairston later commented, "Our pride was at stake because we are the best hitting club in the league." As the uncomfortably cold game had progressed, Hairston sat in the clubhouse waiting for a pinch-hitting appearance. The veteran outfielder, a switch hitter, debuted in the big leagues in 1973. He never recorded more than 227 at-bats in a single MLB season, but was a career .258 hitter, and a tough out off the bench.

Hairston was 0-for-6 on the 1983 season. He told reliever Jerry Koosman that he was going to jump on the first pitch from Wilcox. For his part, Wilcox later told reporters, "I knew he'd be swinging at the first pitch, but I didn't want to fall behind in the count."

The first pitch came in, high in the strike zone, exactly where Hairston liked the ball. "It was the worst pitch I made all night," lamented Wilcox after the game. Hairston jumped on the pitch, lining it solidly into center field for a base hit, ending the perfect game and the no-hitter.

Wilcox fought off the disappointment, got Rudy Law to ground to Leach on the next pitch, and put the finishing touches on a 6–0 win that was so close to perfection. The veteran admitted his disappointment. "If you pitch a perfect game, you go into the Hall of Fame," Wilcox said after the game. "That's the only way I'm going to get there." Instead, Wilcox had his first win of the season and a $1 fine from the team's kangaroo court for giving up a base hit.

Hairston stayed active in the big leagues through 1989, remaining a tough out as a pinch-hitter. LaMarr Hoyt, despite winning 24 games and the 1983 AL Cy Young award, was arrested or detained four times in two years on drug-related matters in 1986 and 1987. He won 98 career big-league games. The 1983 White Sox won 99 games and the division title, although they lost the ALCS to the Orioles.

The Tigers made a good run in 1983, but finished second to the Orioles for the division crown. Wilcox won 11 games and battled some injuries down the stretch. His best—and worst—times in baseball were both still ahead of him, even if he never approached perfection again.

Milt Wilcox's career went both into the stratosphere and ultimately to the dogs as a result of the 1984 season. The two biggest missing items from his résumé entering that season were a world championship and a career-defining season. Both Wilcox and the Tigers started like gang-busters in '84. The Tigers went 35-5 in the first two months of the year, and Milt began the year with a 6-0 mark and a 3.08 ERA on May 20th. Milt fell back to an 8-6 mark at the All-Star break, but went 9-2 in the second half of the year to finish with a career best 17-8 record.

On paper, everything was wonderful. But in reality, Wilcox was breaking down. He never missed a start, but received seven cortisone injections in his right shoulder over the course of 1984. He recalled, "We'd inject the joint with Xylocaine, which deadens the pain, and then follow it with cortisone to quiet the inflammation. It started in May and went through the end of the season. I'd go through withdrawal from the cortisone. I'd get hot flashes, sweat, and my heart would start beating real fast. I kept a lot of symptoms away from the trainers because I didn't want them to refuse me from getting it anymore." Down the stretch, Wilcox also was treated with dimethyl sulfoxide, which is intended for horses and may not be safe for human use.

Unlike the heavy hitters in baseball's 1980s drug war, who doped up recreationally, or the upcoming steroid users in the 2000s, Wilcox wasn't seeking to gain a competitive edge, but just to stay on the mound. "I stayed healthy enough to never miss a start," he said of 1984. "But I had a feeling this was possibly my last year."

Wilcox was especially effective in the biggest games of all. He earned a hard-fought 1–0 win in the clinching third game of the ALCS. With the World Series tied 1–1, Wilcox picked up a gutsy victory in Game 3 over the Padres, scattering seven hits over six innings of one-run ball for the win. Two games later, the Tigers were the champions of baseball.

And Wilcox, for all intents and purposes, was done. "In mid-December [1984], I couldn't lift my arm to brush my teeth," he recalled. "I couldn't even comb my hair. I couldn't do anything." Arthroscopic surgery and extensive rehabilitation followed, but provided little help. Wilcox won one game for Detroit in 1985, pitching just 39 innings, as his shoulder finally forced him out of action. He tried again in 1986 in Seattle, but was 0-8 with a 5.50 ERA before he was released. The last batter he faced in the big leagues was Jerry Hairston. This time, Hairston grounded out.

Wilcox ended up posting a 119-113 career record with a 4.07 ERA in 2,016⅔ big-league innings. He pitched a total of 10 MLB shutouts, with the last coming in the start after his near-perfect game, when he five-hit the Seattle Mariners on April 22, 1983. Wilcox stuck around baseball for a time, pitching effectively for two seasons in the Senior League and spending some time as a broadcaster.

However, at the end of the day, as for most players, there was a vacuum from the competitive fires of baseball to life after the game. Wilcox had always loved animals, and once he was finished with baseball, a friend gave him a black Labrador that he named Sparky Anderson. One day, Wilcox was watching ESPN and saw a dog jumping into water and inspiration struck.

The next thing he knew, not only was Sparky Anderson one of the top jumping dogs in the world, but Wilcox was creating a whole new sport. In 2002, he founded Ultimate Air Dogs, and began traveling around, putting on dog-jumping events. Dogs run down a dock and jump into a pool or lake, with the longest-distance jumps constituting victory. Wilcox was hooked.

Dog jumping became not just a hobby but a livelihood. "I make money by playing again," Wilcox told a journalist. "Baseball was work because there was a lot that went into preparing to pitch in a game, but it wasn't work because it was just fun, and the end result is the same with dock jumping. After all the miles I travel, I have fun with my dogs and with other people, and that's what it's all about." Indeed, Wilcox met his current wife, Cathi, at a dog jumping event in Florida. His son, Brian, is an active part of Ultimate Air Dogs.

After the heartbreak of near-perfection, and then ruining his arm with a great team and title, Wilcox became firmly vested in Ultimate

Air Dogs. His new work found him carrying almost a missionary zeal to share his new findings with dog owners and lovers around America. This was particularly poignant as things turned very sour with the Tigers. Wilcox did not appear for some of the 30th anniversary tributes to the 1984 team, apparently not by his own choice but due to a pending workers' compensation claim arising out of a knee injury in a Tigers fantasy camp. In mid-2015, he made clear where his loyalties stood. "[The Tigers] are not real happy with me, and I'm not real happy with them— not the players, but the management," Wilcox said. "I think they should treat former players a little bit nicer than they do." Wilcox expressed criticism of a perceived lack of organizational support for Whitaker, Trammell, and Jack Morris's bids for the Baseball Hall of Fame. "If any of those players—maybe even Lance Parrish—played on the Yankees, they'd be in the Hall of Fame."

Still, for the most part, Wilcox has been too busy to dwell on hard times or slights. He became involved in a sport that he loves and has participated in almost year-round. "I'm still going to stay young my entire life," he said. "Sometimes people will say, 'When are you going to grow up and be responsible?' Well, I don't want to. I want to stay young and have fun." Wilcox has spoken of retiring soon from Ultimate Air Dogs, but in the meanwhile, he traded in managers and baseball friends for four-legged friends. His philosophy seems pretty nearly perfect.

April 15, 1983
Comiskey Park, Chicago, IL

	1	2	3	4	5	6	7	8	9	R	H	E
DET	0	2	0	0	0	2	0	2	0	6	14	0
CHI	0	0	0	0	0	0	0	0	0	0	1	2

W: Wilcox (1-1)
L: Hoyt (1-2)

The End of Wilcox's Perfect Game:

Bottom of Ninth Inning, Two Outs.
First pitch to pinch-hitter Jerry Hairston.
Hairston lined a single to center field.

CHAPTER 8

THE TRUE CREATURE AND CHARLIE HUSTLE

May 2, 1988
Montreal Expos at Cincinnati Reds
Ron Robinson

Baseball has a long and colorful history of nicknames. From Dummy and Rube to Three-Finger or Vinegar Bend, baseball players—and particularly pitchers—have been saddled with monikers ranging from unusual to unfortunate.

But "The True Creature"? How did Ronald Dean Robinson acquire such a handle?

"I had been called up in August of '84 ... and we went to Montreal," remembers Robinson. "And [Pete Rose] asks me if I know anybody on the Expos. I said, 'Yeah, I know [Montreal outfielder] Jim Wohlford.' And

Ron Robinson, who was given a nickname and an opportunity to pitch by the now-exiled Pete Rose
NATIONAL BASEBALL HALL OF FAME

[Rose] goes, 'You mean "The Creature"?' And I said, 'Uhhhh, I guess so.' And he says, 'No, you're The True Creature.' So, I thought, 'Well ... I have no problem if Pete's making fun of me. As long as I'm in the big leagues, who cares?'"

Shortly after Robinson was promoted to the big leagues, Rose became not only his teammate but his manager. Charlie Hustle's final days in Cincinnati coincided with Robinson's development into an almost-perfect pitcher. But both would be gone before Cincinnati returned to the top of the heap of Major League Baseball. One, to Milwaukee, and the other, to baseball purgatory.

⌒

Ron Robinson could have been "The True Creature" due to his freakish athletic ability. At Woodlake High School, Robinson was not only a top baseball prospect but also a star QB on the football team. Growing to 6'4" in height and always a thick, muscular player, he was good enough that Fresno State sought him out on a football scholarship as well as a baseball scholarship. Robinson's father, Leo, was a legendary coach in California high school football and baseball circles. He won 290 football games over 41 years, good at the time for the third most football wins in California high school history. Robinson admits, "I was around sports all my life." He hoped to be a physical education teacher himself, if his professional sports dreams didn't come true.

Robinson's decision between baseball and football became considerably easier when the Cincinnati Reds drafted him in the first round of the 1980 major-league draft. Robinson climbed steadily through the minor leagues as a starting pitcher. He spent the end of 1980 and the 1981 season in A ball, won 13 games in AA in 1982, and split 1983 between AA and AAA. After pitching solidly in AAA in 1984, he got the call to Cincinnati.

As a big leaguer, Robinson was yo-yoed back and forth between starting and relieving. For a player who had pitched in relief only 10 times in four professional seasons, this was a startling change. Still, as a rookie, for the most part he was happy to be around. He went 1-2 with a 2.72 ERA in five starts and seven relief appearances.

The following season was more of the same for Robinson. He was 7-7 with a 3.99 ERA in 1985. He made 12 starts and 21 relief appearances, totaling 108⅓ innings. In his first full season as a manager, Rose could not determine how to best utilize Robinson. The Reds had a successful season, winning 89 games and finishing second to the NL Champion Cardinals in their division. At 44 years old, Rose not only managed but also had 405 at-bats over the course of the season. On September 11th, Rose broke Ty Cobb's all-time hit record with his 4,192nd hit. Robinson had started the day before.

In 1986, Rose determined that he would turn to Robinson to further shore up Cincinnati's strong bullpen, often setting up relief ace John Franco. Robinson made 70 appearances, all in relief, good for sixth most pitching appearances in the National League. He posted a 10-3 record, a 3.24 ERA, and 14 saves. But he wasn't happy.

In mid-1986, Robinson offhandedly mentioned to writers that he'd like a job description. Rose countered by saying, "Robinson's job is to pitch when I give him the ball." After two other starting pitchers were injured, Robinson admitted that he "kind of thought they'd use me. I've been waiting for the call. My friends and other players ask me, 'When are you gonna start?' I tell them, 'I don't know. I'm in middle relief, I think.'"

If 1986 was frustrating, then 1987 was near torturous. Robinson began the year pitching out of the bullpen, but rapidly developed arm problems that would plague him intermittently for the rest of his career. He moved to the rotation in June, and spent the rest of the season starting. For the year, Robinson was 7-5 with a 3.68 ERA. He started 18 times and pitched out of the bullpen 30 more. On August 10th, Robinson was examined by Dr. Frank Jobe, who assessed him with tendinitis due to a bone spur in his right elbow. Robinson planned for postseason surgery and noted, "In the meanwhile, I'll pitch as long as the ice and aspirin hold out." Arm surgery, ice, and aspirin would accompany Robinson for the rest of his days in baseball. "It complicated the rest of my career," he said in 2015. "We never really got it right." Robinson underwent surgery on October 8th and began the long, slow process of healing. After a lengthy offseason, he was ready to go in 1988.

The Reds had finished second in the NL West in 1986 and 1987, and the young team looked primed for a postseason run. Shortstop Barry Larkin made his first All-Star team in 1988, and showed the form that would one day lead to his induction into the Baseball Hall of Fame. Oft-injured star outfielder Eric Davis slugged 26 homers and stole 35 bases despite battling various ailments and complaints. His fellow outfielders, Kal Daniels and Paul O'Neill, both had excellent seasons. Third baseman Chris Sabo was an All-Star as a rookie. On the mound, Danny Jackson won 23 games and finished second in the Cy Young Award voting. Fellow lefty Tom Browning won 18 games himself, leaving the Reds trying to cobble together a back end of their rotation from several likely candidates, including Ron Robinson.

Pete Rose, still among the most popular men in Cinncinnati, remained the Reds manager. On April 30th, the Reds hosted the New York Mets at Riverfront Stadium. Cincinnati was 11-10, having opened the season in competent, if rather uninspired fashion. Umpire Dave Pallone was working first base that night. Pallone, who had been a strikebreaker as a rookie umpire, had a history of prior issues with the Reds, including an ugly confrontation with shortstop Dave Concepción in 1983, in which Concepción spit in his face. At least one writer further notes that Pallone had been angered by a rumor that he had "tried to pick up a young man in a Cincinnati bar." Pallone later outed himself as a homosexual in his autobiography, but the writer in question maintains that the umpire "had gone out of his way to make life difficult for Rose and the Reds."

Whatever the full history, another chapter was forthcoming. With the game tied 5–5 in the ninth inning, Mookie Wilson hit a grounder to shortstop, where Larkin's throw threatened to drag stretching first baseman Nick Esasky off the bag. Pallone hesitated, and only after the Mets' first base coach signaled safe did he make his call. Safe! Howard Johnson of the Mets had hustled through the play and scored from second base. Rose erupted from the home dugout.

Pallone looked like a matador as the enraged Rose charged him, vociferously making his objection not only to Pallone's call but to how slowly it had been in coming. Pallone went back at Rose, and Rose began pointing his finger for emphasis as the two men stood within inches of each other. Pallone pointed his finger back at Rose, and may or may not have actually brushed Rose's face with his finger. Whether it was that brush, as Rose seemed to suggest later, or Pallone's words, something drove Rose further over the edge, and he shoved Pallone backward. Pallone threw Rose out of the game immediately, and Rose bumped him again during further argument.

The Mets won the game 6–5, but that quickly became secondary as National League president A. Bartlett Giamatti announced on May 2 that he had suspended Rose for 30 days and fined him $10,000. The money was a drop in the bucket, but the suspension was the lengthiest for a manager since Leo Durocher's yearlong suspension in 1947 for consorting with gamblers. Such a severe penalty doubtlessly made some wonder whether Giamatti had it in for Rose. Unfortunately, it would be far from the last meeting of the two.

So as Ron Robinson prepared for his next start, on May 2, the same day that Rose's suspension was announced, his manager would not be Rose but rather Reds coach Tommy Helms, who was handed the interim role. For his part, Rose made good use of his time off, immediately undergoing knee surgery to repair a ligament he had torn playing tennis just before spring training.

With so much talk of Rose, the May 2 game against the Montreal Expos had faded into the background. Cincinnati was 11-12, and the Expos were 10-11. Only 15,107 fans attended the game at Riverfront Stadium in Cincinnati.

Montreal was a talented squad, led by outfielder Tim Raines and first baseman Andres Galarraga. Veteran outfielder Hubie Brooks also approached 100 RBI for the team. On the mound, Dennis Martinez was the Expo ace, and fastballer Pascual Pérez faced off against Robinson to open the series on May 2nd.

Ron Robinson had won his last start, against the Expos on April 26th. He had gone only five and a third innings, throwing 92 pitches. With his injury problems, the Reds certainly did not intend to exhaust Robinson. He had started four games and thrown 22 innings in compiling a 1-2 record and a 4.09 ERA. Robinson, in fact, recalled that he was on a pitch count that night—specifically, 75 pitches. He would eclipse that limit, and as the game went on, Rose's suspension would be forgotten as the lucky few in Riverfront Stadium witnessed near-perfection.

"Warming up that night, I felt terrible," remembered Robinson. "That was probably one of the worst bullpens I had in my whole career. There was a DJ in town and he was not too far from the dugout and he said, 'How are you feeling today?' and I said, 'Stick around. It won't be very long.'"

Teammate Tom Browning would later remember Robinson's effort on May 2, 1988, as remarkable not as much for the results as for what the average fan could not see. "Robby had arm troubles all year," Browning wrote in 2012. "His elbow was in such bad shape that he would have to squat down to pick up the ball from the mound. He just couldn't straighten his arm out to reach down and pick it up. I don't know how he was able to pitch like that. Guts and guile and whatever he could muster, I suppose."

Guts and guile aside, Robinson credited throwing strikes—and the aggressiveness of the Montreal hitters—as the keys to his success. "They were hitting the first pitch, they were hitting the second pitch," he noted.

Indeed, the first inning took only 10 pitches. Tim Raines opened the game by lining out to Paul O'Neill in right field on the second pitch. The second batter, Johnny Paredes, grounded to Larkin on Robinson's second pitch to him. Hubie Brooks then struck out swinging to end the inning. In the bottom of the inning, Kal Daniels homered off of Pérez, staking Robinson to a 1–0 lead, and setting the stage for later controversy.

Robinson was almost as efficient in the second inning as he had been in the first. The frame took a total of 12 pitches, and ended up as a trio of groundouts. Tim Wallach grounded out to second baseman Jeff Treadway. Andres Galarraga grounded to Larkin on the first pitch, and Mitch Webster then grounded to Treadway. Six up, six down.

The Reds didn't score in the bottom of the second, but then Robinson plowed through the third inning in just seven pitches. Mike Fitzgerald grounded out to Sabo, Tom Foley flied out to Kal Daniels in left field, and opposing pitcher Pérez bunted back to Robinson to end the inning.

Robinson featured four pitches—the usual repertoire of fastball, curve, changeup, and slider. He was noted throughout his career for a solid heater with movement. On this night, Robinson and his catcher, Bo Diaz, were in sync. "I remember Bo Diaz catching me and never shaking him off," says Robinson. "I remember everything going my way."

To be sure, Robinson was enjoying an unusually fortunate outing. After Pérez set down the Reds in order in the home third inning, it took Robinson just eight more pitches to complete the fourth inning. Tim Raines grounded to Larkin, Paredes fouled out to Nick Esasky at first base, and Brooks flied out to shallow left field. Four innings had yielded 37 pitches, a couple of routine flyballs, and a heap of grounders. The Reds tacked on an insurance run in the fourth inning, with Eric Davis singling home Kal Daniels, who had previously stolen a base off of Pascual Pérez.

Staked to a two-run advantage, Robinson saw no reason to change a good thing. Tim Wallach lined to Larkin to begin the inning. Andres Galarraga saw seven pitches, working a full count before striking out. Mitch Webster then lined out to O'Neill on the first pitch. The Reds went down in order in the fifth, and Robinson quickly returned to the mound.

Leadoff man Mike Fitzgerald hit a flyball fairly well, but Kal Daniels chased it down easily. Tom Foley had a rare advantage with a 2-0 count, but then flied out to Eric Davis. Pérez finished the frame by striking out, Robinson's third punchout of the game. A second trip through the Montreal batting order had been completed, and more than a few folks in Riverfront Stadium had started to wonder about perfection.

In the bottom of the inning, Chris Sabo led off with a home run off Pérez, extending the Cincinnati lead to 3–0. The next batter was Kal Daniels, who had also homered off of Pérez. Pérez was a respected competitor, but a pitcher with something of a reputation as a showboat and a hothead. An anonymous opponent once said of him, "There's not enough mustard to cover Pérez. He's such a hot dog."

Pérez apparently took umbrage to Daniels and Sabo, and counterattacked by throwing at Daniels. Pérez had played a major role in one of baseball's biggest bench-clearing brawls when he had hit the leadoff batter in a game against the Padres. When the Padres had hit Pérez during his at-bat, a maelstrom had broken loose. Now, the Reds immediately spilled out of the dugout onto the field, and mayhem was again looming. Perfect game or no, the imposing Robinson was one of the first players out of the Reds' dugout. Fortunately, no punches were thrown, and Reds pitching coach Wayne Breeden counseled Robinson not to let the altercation affect him.

Cincinnati did not score additional runs, and Robinson returned to the mound for the seventh inning with a 3–0 lead. Again, it took him just 10 pitches to dispose of the Expos. Tim Raines flied out to Daniels in left field. Paredes, eschewing conventional baseball morality, bunted, but Esasky fielded the ball and fired to Robinson for the out. With two out, Hubie Brooks lined out to Esasky to end the seventh inning.

According to Robinson, the legitimate possibility of a no-hitter or perfect game entered his mind "after the top of the seventh, when nobody would sit around me." While his teammates, in keeping with baseball tradition, were giving Robinson the silent treatment, he was determined not to change his gameplan.

"It was business as usual," he said. "It was going so smooth. The total thing, of just being in a groove, was throwing strikes. I almost hit Tom Foley. . . . But I didn't have any close calls, the whole game." The Reds went down in order in the seventh, and Robinson returned to the mound just six outs from history.

He was so efficient that only late in the eighth inning did Robinson eclipse the 75-pitch mark. Of course, with a perfect game on the line, the pitch count was out the window. Tim Wallach tapped back to Robinson for the first out of the eighth. Andres Galarraga lined to Kal Daniels in left field. Mitch Webster worked a full count, but with the crowd holding its breath, he grounded out to Treadway at second. Three outs to go.

While Robinson's teammates were giving him the silent treatment in the dugout, the home crowd was not. "I got a standing ovation for striking out [in the eighth]," Robinson recalls with a laugh. The Reds went down in order, and in well under two hours, Robinson returned to the mound for his date with history.

Mike Fitzgerald worked a 2-2 count, but then grounded out to Larkin. Two to go. Tom Foley flied out harmlessly to Davis on a 1-2 pitch. Ron Robinson was one out away from history. Manager Buck Rodgers needed a pinch-hitter for Pérez, and he called for Wallace Johnson. A switch hitter with a penchant for contact hitting, Johnson was one of the premier pinch-hitters in the National League. Three hundred of his 569 MLB at-bats came as a pinch-hitter, and Johnson hit .260 in that role. Robinson had faced Johnson once before two years prior, and on that occasion, he had gotten Johnson out.

Pitching carefully, and feeling the weight of the occasion, Robinson worked to a 2-2 count on Johnson. He threw a changeup on the outside corner that he called "really good." Johnson looked fooled, but reached out at the last instant and punched the pitch foul. He wasn't one of the best pinch-hitters in baseball for nothing. The video of the moment shows Johnson looking aggressive, even jumpy. His eyes never leave Robinson for a second. Robinson, on the other hand, takes his time, wipes his hands on the rosin bag, and generally looks like a man trying to find another perfect pitch.

The next offering was a curveball, again on the outer half of the plate. "I thought it was a pretty good pitch," Robinson remembers. Johnson went with the pitch, poking it on a low arc into left field, where it one-hopped Kal Daniels for a solid single. "If I tried to pull that pitch," Johnson told reporters after the game, "I would have hit a groundball." Instead, he hit a soft line drive into history.

Robinson never blames Daniels for failing to catch Johnson's hit, and in fact, went out of his way to credit his teammates for their role in the game, but he does mention that Rose often substituted Dave Collins into games in late-game situations, because he was "a little bit better defensively."

Daniels was not generally noted as a particularly brilliant defensive outfielder, and Collins, much fleeter of foot, was on the active roster. Rose had inserted Collins twice in left field in late-game situations in April 1988. In a contemporary article, Rose was noted as telling Robinson, "You threw that pitch and I saw it was hit to left and I was screaming,

'Get it, get it, get it.'" Johnson's hit was clean, and it is doubtful that even a faster outfielder playing a more shallow position could have made a play. But the nagging question is still there.

Back on the mound, Robinson had no time for such questions. He wanted to complete his shutout. But Tim Raines, hitting next, clubbed a 3-2 pitch for a home run. Suddenly, not only was Robinson not pitching a perfect game, but his lead was trimmed to 3–2. Pitching coach Wayne Breeden walked to the mound and told Robinson, "I'm sorry as hell you didn't get that final out."

John Franco entered from the bullpen and did get the final out, as the Reds won 3–2. Robinson professed to no real disappointment after the game. "I'm just glad a guy with arm surgery could go that far," he told a reporter.

Ron Robinson won only one more game in 1988. His elbow problems returned, and he pitched only six and a third innings after June 24th, finishing the season with a 3-7 mark and a 4.12 ERA. Arm problems caused him to miss the first half of 1989 as well. Robinson did pitch well in the second half of the season, starting 15 games and going 5-3 with a 3.35 ERA.

However, 1989 was a year to forget for the Cincinnati Reds. Around the beginning of the regular season, *Sports Illustrated* dropped the bombshell that manager Rose was being investigated for gambling, including possibly betting on baseball. Rose fought the allegations vigorously, and refused to even appear with newly crowned MLB commissioner Bart Giamatti for a hearing. On August 24, 1989, Giamatti announced a settlement between MLB and Rose. The settlement allowed Rose to neither specifically admit nor deny betting on baseball, but called for Rose to be permanently placed on baseball's ineligible list. Rose was allowed to apply to MLB for reinstatement in a year, but Giamatti denied that there was any sort of secret deal for reinstatement. To make a sad situation worse, Giamatti, who was only 51 years old, died of a heart attack eight days after making the announcement.

Rose's banishment remains an ongoing concern. In a 2004 book, Rose admitted to betting on baseball, but denied betting on Reds games. The BBWAA and the Veterans Committee have each barred ineligible personnel from Hall of Fame selection, and there are many who maintain that Rose, whatever his misdeeds, deserves to be enshrined in Cooperstown. Not surprisingly, Ron Robinson is one of those. "He totally deserves to be in the Hall of Fame," said Robinson. "What supposedly happened . . . was after he played. . . . He's been a good ambassador for baseball. He's done his time. He deserves to be in the Hall of Fame."

The various MLB commissioners who have followed Giamatti have shown no inclination to reinstate Rose. For his part, Rose has rarely shown much contrition. At one point, a memorabilia dealer sold baseballs Rose had signed, bearing a heading, "Sorry I bet on baseball." That said, time may change the situation. Reports have indicated that in 2010, at a celebrity roast, Rose broke down and wept, acknowledging that he had "disrespected baseball." In 2015, when the All-Star Game was held in Cincinnati, MLB allowed Rose to appear with Barry Larkin, Joe Morgan, and Johnny Bench as part of a fan-elected group of the greatest Reds players ever. Rose received a huge ovation, and rumors surfaced again of possible reinstatement following the event, although they were hastily put down by those in positions of authority.

In 1990, the Reds and Ron Robinson began a new era, with Lou Piniella hired to replace Rose as the new manager. The Reds won their first nine games and posted an otherworldly 30-12 mark in the first two months of the season. For Cincinnati fans, it was a welcome respite to the ugliness of the Rose dismissal. But for Ron Robinson, it was something else.

Robinson did not appear in the first 14 games of the season, and when he was finally used, on April 29th, it was as a long reliever after Danny Jackson was injured. In the next five weeks, Robinson made five irregularly spaced starts for the Reds. "I was healthy, but I wasn't pitching," Robinson told a reporter in 1991. "Lou Piniella didn't know who I was."

Finally, on June 9th, the Reds traded Robinson and pitcher Bob Sebra to the Milwaukee Brewers for outfielder Glenn Braggs and infielder Billy Bates. Robinson immediately flourished in Milwaukee. In roughly two-thirds of a season, he went 12-5 for the Brewers with a 2.91 ERA. Perhaps more impressive for a pitcher with durability concerns, Robinson completed 7 of the 22 starts he made for Milwaukee.

The only bad news for Robinson was that the Reds, behind the strength of their brilliant start, went on to beat the Pirates in the NLCS and sweep the favored Oakland A's in the 1990 World Series. Neither Rose nor Robinson got to be part of the most memorable Cincinnati postseason since the days of the Big Red Machine.

For Robinson's part, he professes no real regret. "The best thing that happened to me was getting traded," he said in 2015. "Marge Schott gave me a ring, the players gave me a share [of the pool of money allotted for the series winners]. . . . But I got to play in both leagues."

The financial aspect of the transaction goes unmentioned, but it clearly did not hurt. After years of playing for the penny-pinching Reds, Robinson parlayed his 1990 success into a new contract with the Brewers. He signed a three-year deal for $3.3 million, which was about double his best annual salary with the Reds.

Unfortunately, 1990 was basically the end of Robinson's big-league career. He made one start in 1991, pitching four and a third innings and reinjuring his arm. He came back in 1992, but was still fighting pain, and went just 1-4 with a 5.86 ERA in eight starts. In March 1993, the Brewers gave Robinson his unconditional release, although they paid him the salary due for the final year of his contract.

~

Robinson wisely refuses to see his own story as tragic. Many of the other key personnel from that game have met with worse fates. Rose, of course, remains persona non grata from Major League Baseball, requiring extensive red-tape clearance to even attend a game. Bo Diaz, the veteran catcher who guided Robinson through his historic game, retired after 1989 and died in November 1990 when he was crushed by a satellite dish. Pascual Pérez, the opposing pitcher, battled drug addiction and was killed during a home invasion in the Dominican Republic in 2012.

Robinson says that he spends his time "chasing my grandkids around and doing the things that retired ball players do," particularly spending time with his family. He still gives pitching lessons in California, and freely admits that he enjoyed getting to return to Cincinnati in 2015 for a reunion of the 1990 team and the All-Star Game.

When asked what he learned from pitching an almost-perfect game, Robinson says without hesitation, "That anybody could do it." It has been a long ride for the man that a baseball icon called "The True Creature." Baseball took him from California to Ohio to Wisconsin and back home. The humility and positivity that sprinkle Robinson's remarks have served him well. But if anybody could be almost perfect, maybe it took "The True Creature" to find the perspective to look back fondly on his just-imperfect brush with history.

May 2, 1988
Riverfront Stadium, Cincinnati, OH

	1	2	3	4	5	6	7	8	9	R	H	E
MON	0	0	0	0	0	0	0	0	2	2	2	0
CIN	1	0	0	1	0	1	0	0	X	3	5	0

W: Robinson (2-2)
L: Pérez (3-3)
S: Franco (4)

The End of Robinson's Perfect Game:

Top of Ninth Inning, Two Outs.
2-2 pitch to pinch-hitter Wallace Johnson.
Johnson singled to left field.

CHAPTER 9

TOMORROW I'LL BE PERFECT

August 4, 1989

New York Yankees at Toronto Blue Jays

Dave Stieb

Just another day at the office? Now, Dave Stieb routinely performed at high levels. Always marked as a particularly driven and tough competitor, Stieb in 1989 had been an All-Star in six of the previous nine seasons. But even such a résumé couldn't make Stieb's run at perfection seem perhaps a bit routine. What did was that the hurler, whose 1986 autobiography was titled *Tomorrow I'll Be Perfect*, was seemingly always flirting with historic mound feats—and being denied at the last possible second.

In 1985, Stieb took a no-hitter into the ninth inning before it was broken up. Twice in

Dave Stieb, who recorded the second-most wins in the 1980s and approached no-hitters painfully often (including his 1989 near-perfect game), before finally nabbing one in 1990 TORONTO BLUE JAYS

a week in late 1988, Stieb had again approached a no-hitter. In fact, in each game, he got down to the last out and, in fact, to the last strike on the last batter. But each time, the obstinate hitters thwarted baseball history. So on August 4, 1989, when Dave Stieb accumulated row after row of zeros on the opposing Yankees' half of the scoreboard, he could be forgiven if this seemed like old news. Stieb, his Blue Jay teammates, and a boisterous home crowd hoped that maybe this would be the night when he would break the "almost" trend.

~~

Dave Stieb was born on July 22, 1957, in Santa Ana, California. Stieb and his older brother, Steve, grew up in nearby Yorba Linda. Stieb wrote of the experience, "So far as I can tell, we were no different than any other kids who grew up in any other middle-class neighborhood. In other words, if I had a dollar for every time my mom said, 'Wait till your dad gets home,' I could have retired long before I decided to take up pitching for a living." Stieb recalled being outshined as a youngster by his brother, writing of the experience, "Steve was the one everybody, myself included, expected to make it. As kids, in high school, in junior college, even as far away as Alaska, the attention was on him and, to be honest, rightfully so. He was that good. Keeping up with him, never mind dreaming about the big leagues, was challenge enough for me."

The brothers played together at Southern Illinois University. Steve was a 13th-round draft choice of the Atlanta Braves, and played for three years in the minor leagues. As for Dave, he was an outfielder at SIU, with self-described "decent power and an exceptional arm." He happened to fill a few innings on the pitching mound one day when Toronto Blue Jays scouts were watching—and then he wound up being the Jays' fifth-round draft choice in the 1978 draft. Stieb recalled being approached by scout Al LaMacchia and asked if he would consider pitching—but Stieb told LaMacchia he was an outfielder. Toronto didn't see things quite that way. "The Blue Jays drafted me," Stieb recalled in 1982, "and while we were negotiating, they asked if I would pitch. I said I didn't know. They said, 'Let's put it this way. The quickest way to make it would be pitching.' I said O.K."

Stieb threw a live fastball and had worked up an effective slider. Stieb pitched 26 innings in A-level Dunedin in 1978, 51 more there in 1979, and 51 more innings in AAA Syracuse. With a 12-2 record and an ERA under 3.00, Stieb was promptly called up to the major leagues.

He was 21 years old, 128 innings into his professional career, and wasn't entirely prepared for what he would find in Toronto.

Toronto had followed Montreal as the second MLB franchise ever placed in Canada, and they had debuted in the 1977 season. In the two years before Stieb arrived in the majors, the Jays lost 107 and 102 games. They lost the team's first game during a minor snowstorm. The Jays played in Exhibition Stadium, a football stadium that had been converted only semi-successfully to baseball use. Blue Jays president Paul Beeston unfondly remembered the park in 2015 as "[not] just the worst stadium in baseball, it was the worst stadium in sports." The challenges were not only external; in many cases, they were cultural.

"It was a learning experience, not only for the players, but for the fans also," admitted Stieb. "They knew really nothing about how to root your team on or be part of a game. It was almost like you were playing on the road . . . because they wouldn't respond when you were generating a rally. They wouldn't even recognize it, and start trying to clap and be loud or start trying to bother the other pitcher."

In fairness to those early Blue Jays fans, in the lean early seasons, they didn't have much to appreciate. In 1979, the team lost 109 games, and in 1980 they lost 95 more. But as time went on, and success came, Toronto fans raised their efforts. "They finally caught on," admits Stieb, who fondly recalled 1991, when Toronto broke the single-season MLB attendance mark. "It evolved from fans not really knowing what to do to being really loud . . . so they learned how to do it."

The young Blue Jays on the field learned how to do it too, as manager Bobby Cox led the team to 89 wins in 1983 and 1984, and then to an AL East division title and 99 wins in 1985. A dynamic outfield and an up-and-coming pitching staff made Toronto one of the best teams in baseball for the remainder of the decade—and beyond.

For his part, Stieb had begun to shine even before the team was competitive. His record was only 12-15 in 1980, but Stieb's excellence on a poor team earned him his first All-Star Game appearance. Stieb won 11 more games in a strike-shortened 1981 season, again earning All-Star honors. From then until 1991, aside from a disappointing 1986 campaign, Stieb reached 13 or more wins in each season. He was a work-horse, twice leading the league in innings pitched, and drawing notice for his intense competitiveness, which could lead him to stare down umpires, opponents, or even teammates after a poor play. But more than that, he drew notice for excellence. Bobby Cox once commented, "I can't imagine anyone being a better pitcher than Dave Stieb."

Unfortunately, aside from general excellence, both Stieb and the Blue Jays were notable for almost, but not quite, reaching history. For his part, Stieb had almost, but not quite, reached a no-hitter on three occasions. In 1985, he had gotten to the last three outs, and in August 1988, he twice made it to the last strike. In 1985, he was victimized by a Rudy Law homer, but in 1988, it was a bad-hop single from Julio Franco and a bloop hit from Jim Traber that kept Stieb out of no-hitter history. Stieb was the second winningest pitcher of the 1980s, but as the decade was running down, he still had a sizable monkey on his back.

Likewise for the Jays, whose 1985 division title was followed by a 3–1 lead in the ALCS. But the Kansas City Royals won the last three games of the series, and then went on to take the World Series. In 1987, Toronto had a three-and-a-half-game lead in their division with a week to go, but lost their last seven games and missed the playoffs. In 1988, the team finished a couple of games behind the Boston Red Sox.

But there was reason for optimism in 1989, for both Toronto and for Dave Stieb. The first piece of good news for all was the midseason opening of the Skydome, Toronto's convertible domed stadium that immediately moved the Blue Jays from the bottom to the top of the heap in terms of facilities. The 1989 season began in misery, as Toronto opened the year with a 12-24 mark before manager Jimy Williams was fired. Williams was replaced by Cito Gaston, and everything turned around almost overnight. The team caught fire, and by August 4th, had fought their way back into the AL East race.

The Blue Jays fielded a talented lineup, led by sluggers Fred McGriff and George Bell. McGriff slugged 36 homers in 1989, and Bell knocked in 104 runs. Defensive standout shortstop Tony Fernandez and up-and-coming third baseman Kelly Gruber both had fine seasons as well. On the mound, Stieb was supported by lefties Jimmy Key, John Cerutti, and Mike Flanagan. The Jays bullpen was led by dominating closer Tom Henke.

And Stieb was very much on his usual form. He missed the All-Star team in 1989, but he had posted a solid 10-6 mark by August 4th. Stieb was pitching well in the new stadium, allowing just one earned run in his first 18⅓ innings at Skydome. The stage was set for Stieb to again flirt with baseball history.

He would be opposed on August 4, 1989, by the Yankees. The traditional pride of baseball, New York was moving toward a second consecutive fifth-place finish. The Yankees had not reached the postseason since 1981, and had not won a championship since 1978. Perennial All-Star Don Mattingly was still a Yankee, and some other big names like second baseman Steve Sax and outfielder Jesse Barfield still filled the roster. But the Bronx Bombers had traded future Hall of Famer Rickey Henderson and were handicapped by a porous pitching staff that weighed the team down. New York had been surpassed by Toronto in the standings, and Yankee manager Dallas Green was in the last month of his tenure.

The Yankees were making their first trip to Skydome. Rookie Clay Parker, who had made only 27 career big-league starts, would take on Stieb in the first game of their series. And Dave Stieb was about to make the Yankees look completely clueless.

For Dave Stieb, he knew that evening in the bullpen that he might well have a special night up his sleeve. "That particular day, I went out to warm up, I'm throwing my fastball, and it's moving nicely. And then I'm throwing my slider and it just wasn't really breaking that good. . . . So I said to myself, 'I'm going to hold the ball like back when I played Little League.' If you tried to throw a curveball [then], you hold it with the seams. . . . You hold your fingers right along those seams and then just break your wrist. . . . I threw one of those, and it broke like two feet. I kept throwing those, and I'm going, 'I'm using *that* this game.'"

Stieb laughingly admits that this wasn't his typical slider, but whatever this slider/curveball hybrid was, he suddenly had found a new weapon, and the Yankees' evening would be the worse for it. Stieb needed just eight pitches to work through the first inning. Steve Sax took a pitch and then lined out to Lloyd Moseby in center field. Luis Polonia grounded harmlessly to second base, and Don Mattingly then also easily flied out to Moseby to end the inning. The Blue Jays went down in order in the home half of the first.

With an inning under his belt, Stieb got even more comfortable, and had the Yankees overmatched and guessing. Lefty slugger Mel Hall whiffed to begin the inning. Right fielder Jesse Barfield followed up by doing the same, and then catcher Bob Geren grounded out to Fernandez at shortstop. In the bottom of the inning, Toronto parlayed singles from Bell and McGriff into a run, and staked Stieb to a 1–0 advantage.

By the third, Stieb was showing the full extent of his mastery, and was enjoying his monster slider concoction. In discussing the game, he recalled, "I went out there and I had right handers frozen, because I would start [the unusual slider] at their hip and it would just break over the plate. Then I'd throw it down the middle and it would break like two feet outside, and they were bailing and swinging and were not even close to it." In a nutshell, that was the third inning. Randy Velarde struck out swinging. Fellow righty Alvaro Espinoza fell behind and grounded out meekly to McGriff at first. And rookie Roberto Kelly fouled off one strike, and then watched two more to end the frame. After three innings and 31 pitches, Stieb had four strikeouts and the Yankees had not even threatened. The pattern was set.

The Blue Jays did not extend their lead in the home third, but Stieb continued baffling the Yankees into the fourth inning. Steve Sax grounded to second. Luis Polonia then lined easily to shortstop Fernandez. The ever-dangerous Mattingly fell behind in the count and lined to Bell in left field to end the inning. Even on the rare occasions when the Yankees made something resembling solid contact, they were not threatening for base hits. Stieb recalled it as like his other no-hit bids. "There were never any great, hit-saving plays," he remembers. "They were all just pretty much routine outs."

After a scoreless fourth inning, Stieb set about creating another round of routine outs. Hall and Barfield had realized that the protracted approach had not worked in their second-inning strikeouts. In the fifth, they came up hacking. Each grounded the first pitch he saw to the sure-handed Fernandez. With two out, catcher Bob Geren jumped ahead of Stieb by watching three balls. It was the only time all game that Stieb went to a three-ball count. Geren then watched strike one, and swung and missed on the next two pitches to end the frame and preserve perfection. Parker, who was pitching a fine game for New York, set the Blue Jays down in order in the bottom of the inning, leaving the score 1–0.

Stieb was dominant in the sixth. He threw just seven pitches. Verlarde grounded Stieb's first pitch to Fernandez for a quick out. Espinoza and Kelly both watched first strikes, and then missed the next two pitches to become Stieb's sixth and seventh strikeouts of the night. Stieb related, "I just kept going with that breaking ball, throwing a lot of that slide-arm-curveball thing, just wearing it out, probably overexposing it. But I didn't care, because it was working and I was liking it. It was probably not until the sixth or seventh inning that I'm thinking, 'I'm close to not only a no-hitter, but a perfect game.'" Unlike most pitchers, Stieb had a veritable wealth of experience to draw on in these situations as he continued to chase history.

Stieb also benefitted from an extended lead, as Nelson Liriano singled and then came in to score on a Mookie Wilson double in the bottom of the sixth inning. With a 2–0 advantage, Stieb took the mound in the seventh inning to begin his third round of the Yankee lineup. Steve Sax swung at the first pitch and hit a routine fly to Wilson in right field. Luis Polonia watched two pitches and then grounded to Liriano at second base. Mattingly followed the same template, and ended the inning with his grounder to second. The Skydome crowd was increasingly aware of the historic effort Stieb was putting together.

The Jays went down in order in the seventh against the Yankee bullpen, and Stieb returned to the mound. Mel Hall watched two strikes and then whiffed at a third one. Jesse Barfield cut and missed at strike three as well. Barfield told reporters after the game, "[H]e threw me mostly sliders, and he had a wicked one. When he's like that, he's almost unhittable." Catcher Bob Geren watched a strike and then grounded harmlessly to Fernandez to end the frame. Here Stieb was again, one inning from history.

After a perfunctory bottom of the eighth, Stieb took the mound for the final time. He had used only 73 pitches to work eight perfect innings, and the Skydome was rocking with anticipation. Lefty pinch-hitter Hal Morris came to bat for Randy Velarde. Morris took a strike, then a ball, whiffed at strike two, fouled another pitch away, and then chased a high outside fastball from Stieb for strike three, Stieb's tenth strikeout of the night. One down. Lefty Ken Phelps, who would break up a ninth-inning perfect game bid a year later, was sent up for Alvaro Espinoza. Stieb got ahead of Phelps on a 1-2 count, and then threw a nasty breaking ball that Phelps swung over for another strikeout. Two down.

Roberto Kelly stood between Dave Stieb and not only perfection, but the end of his no-hitter jinx. Stieb started Kelly with one of the wicked slider/curve offerings that he had increasingly relied upon. "I threw that sidearm-curveball thing, and I left it about an inch inside," recalled Stieb. "[Home plate umpire Terry Cooney] called it a ball. . . . It sat there so close. He could've called it, because of what's going on." So for one of the few times that night, Stieb fell behind. "When he called it a ball," admitted Stieb, "that changed everything."

Stieb threw another breaking ball to Kelly, but this one missed inside, and suddenly he was behind in the count 2-0. Behind in the count, Stieb had to adjust his strategy. "I surely don't want to throw him a fastball," Stieb said. "I think, 'I'm going to throw him a slider.' So I threw him a slider and it broke nicely. I just left it over the middle of the plate."

For his part, Kelly saw an opening. "He threw me a slider, which I saw all day. So I was just looking for the slider," he said after the game. Kelly stayed on the pitch and pulled it sharply into left field, dumping it in front of George Bell. When Bell was slow to move on the ball, Kelly hustled into second with a double. Perfect game over, no-hitter again missed for Stieb.

More than a quarter century on, Stieb second-guesses himself. "It was probably a mistake. I should have probably thrown a fastball. . . . I could have thrown it in on him and jammed him. . . . It was just total heartbreak."

Stieb refocused on the mound, and went back to the business of getting the last out. But Steve Sax singled to right and Kelly scored, to cut the Jays' lead to 2–1. Manager Cito Gaston came to the mound to talk to Stieb, who wanted to finish the game. Luis Polonia then grounded to third, where Kelly Gruber made a diving play, forcing Sax at second and ending the contest. Stieb admitted that he drew comfort from the fact that he was able to finish the game and get his team a win. That said, another near-miss was singularly frustrating. After the affair, he told the media, "If I haven't gotten a no-hitter . . . I doubt I ever will."

Looking back with hindsight, Stieb easily sums up his near-miss experience.

"I got so close so many times, it was a thing where everybody was pulling for me to get one, and that's all they would talk about," he said. "I just got tired of hearing it. Because I understand, it takes a lot of luck to pitch a no-hitter or a perfect game. It really has nothing to do with you as a pitcher, if you don't get one, you're not that good or anything like that. It's just a personal accomplishment."

⌒

While Dave Stieb missed the personal accomplishment of a perfect game, Toronto again came up short in the postseason. The Jays rallied to win the AL East, as Stieb finished the year 17-8, but the team then lost the ALCS to Oakland in five games.

In 1990, Stieb was again in fine form. Toronto lost the division to Boston, but Stieb could hardly be blamed. He went 18-6 with a 2.93 ERA, was named to his seventh (and final) All-Star team, and finished fifth in AL Cy Young voting. And on September 2, 1990, Stieb found himself again approaching a no-hitter, this time against the Indians in Cleveland. Not quite two years prior, Stieb had gone to the last batter with his no-hit bid before a bad-hop single ruined the day. But this time, Jerry Browne ended the game with a line drive into right field—and into the waiting glove of Toronto's Junior Felix. After the game, Stieb told the press, "I had much better stuff the other times, much better control."

Stieb admits to a certain degree of satisfaction that he finally closed the deal. He recently recalled, "The biggest thing about it . . . they put me up on their shoulders, and I'll never forget that. In a team sport, when your teammates lift you on their shoulders, that's got to be the highest accolade in the world. . . . But after about 20 seconds, I said, 'Put me down now, I'm embarrassed.' But it was an awesome feeling. It was an awesome day. And it was an awesome thing to get off my back."

In 1991, Stieb opened the season with a solid start, posting a 4-3 record and a 3.17 ERA. But then he had some tendinitis in his shoulder, which sent him to the disabled list. Once that was improving, he suffered a disc herniation in his back, which necessitated postseason surgery. He came back in 1992, but pitched relatively poorly, in part because he rapidly developed elbow tendinitis that shut him down for the 1992 stretch run.

Unfortunately for Stieb, who had starred for some awful Toronto teams at the beginning of his career, this meant that he couldn't pitch for a historically great Toronto team. Before the season, the 1992 Blue Jays had added veterans Jack Morris and Dave Winfield, and, in part due to Stieb's injury issues, they traded for David Cone during the pennant race. Toronto won the AL East, and found itself facing Oakland again in the ALCS. The Jays led 2–1, but were facing a tied series when Roberto Alomar hit a two-out ninth-inning two-run homer off of A's closer Dennis Eckersley to tie the game. Toronto went on to win the game and the series. The World Series was a nail-biter, with four of the six games decided by one run. But when Mike Timlin threw out Otis Nixon on a bunt in the 11th inning of Game 6, the Toronto Blue Jays were the champions of baseball. And Dave Stieb had watched it happen from the bench.

"It was very bittersweet," admits Stieb. "I was with that team for 15 years. . . . Now finally, to watch these guys spend a ton of money and buy all these veterans, and we've got a killer team in '92, and I'm not on top of my game . . . it would've been nice to have been a starter that year and gone to the World Series and seen what I could have done.

"Obviously, I was one of the biggest fans in that dugout," remembers Stieb. "I wanted us to win so I could get that damn ring! I knew my days there were numbered. . . . We win and I was the first guy on the field and celebrated like I won the last game. I enjoyed it for what it was, but deep down, it was very bittersweet. I'm happy to have a ring and have a little trophy, but I don't look at it like somebody that played in it and won it."

Indeed, Toronto no longer was willing to hold a starting rotation spot for Stieb, and he inked a free-agent deal with the Chicago White Sox for 1993. Stieb continued to battle elbow issues, and after four starts with a 1-3 record and a 6.04 ERA, he was released. Picked up by Kansas City on a minor-league deal, Stieb struggled there, and retired from baseball.

Four and a half years later, he staged an incredibly unlikely comeback. Stieb was guest coaching for the Blue Jays at the time, and went to spring training in 1998. He found himself throwing for batting practice or games of catch, and surprised himself by finding that his lingering elbow issues were gone. Intrigued, Stieb threw an actual bullpen session, and some of the team, including Roger Clemens and Woody Williams, dropped by to watch. Stieb recalls Clemens telling him, "Man, you should still be pitching. Your stuff is nasty." Bullpen catcher Sal Butera was impressed, and on their next session a few days later, Butera stopped the warmup to tell Stieb that he needed to talk to the Jays management about pitching. Stieb remembered being incredulous, thinking, "Man, I'm 40 years old. I'm not going to do this again."

But the lure of pitching was still there for Stieb, and when he approached Jays manager Tim Johnson, who had been a teammate on the 1979 Toronto team, he was encouraged to try a comeback. Stieb was sent to A-level Dunedin, where he had pitched in 1978 and 1979. Stieb was older, but no less effective. He went 2-0 with a 3.00 ERA in three starts, and funny enough, was again promoted past AA to AAA Syracuse, just as he had been 19 years before. In nine starts at Syracuse, Stieb was 5-4 with a 2.73 ERA. Stieb then got the call from the big-league club. Stieb's contract was structured so that if anyone else wanted him on a major-league roster, Toronto could keep him only by allowing him space on their roster. When Texas attempted to sign Stieb, the Blue Jays had no choice but to bring him up or let him go. Stieb admits to mixed feelings, noting that Texas was competitive for a playoff spot, and that he would have enjoyed pitching in a ballpark with a natural-grass surface.

In Toronto, Stieb found himself starting a bit, relieving a bit more, and going 1-2 with three saves and a 4.83 ERA. The Blue Jays encouraged Stieb to return for 1999—as a reliever. Stieb told them he wasn't interested, saying, "I realize I've come full circle. . . . I ended up my career with the team I started with in the big leagues, so I'm done."

Nearing 20 years later, Stieb has no regrets. "It was an awesome thing," he says of the comeback. "I'm so glad I did it, because it was such a rare story. . . . I'm proud to say that in my last year in the big leagues, I was 41 years old and I could still do it."

 ⌒

The Toronto Blue Jays, the franchise that began their professional life at the same time that Stieb began his professional career, are approaching their fourth decade as of this writing, and they are still doing it as well. The Jays won the World Series again in 1993, this time courtesy of a walk-off home run from free agent pickup Joe Carter. The team broke its own MLB attendance record for three consecutive years in the 1990s. While the Jays have been up and down since, the 2015 season was an electric one, and young stars like AL MVP Josh Donaldson have the Blue Jays hoping for further World Series titles.

Dave Stieb posted a career record of 176-137 with a 3.44 ERA in 2,895⅓ MLB innings. His 140 MLB victories in the 1980s were the second-most accumulated in the decade. He has been chosen for the Canadian Baseball Hall of Fame.

Stieb has been out of coaching for years, and in fact has spent the last few years as a partner in a construction company, building homes in and around Nevada. He spends most of the rest of his time with his family, enjoying the company of children and grandchildren. When asked about his legacy, Stieb is direct. "I want to be remembered as one of the most competitive pitchers that ever toed the rubber," he says. Stieb hopes that those who remember him will say, "His objective was to win."

On both accounts, Dave Stieb made his mark. He began with an expansion team that was losing 100 games a year, and helped turn that organization into a perennial contender, even if he wasn't able to pitch through the crowning years of World Series glory. As far as competitiveness, the courage to face down no-hit history four times in five years and come up *just* short, but yet bounce back to make the fifth time a success is unmatched in MLB history. At the end of the day, what else could Stieb do? The path to pitching excellence, to making the Jays a champion, happened to pass through several no-hit near-misses, including the near-perfect game on August 4, 1989. Despite several near-misses, the Jays eventually got to their ultimate prize, and Stieb ultimately completed a successful no-hitter. If at first (or second, or third, . . .), Toronto or Stieb didn't completely succeed, it just made the story that much sweeter when they did.

August 4, 1989
Skydome, Toronto, Ontario, Canada

	1	2	3	4	5	6	7	8	9	R	H	E
NYY	0	0	0	0	0	0	0	0	1	1	2	1
TOR	0	1	0	0	0	1	0	0	X	2	5	0

W: Stieb (11-6)
L: Parker (3-2)

The End of Stieb's Perfect Game:

Top of Ninth Inning, Two Outs.
2-0 pitch to center fielder Roberto Kelly.
Kelly doubled to left field.

CHAPTER 10

"IT'S JUST BASEBALL"

April 20, 1990
Seattle Mariners at Oakland Athletics
Brian Holman

Six weeks before his April 20, 1990, start against the Oakland A's, Seattle Mariners pitcher Brian Holman might've wondered if the game would be played at all. After the 1989 season, the collective bargaining agreement between the Major League Baseball Players Association (MLBPA) and the baseball owners had been allowed to expire. With negotiations going unsteadily, on February 15, 1990, the owners locked the players out of spring training. Despite howls of outrage from baseball fans from Seattle to New York, there was no baseball, and it was unclear when there would be any. Had Brian Holman been able to see his future, he would've known

Brian Holman, who has used his near-perfect outing and off-field adversity to craft a message of resilience that he shares as a motivational speaker

NATIONAL BASEBALL HALL OF FAME

that life issues that dwarfed baseball would haunt his days and nights. As it was, he simply waited to get back to work.

123

The 1990 lockout was another move in the ongoing chess match between the MLBPA and the owners who controlled baseball. In the early days of baseball, players were essentially stripped of any bargaining power for their services due to a reserve clause in the standard players' contract that bound them to their current team with a one-year renewing option into perpetuity. The clause sapped the power of the players to negotiate labor conditions, and had been around for decades. On December 24, 1969, outfielder Curt Flood, having been traded from the Cardinals to the Phillies, wrote to Major League Baseball commissioner Bowie Kuhn, in a letter that would begin a baseball revolution. "After twelve years in the major leagues, I do not feel I am a piece of property to be bought and sold irrespective of my wishes," Flood wrote. "I believe that any system which produces that result violates my basic rights as a citizen and is inconsistent with the laws of the United States and of the several States."

Flood fought the reserve clause all the way to the US Supreme Court, where he lost, but in 1976, arbitrator Peter Seitz declared two pitchers to be free agents, and essentially changed the face of baseball forever. Free agency did lead to wild increases in salary, as the owners had predicted for years. In 1970, when Curt Flood had sued Major League Baseball, the game's top earner was Willie Mays, who was paid $135,000 that season. By 1980, Nolan Ryan eclipsed the $1 million mark. By the mid-80s, top salaries had surpassed $2 million per season, and after the 1989 season, players like Kirby Puckett and Rickey Henderson were signing contracts for more than $3 million per year—more than six times the value of Willie Mays's 1970 salary even after adjustment for inflation. Of course, with television revenues soaring and expansion adding additional teams, baseball made more money than ever before.

The players' payday, however, was often met with significant bitterness from the baseball owners. Following the 1985, 1986, and 1987 seasons, the owners engaged in illegal collusion against free agents. After MLBPA president Donald Fehr filed three successful grievances against baseball ownership, a final settlement of $280 million ended up being paid from the owners to the players due to the collusion activities. Those grievances were still being sorted out when the 1990 lockout began. While baseball had undergone a brief strike in 1972 that canceled a handful of games and a more serious strike in 1981, which gutted about a third of the MLB season and wreaked havoc on the playoff situation, the 1990 lockout had the potential to be a much more serious event. What if, baseball fans wondered, there were no games, no All-Star Game, maybe even no World Series? It had never happened. But as the two sides battled over revenue sharing and the terms of free agency, it began to look possible.

The inactivity of the lost 1990 spring training was hardest on young players like Brian Holman, who had just turned 25 and had spent a year and a half in the major leagues. He was a significant prospect in his high school days in Wichita, Kansas. A Montreal scout and former MLB pitcher, Dick LeMay, saw the potential in Holman, and apparently liked the rest of the family, because not only did LeMay convince the Expos to draft Holman with the first-round pick (16th overall) in the 1983 MLB Draft, but he subsequently married Holman's mother. Holman turned down a scholarship from the University of Nebraska to enter professional baseball. For a couple of seasons, he struggled to learn control in the minor leagues—for instance, walking 119 batters in 98⅔ innings of work at the A level in 1984. But by 1987, he was an All-Star in AA, and in 1988, a similar start in AAA propelled him to the parent club.

Holman went 4-8 for the Expos in 1988, but posted a solid 3.23 ERA. He began the 1989 season at 1-2, but on May 25th, he was included in a package of young pitchers who were shipped to Seattle for Mariners left-hander Mark Langston. Langston was 12-9 for Montreal before signing a hefty free agent contract with the California Angels after the 1989 season. In exchange, the Mariners had netted Gene Harris, who went 2-6 for the club before being traded; Holman; and another young pitcher named Randy Johnson, who went on to earn a Cy Young Award, win 130 games, and strike out 2,162 batters as a Mariner.

Holman recalled, "When Dave Dombrowski called me in . . . to tell me about the trade, he said, 'There's been a trade, you're involved. I traded you to Seattle for Mark Langston.' I was kind of like, 'I'm sure you didn't trade me straight-up for Mark Langston.' And he said, 'No, we traded Gene Harris,' and then in a lower voice, 'and Randy Johnson.'"

Holman further explained, "What was great about [the trade] was that we went from rookies that were just prospects to [pitchers]. . . . Jim Lefebvre came up to us and put a ball in our hands and said, 'You're going to pitch every five days whether you get your brains beat in or not.'"

Holman's 1989 season had gone better than Johnson's. He was 8-10 with Seattle, but posted a 3.44 ERA, with a couple of shutouts, and showed great promise. The Mariners, having been added to the major leagues via expansion in 1977, looked to field a talented if inexperienced squad behind Holman in 1990. The franchise had never enjoyed a .500 season and ended 1989 with a 73-89 mark, but better times were on the way. In addition to Holman and Johnson, pitcher Erik Hanson was a solid young starter. Slick-fielding shortstop Omar Vizquel was just breaking into the major leagues, as were talented first base prospect Tino Martinez and right fielder Jay Buhner, whom the team had acquired from the Yankees for aging slugger Ken Phelps. The crown jewel of the Seattle organization was center fielder Ken Griffey Jr., who had turned 20 years old just after completing his 1989 rookie season in Seattle by finishing third in the American League Rookie of the Year voting. Griffey was a multi-tooled star, excelling at hitting for power and average, making acrobatic defensive plays, and running well.

But as February 1990 turned into March, the labor dispute intensified, and threatened to sideline the 1990 Mariners before the team ever got started. Brian Holman was the Mariners' player representative, so he had a front row seat for the sideshow. The odd days of labor stoppage stick with Holman a quarter century later. "I remember in 1990 sitting on my ranch in Kansas and the owners locked us out of spring training," Holman said. "I remember fishing and just hanging out and rolling up at the little school gym every day and throwing my bullpens. . . . It's scary anytime you go through labor negotiations and disputes. You're trying to do the right thing not only for the guys currently, but the future of all players coming up. Unfortunately, that year, we had a real struggle on our hands."

There were several major stories in the news in the late winter and early spring of 1990, as Nelson Mandela was released from prison and the Soviet Union prepared to stage democratic elections for a president. But in sports news, lockout coverage dragged on ESPN, as every day seemed to bring the same message: still no baseball.

MLB commissioner Fay Vincent continued to work in negotiation with both sides, ultimately chastising the owners to the extent that two years later, he would receive a no confidence vote and be removed as commissioner. However, on March 19th, he announced the news that millions had hoped for: The strike was over. Both sides had made concessions, and a four-year deal settled little but postponed the major fight for another day. Under the circumstances, no spring training games were played, the regular season was delayed until April 9th, and the season was extended by three days to fit all games. But baseball was back!

On Opening Day, Brian Holman was chosen to start for the Mariners. He went only five innings, but picked up a win as the Mariners beat the Angels. Six days later, on April 15, Holman made his second start of the season, against Oakland. He pitched solidly, but lost the game 3–0 to the A's Bob Welch. Five days later, the Mariners played at Oakland, and Holman found himself again matched up with Welch. This time, the results were quite different.

The Oakland Athletics were the defending World Series champions, and a look at the A's lineup showed the team's strength. The roster that faced Holman on April 20, 1990, featured future Hall of Fame out-fielder Rickey Henderson as well as slugging sensations Jose Canseco and Mark McGwire, who had combined for 204 home runs in the past three seasons. Young talents like catcher Terry Steinbach and shortstop Walt Weiss also started for Oakland, which had a fearsome pitching staff featuring Dave Stewart, the aforementioned wily veteran Bob Welch, and closer Dennis Eckersley, who would join Henderson in the Hall of Fame.

The A's had throttled the competition in 1989, beating the Toronto Blue Jays four games to one in the ALCS, and then sweeping the San Francisco Giants in a World Series that was interrupted by an earthquake before Game 3. They had opened 1990 on a similar tear, showing why they were favored to repeat as champions with an 8-1 start. The Mariners, on the other hand, were 2-8, and were in last place in their division. The April 20th game was the second in the series, and was played on a cool night in Oakland with temperatures starting off in the high 50s.

Before the game, Holman bumped into A's manager Tony La Russa at an Italian restaurant for lunch. Holman remembers La Russa stopping by to make small talk, complimenting him on the game five days before, and wishing him good luck.

Warming up in the bullpen, Holman thought he might need a lot of luck. "I didn't have it," Holman recalls. "I felt terrible in 'pen. Nothing was working. I couldn't spot my fastball, my breaking ball was flat, my changeup was flat. I was so terrible that my relievers . . . were taking bets on how long I was going to last and who the first guy out of the bullpen was going to be." Holman did his best to get ready, trying to remember the basics of pitching.

The game moved quickly. Seattle did not score off Welch in the first inning, and Holman took the mound to face Oakland. Rickey Henderson, who was known for hitting leadoff home runs, very nearly did so on a 2-2 offering from Holman, but right fielder Greg Briley chased down the drive. Holman recovered to strike out Stan Javier and Canseco to end the frame.

The two pitchers battled early, with Holman needing only seven pitches to dispatch Oakland in the second inning. McGwire grounded out to Edgar Martinez at third base. Ron Hassey flied the first pitch out to left fielder Jeffrey Leonard, and Terry Steinbach then popped up to Harold Reynolds.

The third inning yielded only a flyball to Griffey in center field and a pair of harmless groundouts. It became apparent to catcher Dave Valle that Holman was doing something special. "I talked to him early on," recalled Valle. "But after the first three innings, I didn't have to make any corrections. He was doing it all by himself."

In the fourth inning, after Rickey Henderson led off with a popup to shortstop, Stan Javier tried to bunt his way on base, but Holman threw him out, and then fielded Canseco's grounder back to the mound to end the inning.

In the visitors' half of the fifth inning, Seattle finally got to Welch. After Mike Brumley tripled, second baseman (and future ESPN commentator) Harold Reynolds tripled him home, with Reynolds then scoring on a double from Greg Briley. The 2-0 lead would prove to be all the help that Holman needed on this night.

In the Oakland half of the fifth inning, McGwire hit a towering flyball to center field, but Griffey flagged it down easily. After Ron Hassey flied out, Holman struck out Terry Steinbach and the game moved on. In the sixth inning, 11 pitches yielded three Oakland groundouts, and Holman had completed his second perfect jaunt through the A's lineup.

The tension became palpable in Oakland's Alameda Coliseum as Rickey Henderson fought through an eight-pitch at-bat to begin the seventh inning, before finally popping out to Griffey. Javier grounded out and Canseco, after blasting a vicious line drive just foul past third base, whiffed on a 3-2 pitch to end the inning.

With history looming, Holman found himself getting the cold shoulder. "As I come off the field, I sit down and everybody got away from me," he recalled. "Nobody would look at me, nobody would talk to me. Nobody would get me a drink of water, nobody would get me a towel. And I'm [thinking], 'Why is everybody acting this way?' Then I look at the scoreboard and it dawned on me that not only had I not given up a hit, but I had a perfect game through seven innings."

Of course, now that he was aware of his shot at perfection, Holman admits that his focus changed. "The crazy thing was I was just out doing my thing, pitching, having fun, and I wasn't nervous at all or worried at all until I looked up and realized what I could possibly lose."

In the eighth inning, Seattle manager Jim Lefebvre made an odd move when he pulled first baseman Alvin Davis as part of a double switch, shifting designated hitter Pete O'Brien to first base in his place. While Lefebvre was doubtlessly trying to make sure that his best defensive unit was behind Holman to protect his shot at perfection, in removing the DH, he caused Holman to have to assume Davis's spot in the batting order—far from a normal circumstance for an American League pitcher.

Holman was unfazed in the eighth, as McGwire flied out, Hassey struck out on three pitches, and Steinbach worked a 3-1 count before grounding out to Brumley at shortstop, leaving Holman three outs away from baseball immortality.

In the top of the ninth, Seattle tacked on four runs. In the midst of the damage, Holman did indeed have to bat. The distraction was an unwelcome one for Holman, who remembered, "Henry Cotto went up with two outs and I yelled, 'Turbo, DO NOT get on base. I do not want to hit.' So he gets walked . . . and he's looking at me like, 'I'm so sorry, Brian.'" Holman, in his only career American League at-bat, grounded to second baseman Mike Gallego, who promptly committed an error. Holman was on second base when the inning ended, and had to get back to the mound for one last battle with Oakland.

Pinch-hitter Félix José led off the inning by striking out on a 1-2 pitch. Holman missed with two pitches in the next at-bat, but Walt Weiss then grounded out to Harold Reynolds, leaving Holman one out away from perfection. Mike Gallego was due up for Oakland, but the light-hitting second baseman was batting .111 on the season, and so—even with the score at 6–0—Tony La Russa went to his bench for pinch-hitter Ken Phelps. Phelps was a left-handed slugger, who at age 35 was mostly a fill-in player for Oakland. He had briefly been a teammate of Holman in 1988 with Seattle, before he was traded to the Yankees for Jay Buhner. Phelps was 3-for-14 on the season and had not faced Holman in the game five days before in Seattle.

For Holman, the reaction of the Oakland crowd as Phelps prepared to hit was memorable. "I think the most special thing of the night was before they announced the pinch-hitter, 43,000 people in Oakland Coliseum stood up and began to cheer for an opposing player and what that player was doing," Holman remembered. "It was as loud as a 747 and the whole place was shaking. For an opposing pitcher, there is no better compliment."

For his part, Holman admits that his mind was wandering. "I'm literally thinking, 'I'm going to be in the Hall of Fame. They're going to want my jock and my underwear and my jersey and my cup and my hat and they're going to erect this locker in Cooperstown and I'll be immortalized for all time.'" But there was one obstacle between Holman and that dream.

Ken Phelps told reporters after the game, "I was looking for something to get a basehit, that's all." Holman noted. "I'd been getting ahead of hitters all night. . . . I was just trying to do that again."

Holman's first-pitch fastball caught a good chunk of the plate, and to his surprise, Phelps did swing. The ball rocketed off the bat into the Oakland night, as the California crowd was unsure of what to wish—that the ball would soar on or be caught. Henry Cotto raced to the right field wall, ready to leap. But the ball flew too high, too far, dropping a few feet beyond the wall for a home run.

"At the moment, when you see the ball fly over the fence, you're kind of pissed off because you gave up a home run," Holman admitted. "I used to laugh and say you want to crawl into the fetal position and start sucking your thumb, because you know you'll never get another chance."

Perfect game, no-hitter, and shutout were gone when Phelps circled the bases. Holman recovered to strike out Rickey Henderson and end the game with a 6–1 victory. "We needed something spectacular,"

Lefebvre told reporters after the game, "and he gave us the most spectacular performance of his career."

For his part, Holman initially professed only mild disappointment. "Give him [Phelps] credit," he told reporters. "He hit the you-know-what out of it. . . . I'm glad it happened that way and not a bloop single or something."

Phelps claimed no regret. "I was glad I broke it up," he said after the game. "I don't feel like a villain."

Holman acknowledges that it took a few hours for the game to sink in. He explained, "About 4:40 in my hotel room, I remember sitting up in bed and screaming, thinking, 'I can't believe I just missed that!'"

Holman is grateful for the multitude of stories that he has picked up over the years from fans who experienced the near-miss vicariously with him. His daughter told him in college that another student overheard her name called during the class roll call, asked if she was related to Brian Holman, and then told her, "I'm from Duvall, Washington. . . . My dad watched that game when I was a little kid and when your dad gave up the home run, he got up and kicked a hole in the living room wall. To this day, he will not fix it, because he says it's part of Mariner history, so we still have a hole in our wall."

Holman laughs and admits, "Of all the crazy things, I think I'm probably more remembered for not getting it than I would've been had I gotten it."

In a more philosophical vein, Holman continues, "No matter what happens, you can be at the top of the world one moment, and you can make one mistake, one bad pitch, one dumb move, and you come crashing down. . . . But the choice is you either wallow in it and feel sorry for yourself or you get back up on the mound."

⸺

Unfortunately, Holman's days on the pitching mound were numbered. He finished 1990 with an 11-11 mark and a 4.03 ERA. The following year was another workmanlike season, as he managed a 13-14 record and a 3.69 ERA. However, arm injuries turned into multiple shoulder surgeries, and Holman never threw a professional pitch after 1991. His career record stands at 37-45 with a solid 3.71 ERA.

The Mariners were 77-85 in 1990, breaking the .500 mark in 1991 with an 83-79 record. As Griffey and Johnson became two of the most feared players in baseball and Buhner developed an impressive power stroke, Seattle soared. The team made four playoff appearances between 1995 and 2001. Shortstop Alex Rodriguez also became a star in Seattle, with the team posting a 116-46 mark in 2001, but losing the ALCS to the Yankees. Of the four playoff runs, none ended in a World Series, meaning the Mariners are approaching a four-decade drought without a Fall Classic appearance.

Ken Griffey Jr. hit 398 home runs in his tenure with the Mariners before signing with Cincinnati before the 2000 season. He ended his career back in Seattle, finishing with a total of 630 career home runs and 13 All-Star appearances (10 as a Mariner). Randy Johnson was in five All-Star Games as a Mariner, and won 130 of his 303 games with the team before he was traded to the Houston Astros, from which he signed a huge free agent contract with the Arizona Diamondbacks. He was MVP of the 2001 World Series, finally winning an elusive championship ring. Alex Rodriguez also left Seattle for the greener (financially speaking) pastures of the Texas Rangers, before becoming infamous as a New York Yankee. Seattle's 13-year postseason drought has been mostly caused by an inability to keep young stars due to financial constraints.

As for Oakland, they repeated as American League pennant winners before being swept in the World Series by the Cincinnati Reds. They also lost their bevy of stars due to age and financial difficulties by the mid 90s, and the franchise had a lengthy slump before general manager Billy Beane remade the team with his emphasis on statistical knowledge and careful spending.

Ken Phelps had hit his 123rd career home run to ruin Brian Holman's perfect game. It was his last major-league home run. He hit .150 in 1990, and had only 14 more major-league hits after the blast off Holman. He'd earn a second measure of fame in an episode of *Seinfeld* during which character George Constanza ridiculed George Steinbrenner for trading Jay Buhner for Phelps. Buhner blasted 307 home runs in Seattle and retired as a Mariner after the 2001 season. "My baseball people . . . kept saying, 'Ken Phelps, Ken Phelps,'" Steinbrenner said on the television show. One could forgive Brian Holman if he did not do the same.

⸺

While Major League Baseball had averted a disastrous strike in March 1990, it did so only for a short time. When the 1990 lockout settled, Mariners owner Jeff Smulyan was direct in his thoughts. "Nothing in the negotiations helped baseball in Seattle," Smulyan said. "Maybe this was a waste of time, but in four years, if the same approach applies, it's going to be worse than a waste of time, it's going to be a disaster."

Smulyan was prophetic. The agreement ending the 1990 lockout was much less a solution than a Band-Aid, allowing baseball to return but doing little to address the festering profit-sharing issues. Baseball's biggest labor storm was brewing, and the results, four years in the making, nearly crippled the game. On August 12, 1994, with the players and owners unable to reach any consensus regarding a long-term labor agreement—or even to resolve the most fundamental issue, a potential salary cap—the players went out on strike. A month later, MLB commissioner Bud Selig made an announcement that was unthinkable. The World Series was canceled.

While baseball returned in 1995, the damage to the sport was incalculable.

Never before had fall meant universal disappointment for *everyone* in and around baseball—players, owners, and fans.

⸺

With his own career over well before the 1994 strike, Brian Holman adapted to life after baseball. He and his wife, Jami, had three children and lived near Seattle until 2005, when they returned to Kansas, near the town where Brian had grown up. He worked as a financial advisor, and now runs a baseball school and works as an agent.

Time and tragedy have given Brian Holman a sense of perspective on his near-miss that few could comprehend. In 2010, he told an interviewer, "A perfect game is a great thing, and wonderful, but it's just baseball. We've certainly dealt with a lot harder things than baseball."

In February 1999, on a snowboarding trip, Brian's son David, age eight, fell 31 feet out of a chairlift and sustained a broken leg, broken wrist, concussion, and lacerated kidney and liver. As if that were not enough, subsequent testing showed a small spot on David's brain, which turned out to be a tumor. At age 11, he underwent brain surgery. Mariners star Jay Buhner shaved his head in solidarity before the boy's procedure.

"You can't describe lying in bed with David and hearing him say, 'Daddy, will this be my last birthday?'" Holman told an interviewer.

David Holman would survive, but his battle was not the family's last with adversity.

Also in 1999, the Holman family traveled first to Hawaii and then to the Marshall Islands, where Brian and Jami hoped to adopt a daughter. "We had three kids, but we wanted to give a child an opportunity they never would have had," Jami Holman told the *Seattle Times* in 2004. "We wanted to go to a place where girls don't have opportunities and give one girl an opportunity."

They met a girl, but after three days the birth mother backed out of the adoption. A few days later, the Holmans met three-year-old Kassidy on the streets.

"It took her about fifteen minutes to become a Holman," remembered Jami. They adopted Kassidy.

In January 2000, Kassidy Holman was diagnosed with leukemia. After a lengthy and courageous battle, she passed away in July 2006. Holman described her as a "very special kid."

"When Kassidy got sick, one of the things she used to tell me was, 'Dad, I would rather be sick and have a family than be well and not have a family,'" Brian remembered. "We had her for almost six years before she passed away . . . and you think about how hard that is, but now, my daughter Jennifer, through all that stuff, that really gave her a dream and motivated her, and now she is a nurse at the children's hospital in Fort Worth, Texas, and is going to be working on the pediatric oncology unit before long, we hope. All of that worked out because of being with Kassidy."

Holman pauses. "There's always a plan and things always work, even if it's hard."

In fact, in the early 2000s, Brian Holman faced an aching heart not only emotionally but literally. While Kassidy's treatment was ongoing, he was diagnosed with a leaking mitral valve, which had caused his heart to be enlarged. Brian himself underwent cardiac surgery in the midst of the family troubles.

Compared with the illness and heartbreak that struck the Holman family after Brian's retirement, having missed out on baseball perfection was insignificant.

David Holman not only recovered from his brain tumor, but he also became a pitcher. He was drafted by the Mariners out of college in 2011 and—as of this writing—is still pursuing his own baseball dreams with the independent league Kansas City T-Bones.

"I'm extremely proud of David, not just because he's a baseball player, but because he's a great young man. He went through a lot."

Part of the removal of David's tumor resulted in a stroke that temporarily paralyzed his left side. But Brian recalls, "He never complained. He went through rehab every day, couldn't even move his fingers. It took a long time, and then he began playing baseball again."

These days Brian Holman delivers motivational and inspirational speeches, sharing his story around the nation. In 2004, the almost-perfect pitcher told a writer, "To be so high one moment, and then to be knocked off your pedestal the next, that to me is what life is. So you enjoy your life. Take it as far as you can, knowing that it can change at any time."

April 20, 1990
Oakland–Alameda County Coliseum, Oakland, CA

	1	2	3	4	5	6	7	8	9	R	H	E
SEA	0	0	0	0	2	0	0	0	4	6	11	0
OAK	0	0	0	0	0	0	0	0	1	1	1	1

W: Holman (2-1)
L: Welch (2-1)

The End of Holman's Perfect Game:

Bottom of Ninth Inning, Two Outs.
First pitch to pinch-hitter Ken Phelps.
Phelps homered to right-center field.

CHAPTER 11

LITTLE BROTHER NO MORE

June 3, 1995
Montreal Expos at San Diego Padres
Pedro Martinez

Even later, during the prime of his manhood, the boy would struggle to pass the eyeball test. He just did not look like a great pitcher. He was compact and lithe. As a teenager, his pitches, while quite respectable, did not yet explode at the plate. The boy was no Clemens, no Gooden. For that matter, he wasn't even the best pitcher in his own family. And in the spring of 1990, as he participated in a drill, when he mishandled a throw, even his own coach had seen enough.

"This is Ramon's little brother," the coach announced to the rest of the players partici-pating in a drill. "[S]o he knows

Pedro Martinez, in his early days as a Montreal Expo, before the team was disbanded and Martinez pitched his way into the Baseball Hall of Fame
NATIONAL BASEBALL HALL OF FAME

better than everybody else. He spent two years [in the Dominican] doing fundamentals, and he comes over here and does them the wrong way. This is a good example of what *not* to do."

The coach then prepared to deliver his parting shot, "I'll see you in a couple years cutting sugar cane in the Dominican," he told the boy. "You're not going to make it here—you're a pile of shit."

Throughout not just 1990, but for much of his young life, the boy had heard some variation of the same story. He wouldn't make it. He wasn't big enough, strong enough. He was just Ramon's little brother. But he knew better. Pedro Martinez would change the game, and one night he would pitch the best game ever thrown by a Montreal Expo, shortly before that team disappeared from the map. He would go on to change not just his reputation but his country, and his sport. He would stand alongside Juan Marichal as the second Dominican pitcher in the Hall of Fame. But first, he was just Ramon's little brother.

In all fairness, Ramon wasn't exactly a poor prospect. Pedro was the little brother not only physically but chronologically, and so by the time he was more than a blip on the Dodgers' big-league radar screen, his brother was a star. Ramon was always thin, but he grew to 6'4", and blew hitters away with an overpowering fastball. In 1990, he was an All-Star, won 20 games, and finished second in the National League Cy Young voting.

In 1990, Pedro was still shy of the 5'11" that he would eventually reach. He was 18 years old, frequently homesick for the Dominican Republic, and adjusting to American baseball in Great Falls, Montana, home of the Dodgers' rookie league team. To say that some cultural differences manifested themselves would be putting things lightly. Martinez specifically recalled his manager admonishing Raul Mondesi and him for wearing their uniforms after a game onto the team bus, calling them "f—ing dirty bastards," and telling them, apparently for the first time, "you don't do that in the States, this is not the Dominican Republic."

An embarrassed Pedro Martinez was left in tears. America was not the Dominican Republic. Even Great Falls, Montana, was a long way from Manoguayabo, where the Martinez brothers were part of a decidedly baseball-loving family. It is still home to Pedro—as of this writing—and as the starting place of his baseball odyssey, carries deep meaning to him. That does not mean he easily forgets that his father missed trying out for the San Francisco Giants because he could not afford a pair of spikes. Or that he himself missed the Little League World Series because the cost was prohibitive to the family's limited income. Or that baseball became a way out for so many Dominican youths because the educational opportunities were severely limited. Martinez would draw inspiration from his past where he could, and work to fix the rest.

He had a great tutor in learning the ropes in his big brother, even from their early days. Ramon recalled, "When Pedro was very little, he would follow my dad. But when I began to play ball, he would follow me. Sometimes I would tell him that he couldn't play with us, because we were using a hard ball and he was so little. He would cry. I would try to explain to him that it was dangerous, but he always wanted to play."

The relationship hit a different level when the boys' parents divorced. "It was time to take charge of the family," said Ramon years later. "I had to accept that responsibility." With that responsibility came a healthy respect—which Ramon generally earned. When Ramon signed with the Dodgers, he used his signing bonus to buy things for the family's home and clothes for himself and his siblings, and then he saved the rest of the money. Pedro tagged along to the Dodgers' academy in San Pedro de Macoris. When Ramon learned English, Pedro mastered it. "I can't describe, really, how much it meant to me what Ramon had to go through before I did," Pedro stated in 2000.

While Pedro could never hope to match Ramon's size or velocity, he pitched with an abundant supply of raw emotion and heart. In only two and a half years, he went from Great Falls to Bakersfield to San Antonio to Albuquerque, and then . . . to the big leagues. He pitched eight innings for the Dodgers in 1992, but after the team demoted him back to Albuquerque to begin 1993, he nearly quit baseball. Yet instead, relying heavily on Ramon's advice, he battled through the temporary setback, stuck with Los Angeles, and went 10-5 with a 2.61 ERA in a mixture of starts and relief appearances in 1993. He was ninth in the Rookie of the Year voting, he was teammates with Ramon, and he seemed destined to succeed. Just not in Dodger blue.

A month after the season ended, Pedro got a call from general manager Fred Claire. The pitching-rich Dodgers had decided to trade Pedro to the Montreal Expos for second baseman Delino DeShields. It is just under 2,000 miles from Manoguayabo to Montreal. To Pedro, it seemed much farther. "I didn't know any French," he wrote. "I thought Montreal was a nice place for a city, but as a baseball town, it was a dump, the furthest thing from Los Angeles in terms of exposure and payroll."

It was not without reason that Pedro evaluated the Montreal Expos as some sort of baseball Siberia. From the beginning, the Expos faced an uphill climb. In 1969, the expansion Expos went 52-110 and drew just 1.2 million fans to Jarry Park, a temporary rebuild which had seated just 3,000 fans in 1968 and was a poor stopgap of a baseball stadium. One author termed the stadium to be "a minor league facility," citing horrific winds, blinding sun, awful field conditions, and for fans, some of the worst sight lines imaginable.

The team moved to Olympic Stadium in 1977, a lengthy six years after it was due to be completed. In fact, Major League Baseball had become so tired of Montreal's failure to provide a permanent solution to the lack of an appropriate stadium that quiet conversations had occurred regarding relocating the team or revoking the franchise. In spite of the turmoil, the Expos assembled a talented young team with players like Gary Carter, Andre Dawson, and Tim Raines. The Expos even reached the playoffs in 1981, losing the NLCS to the Dodgers. They never returned again. After the brief run of prosperity, the team was forced to part with its best players and fell back in the standings (as well as the league's attendance figures). By the 1990s, the club had committed to young, cheap talent, as it was all they could afford.

In spite of his expectations about Montreal, or lack thereof, Pedro had finally arrived. He had a spot in the Expos rotation, and had arrived in time for the last great burst of Montreal baseball glory. In 1994, manager Felipe Alou fielded a great team—hitters Marquis Grissom, Moises Alou, and Larry Walker, and Ken Hill, John Wetteland, and Pedro on the mound. The team posted a 74-40 record, the best in MLB. Pedro was 11-5 with a 3.42 ERA.

Then the players' strike ended the season—as well as the Expos' last real chance to make baseball work in Montreal. Despite posting the top record in the game, the Expos ranked just 11th in the 14-team National League in attendance in 1994, and when the great underdog run of the

Expos was busted up by the player strike, the result was barely organized chaos.

In 1995, the Expos had already traded Hill, Wetteland, and Grissom. A young team got even younger, with no everyday starter having yet reached age 30. Despite the payroll dump, there was still enough talent on board to keep the Expos competitive. Pedro, still an Expo due to his meager* $275,000 salary, became the team's ace. As the up-and-coming face of the Expo franchise, Pedro found himself drawn into a mini-controversy. Pedro always willingly admitted his appreciation for the fine art of pitching inside. In 1994, despite pitching just 144⅔ innings, Martinez led the league in hit batters. Accurately or not, Pedro gained a reputation as a guy who had no problems with hitting the occasional batter . . . or even more. In his second start of 1994, Pedro was perfect for seven and a third innings before he hit Reds outfielder Reggie Sanders with a pitch. So strong was Martinez's reputation for headhunting that Sanders charged the mound, doubtlessly making him the only batter to break up a perfect game and immediately charge the mound. Pedro gave up one hit and won that game, 3–2.

The controversy was still active in June 1995. In his start on May 29th against San Francisco, Martinez went inside on his first three pitches to leadoff batter Darren Lewis. Incredibly, home plate umpire Bruce Froemming issued Pedro a warning on the spot. Deprived of the ability to pitch inside, Pedro gave up five runs in five and a third innings to the Giants. Martinez got no decision in the game, but heading into his next start, he was 3-1 with a 3.05 ERA, and a reputation for brushbacks. Pedro blamed much of his problem on poor control, but regardless, if nothing else, his control issues (18 walks and two hit batters in his first 44⅓ innings in 1995) made perfection an unlikely goal.

For Pedro's next start, on June 3, 1995, the Expos were in San Diego. The team was 21-15, then good for second place in the NL East. The Padres were 14-20, barely out of the cellar of the NL West. San Diego was hardly a punchless group, though. The team would go on to win their division the following season, and much of that core was in place.

* Or "affordable," depending on whose side you're on.

Veteran outfielder Tony Gwynn was winding down a Hall of Fame career by hitting .368 in 1995. Third baseman Ken Caminiti, who went on to be the NL MVP in 1996, was having an All-Star caliber season in 1995. The Padres hit .272 as a team in 1995, good for third in the National League. Young pitching star Joey Hamilton, who had finished fifth in NL Rookie of the Year voting in 1994 (compared to Pedro's ninth place results in 1993), would oppose Martinez on June 3rd. The two had faced off on May 24th in Montreal. Both pitched well—Martinez allowing two runs in six and a third innings, and Hamilton giving up just two unearned runs in seven and two-thirds. But neither had earned a decision. Both would pitch well again on June 3rd.

It was a comfortable night in San Diego, although a few less than 10,000 fortunate souls were in attendance for the game. Montreal loaded the bases against Hamilton in the first inning on an error, a single, and a walk, but outfielder Tony Tarasco grounded out to end the top half of the frame, squandering Montreal's best chance to score against Hamilton. Martinez then took the mound. Pedro featured a live fastball, either of the rising or the cutting variety, as well as a slider and a changeup. A 1994 scouting report indicated that Martinez's fastball ran from 89 to 92 miles per hour, but when it was moving well, it was a tough pitch not only to control but to hit. Leadoff hitter Bip Roberts fouled off a couple of pitches, and eventually hit a routine flyout to center field. Center fielder Steve Finley hacked and missed at a third strike, and the eternally dangerous Gwynn flied out easily to left field. Thirteen pitches had completed an inning for Pedro.

The Expos' half of the second inning yielded a walk and no runs. Beginning the bottom of the second inning, Caminiti worked a full count, fouling off three pitches, before he swung and missed to become Pedro's second strikeout victim. Rookie Roberto Petagine then flied to left field, and catcher Brad Ausmus got ahead in the count before grounding harmlessly to shortstop Wil Cordero.

Hamilton set down the Expos on a trio of infield grounders, and Pedro returned to the mound to complete his first jaunt through the batting order. Jody Reed popped up Martinez's first pitch to second base.

Shortstop Ray Holbert and Hamilton both then chased third strikes, and with just nine more pitches, three perfect Pedro innings were now complete.

For his part, Joey Hamilton was in no hurry to be on the back side of history. It took Hamilton just 12 pitches to dispose of the Expos in the top of the fourth inning. As for Pedro, leadoff batter Bip Roberts provided a challenge to begin the fourth. Roberts worked a 2-2 count and then lined Martinez's next offering toward right-center field, but second baseman Jeff Treadway got a good jump on the ball and hauled in the line drive. After that, Steve Finley popped up the next pitch to Treadway, and Tony Gwynn took just two pitches to fly out to center field.

Hamilton retaliated by setting down the Expos in order on eight pitches in the fifth inning. Through five innings, he had hit a batter, walked two, and allowed a single. Martinez was perfect, but Hamilton was certainly good enough to hold Montreal at bay. In the home half of the fifth inning, Martinez was as strong as he had been all game. He struck out Ken Caminiti in four pitches, got ahead of Roberto Petagine by two strikes before inducing an easy groundball to second base, and then struck out Brad Ausmus in four pitches. Through five innings, Martinez had struck out six batters and used just 56 pitches to turn back the Padres.

In the sixth inning, Montreal received the gift of a San Diego error, but otherwise provided a trio of routine flyballs to end another scoreless frame. In the bottom of the inning, leadoff batter Jody Reed hit the ball hard, but right at third baseman Mark Grudzielanek for the first out. From there, Ray Holbert grounded out easily to Treadway, and Hamilton was unable to help his own cause, instead whiffing for Martinez's seventh strikeout of the night. Pedro's second round through the San Diego lineup was complete.

Joey Hamilton would not blink. His seventh inning consisted of a groundball, a strikeout, and another groundball. Pedro would have to work not only to stay perfect, but to earn a victory in the game. Martinez briefly fell behind leadoff man Bip Roberts by missing with his first two pitches. Roberts made good contact with the next pitch and drove a flyball to left-center field, but not deep enough to challenge Expo Lou Frazier. Pedro then jumped ahead with two strikes on Steve Finley. After one foul, the next pitch yielded a foul popup that catcher Darrin Fletcher tracked down for the second out. That brought up Gwynn, the future Hall of Famer and one of the toughest outs in baseball. After the game, Gwynn called Martinez's performance "big league pitching at its best" and described Pedro as "superb" and "awesome." He watched a strike and then grounded to first baseman Shane Andrews to end the inning.

The San Diego crowd was growing excited by Martinez's masterpiece. After the game, Martinez admitted that he first realized he was working on a perfect game right at that time. "When I heard the crowd . . . I looked at the scoreboard and saw the zeros," he told reporters.

Unfortunately for Pedro, there was soon another zero added to the board. Despite a one-out single from Lou Frazier, Hamilton again shut down the Expos in the top of the eighth inning. Having thrown only 75 pitches, Martinez went back to work for a potential eighth consecutive perfect inning. Cleanup hitter Ken Caminiti worked a full count, making the second and final time Martinez would throw three balls to a hitter all night. On the seventh pitch of the at-bat, Martinez left the slugger cutting helplessly at strike three. Rookie Roberto Petagine went with the opposite strategy, going after the first pitch only to pop it up gently to Mark Grudzielanek at third base. Catcher Brad Ausmus took a ball, fouled off a pair of pitches, and then rocketed a solid line drive right into the waiting glove of right fielder Tony Tarasco. Eight perfect innings were complete.

The San Diego crowd was faced with the rare choice of whether to root for the home team or to root for history. Of course, Martinez needed a run. Otherwise perfection in the bottom of the frame, if not meaningless, certainly would be less significant. Moises Alou singled to lead off the inning for the Expos. Although Hamilton had passed 120 pitches, manager Bruce Bochy stayed with him. Bochy's faith was rewarded when Darrin Fletcher flied out and Tony Tarasco grounded into a double play to end the inning. In nine innings, Hamilton had surrendered just three singles, two walks, and a hit batter. Not a bad night for the second-best starter in that particular game.

Despite the fact that perfection guaranteed nothing, history weighed on Martinez as he took the mound for the home half of the ninth inning. Jody Reed took a ball and then flied to Tarasco in right field for the first out. Pinch-hitter Scott Livingstone jumped on Pedro's first pitch and made the best contact of any batter all night, driving a flyball deep into right field. Tarasco headed for the wall, leaped, and—banging into the wall—managed to head off Livingstone's drive before it could land. Martinez later called the catch "great" and stated, "I saw that, I thought I was meant to do it."

With 26 consecutive outs, Martinez prepared to face pinch-hitter Eddie Williams. Williams was a 30-year-old journeyman who never managed more than 296 at-bats in a major-league season, which happened in 1995. For his career, Williams would go 4-for-13 against Martinez, and the .308 mark suggests better success than many more productive hitters could manage. But on this night, he was overmatched. Strike one. Strike two. And with history in the balance, next came a belt-high fastball on the outer half from Martinez. Williams swung right through it—10 strikeouts for Martinez, and nine perfect innings.

Unfortunately, there remained the issue of winning the game. Reliever Brian Williams took over for Hamilton on the mound. Williams was 0-2 with a 5.89 ERA, and looked considerably less daunting than Hamilton. Still, he fanned Mark Grudzielanek to begin the 10th inning. Would anyone ever score? Shane Andrews singled, but Pedro popped out trying to bunt Andrews over. Williams walked Lou Frazier on four pitches, and with runners at first and second, Jeff Treadway lined a single to right field, scoring Andrews with the first run of the game. After Wil Cordero flied out, Pedro returned to the mound with a lead and in pursuit of history.

He had used only 93 pitches to complete nine perfect innings. Pedro began the 10th inning by throwing a ball and a strike to Bip Roberts. He had fallen behind Roberts in the seventh, and then induced a flyout. Roberts was a 5'7" sparkplug of an outfielder who was a pesky contact hitter. In the May 24th game against Pedro, he had cracked two hits, making him 4-for-9 career against Martinez coming into the game. On a 1-1 count, Martinez threw a changeup. It may have caught more of the plate than Pedro wanted, and Roberts turned on the ball and hit it hard into right field. Tony Tarasco chased it, but the ball fell cleanly in front and to his left. Roberts was hustling on contact, and when the bounce dragged Tarasco into the corner, he sprinted into second with a double, ending the perfect game.

"I don't regret throwing that pitch," Martinez insisted after the game.

For his part, Roberts was appropriately humble. "It was a lucky hit to a lucky spot," he told reporters. "I was just able . . . to get it to where they weren't standing."

With the perfect game gone, Felipe Alou managed for the win. He went to the mound to get Martinez, who was given a spirited ovation from the tiny San Diego crowd, which he acknowledged with a raised glove hand. Alou went to closer Mel Rojas, who promptly wild-pitched Roberts to third. But from there, Rojas shut down the Padres. He coaxed a grounder to first by Steve Finley, on which Roberts held at third. Gwynn then grounded to second base. Roberts broke for the plate and was thrown out easily by Jeff Treadway. Caminiti then fouled out to Grudzielanek, and the game was over. Pedro had lost the perfect game and the no-hitter, but won the contest.

After the game, Martinez was asked about Harvey Haddix, the only other man to complete nine perfect innings and then lose the perfecto. Reporters told Martinez of Haddix's nearly perfect day. "Oh, that's tough," Pedro admitted, before cracking, "but I still don't know who he is."

Everybody at the park knew who Pedro was. Padre manager Bochy called the game "one of the best I've ever seen," before indicating, "We only hit a couple of balls all night. It was a hell of a game to pitch."

It was the kind of game that made being the Little Martinez Brother irrelevant. And it was the kind of game that Pedro would pitch many, many more times before he was finished. Just not many of those would be in Montreal.

In 1995 the Expos fell from their first-place spot in 1994 to last in their division with a 66-78 mark. Attendance was down by nearly a quarter, and Pedro's solid season (14-10 record, 3.51 ERA) made clear that he would be among the next round of salary casualties. Martinez actually stuck it out for two more seasons. The Expos rebounded into a second-place finish in 1996, and Pedro won 13 games that year. In 1997, the team fell below .500 and finished a distant fourth in their division. But at age 25, the season was Pedro's coming of age. He finished with a 17-8 mark, a sparkling 1.90 ERA, and his first Cy Young Award. A week later, he was traded to the Boston Red Sox for pitcher Carl Pavano and a prospect.

It was all downhill for Montreal. In their remaining seven seasons, they accumulated six fourth- or fifth-place finishes in their division. The team appeared likely to be contracted after the 2002 season, but was saved briefly by a quirk of the collective bargaining agreement, which took any contraction off the table until 2006. Still, Montreal officials were unwilling to contribute to a new stadium, owner Jeffrey Loria had been a complete failure, and the Expos were doomed. After the 2004 season, the franchise moved to Washington and became the Washington Nationals.

As for Pedro, he never looked back. In the three seasons after the trade, he finished second, first, and first in the American League Cy Young voting. In 1999, his 23 wins and 2.07 ERA were so dominant that he actually finished second in the AL Most Valuable Player vote. On a personal level, Pedro's time in Boston was also memorable because he was again reunited with Ramon. Unlike their early years with the Dodgers, when Ramon was the budding star and Pedro was something of an enigma, in 1999, Ramon was on the back end of his career when he signed with the Sox. Injuries were finishing Ramon's career and he won 12 games with Boston in 1999 and 2000, at the same time that Pedro had become the most renowned pitcher in baseball.

Pedro was a Red Sox star through 2004, going 117-37 with a 2.52 ERA in his years in Boston. More importantly, his competitive fire extended into the postseason, where Boston's eight-decades-plus string of misery hung inviolate. Pedro was 6-2 with a 3.40 postseason ERA in Boston, and in 2004, he contributed seven shutout innings and a victory to the first Red Sox World Series victory since 1918.

Down the backstretch of his career, Pedro was a Met and a Phillie. When he retired after the 2009 season, his career totals included 219 wins, three Cy Young Awards, and 3,154 strikeouts. Not only had Pedro eclipsed Ramon, he had eclipsed all but a handful of pitchers ever.

In his time after baseball, Pedro demonstrated that he had not forgotten what it was like to be dismissed as a little brother or as a Dominican outcast in the land of American baseball. He and his wife, Carolina, established the Pedro Martinez and Brothers foundation, and in an official or unofficial capacity, the couple are moving relative mountains in the Dominican Republic. They have established schools and built churches, a recreational park with a day care attached, and a baseball academy. Martinez told the media in 2011, "I want children in the Dominican to have the educational opportunities that people in the United States are afforded, so someday college teams from the Dominican Republic can play against the great colleges and universities in the United States. In the end, education means opportunity."

Martinez achieved perhaps the ultimate baseball honor in 2015, when he was elected to the Baseball Hall of Fame. In one brief speech, Martinez showed the candor and emotion that had characterized his playing career. More than most players, he spoke freely and lovingly of many familiar people and places. He talked of Montreal, thanking the franchise and admitting, "I hope you get a team pretty soon." He remembered Ramon, saying, "I followed his footsteps and it led me where I didn't expect to be today," and thanked his big brother for "clearing the way." But most of all, the little brother, the perennial underdog, talked about the Dominican Republic, about his pride in being only the second Dominican Hall of Famer at the time, about his gratitude for the land and people that gave him his identity. Pedro lapsed into Spanish, speaking to the game's "future generation." The future generation would be wise to listen. Color or nationality didn't matter, size didn't matter, even being the second-best prospect in his own family didn't matter. Pedro Martinez would not be denied. For nine innings one night in 1995, he was perfect. And thanks to a huge heart, a repertoire of paralysis-inducing pitches, and a dominant competitive spirit, he became a legend forever.

June 3, 1995
Jack Murphy Stadium, San Diego, CA

	1	2	3	4	5	6	7	8	9	10	R	H	E
MON	0	0	0	0	0	0	0	0	0	1	1	5	0
SD	0	0	0	0	0	0	0	0	0	0	0	1	2

W: Martinez (4-1)
L: Williams (0-3)
S: Rojas (11)

The End of Martinez's Perfect Game:

Bottom of Tenth Inning, No Outs.
1-1 pitch to left fielder Bip Roberts.
Roberts doubled to right field.

CHAPTER 12

MR. ALMOST AND AMERICA'S TRAGEDY

September 2, 2001

New York Yankees at Boston Red Sox

Mike Mussina

Adversity is a fact. Pitchers are especially attuned to it. Whether adversity takes the form of arm trouble, lousy defense, or an inability to coax the best hitters in the world to consistently just miss solid contact, for the vast majority of pitchers, it's a matter of when and not whether. Life really isn't any different. Even when a pitcher leads a charmed existence—even when he pitches out his career without major injury, in a consistently effective manner, for two very good teams, the world outside baseball can still wreak havoc on a pitcher. For Mike Mussina, it wasn't his arm, or his ERA, or his record that were threatened. It was two towns—one the small and sleepy village he calls

Mike Mussina, warming up in the bullpen before a 2001 start. That season included his near-perfect game, a trip to the World Series, and helping restore normalcy to New York City baseball fans after the 9/11 terrorist attacks. NATIONAL BASEBALL HALL OF FAME

home, the other the sprawling giant that he learned to love. These places endured two very different events, but twice, the normalcy of Mussina's world turned upside down; and twice, communities looked to the man known as Mr. Almost to help assuage grief and define life after tragedy—through his pitching.

The story of Mike Mussina's pitching begins in Mountoursville, Pennsylvania. Before Mussina, Mountoursville was on the map because of its relative proximity to Williamsport, another small Pennsylvania town that just happens to host the Little League World Series. Mussina told a journalist in 1996 that Montoursville was "not large by any means. You can get from one side of town to the other in about five minutes by car—maybe three minutes, if you don't hit any lights."

Mussina grew up in that quintessentially American small town, and by all accounts, lived a happy and well-adjusted life. He is the son of an attorney and a registered nurse, and was a top student as well as a three-sport athlete. It has been reported that Mussina just missed being the valedictorian of his high school class—and that he missed at all only because he didn't want the attention of giving a speech. Baseball was his best game, and Mussina turned down the Baltimore Orioles (who had drafted him in the 11th round) to pursue his further education about as far away from Montoursville as the American baseball scene would allow, at Stanford University.

Nothing much changed at Stanford. Mussina was a golden boy. He became an All-American, completed a degree in economics, and authored a thesis on the wisdom of amateur baseball players signing professional contracts out of college rather than high school. After three seasons of college baseball, the Orioles again drafted Mussina, this time in the first round, and quickly signed him. After about 180 innings and a year in the minor leagues, Mussina broke in with the Orioles and immediately developed into one of the best pitchers in baseball.

In 1992, in his first full major-league season, Mussina was an All-Star, won 18 games, and finished fourth in the American League Cy Young Award voting—all at the age of 23. Mussina pitched eight more seasons in Baltimore. He failed to pitch 200 innings only twice, once due to minor injury and once due to a player strike. And he won—his win totals were 14, 16, 19, 19, 15, 13, 18, and 11. Five times Mussina was an

All-Star; four times he was in the top five in Cy Young voting. In 1997, Mussina nearly pitched a perfect game, setting down the first 25 Cleveland batters he faced before yielding a one-out single to Sandy Alomar in the ninth inning in what former Oriole ace Jim Palmer termed "the most dominant pitching performance I've ever seen." In the end, Mussina won virtually every individual honor possible for a pitcher, but his Orioles reached the postseason only twice, and both times fell in the ALCS.

Yet no matter how big-time Mussina's pitching became, he remained the boy from Montoursville on many levels. In his offseasons, Mussina returned to town and served as volunteer secondary coach for his old high school's football team. He married a local girl who had been the student manager of his high school baseball team. Mussina was such a fixture at Cellini's Submarine Shop in Montoursville that he routinely entered the restaurant through the kitchen, and would sometimes fill orders for owner Charlie DeSanto. He told a journalist in 1997, "I'm comfortable. I like the pace. . . . I can go anywhere I want and people don't come up to me and hassle me. I'm just Mike."

If there is a cost in small-town life, it may lie in the fact that the daily interconnection makes a common tragedy that much more heartbreaking. Mussina was in Boston in July 1996 when his brother called with trouble from home. An airplane carrying the Montoursville High French Club on a trip to Paris had exploded in midair, and 16 MHS students and five chaperones were among the 229 casualties. Mussina was devastated. He attended as many of the funerals as his baseball schedule allowed, and flew home from Oakland for a memorial on August 17. As usual, Mussina was relatively private, and preferred to share his grief among his family and friends rather than in public. "It's not going to be easy and it's not going to be quick, but the people have a way of sticking together and will pull through this," Mussina told a reporter. Down the stretch of the 1996 season, Mussina had written the names of the 21 deceased former residents of Montoursville inside his cap, as a way of remembering the dead. Slowly, over time, Montoursville went about the painful and difficult business of healing, but the memories of the departed—including a worker from Cellini's whom Mussina knew and a boy whom he had coached—testified to the heartbreak and tragedy that the town had suffered.

Mussina's deep and abiding ties to the small-town world of Montoursville were one reason many were surprised that after the 2000 season, when he became a free agent, Mussina was willing to leave Baltimore for New York City. Mussina turned down a six-year, $72 million offer from Baltimore in September 2000 and eventually signed a six-year, $88.5 million deal with the Yankees. But New York was, at least geographically, only a few miles farther from Montoursville than Baltimore had been. Mussina admitted, "I think everybody assumes I had something against New York simply because I never saw myself playing there. Shoot, if I can ride the subway to the ballpark every day, which I did when I was pitching there for Baltimore, I've got to be OK with New York." And surrounded by pitching talent like Roger Clemens, Andy Pettitte, and Mariano Rivera, Mussina had a significant chance to be much more than OK with New York—maybe even to earn a World Series ring, and perhaps also make some baseball history.

The 2001 Yankees, unsurprisingly, were a juggernaut, posting a 95-65 record, and easily winning the AL East division. Roger Clemens won 20 games, Andy Pettite was superb in the clutch, and Mariano Rivera posted 50 saves. Offensively, Tino Martinez led the team with 34 homers and 113 RBI, but familiar names like Jorge Posada, Derek Jeter, Bernie Williams, and Paul O'Neill each contributed at least 20 homers and 70 RBI. As for Mussina, he was in fine form himself, finishing the season with 17 wins and a fifth-place finish in the league's Cy Young balloting.

On September 2, 2001, Mussina was 13-11 with a 3.55 ERA, and the Yankees were in Boston, leading the second-place Red Sox by eight games and looking ahead to the postseason. Of course, any time the Yankees and Red Sox play, something extra is invested in the game, and the 2001 Sox, if not on the Yankees' level, were a very tough opponent. Slugger Manny Ramirez led a dangerous Boston lineup of veteran players. Boston's pitching was spotty, but wily veteran and former Yankee

David Cone was ready to oppose Mussina that September game. It was a night affair at Fenway Park, and if the weather was turning toward fall, it still wouldn't keep over 33,000 from the ballpark.

Despite an error behind him, Cone set down the Yankees in the top of the first, and Mussina took the mound. Watching Mussina warm up in the bullpen, pitching coach Mel Stottlemyre was struck by the sharp break on his curveball. Not that Mussina had to rely on just the curve. Mussina threw as many pitches as anybody in baseball—two-seam and four-seam fastballs, a cut fastball, a knuckle-curve and the sweeping curve, a slider, and a changeup. Mussina finished third in the AL in strikeouts in 2000 and would end up second in 2001. And on this night, he was untouchable.

Leading off, Red Sox outfielder Trot Nixon whiffed to end a five-pitch at-bat. "You never got a good pitch to hit," Nixon commented after the game. Shortstop Mike Lansing watched a third strike, and outfielder Israel Alcantara lined harmlessly to Jeter to finish an 11-pitch first inning.

With the help of a double play, Cone set down the Yankees in the second. Mussina followed with the type of inning of which pitchers dream. Manny Ramirez led off and struck out on three pitches. Dante Bichette followed and did the same. When Mussina fired two strikes past Brian Daubach, he was a pitch away from striking out the side on nine pitches. Instead, Daubach worked the at-bat, drawing to a full count, and fouling off a couple more pitches before watching strike three, as well. Mussina trotted back to the Yankee dugout. Stottlemyre later admitted that conversation on the night was minimal. "I never said a word to him other than, 'Nice going,' stuff like that. . . . His pitch count was good, so I didn't need to ask him how he was feeling. It was pretty obvious he was feeling good."

Despite Mike Lansing's second error of the game, David Cone needed just 12 pitches to set down the Yankees in the third inning. Mussina took only seven pitches, coaxing two grounders to Jeter and one to rookie second baseman Alfonso Soriano. Mussina was dominant, but Cone hadn't trailed far behind. In three innings, the teams had combined for a single hit. Cone, who had himself pitched a perfect game, would prove to be a worthy foe for any pitcher.

Cone walked a Yankee in the fourth, but quickly worked through the inning, and turned the focus back to Mussina. Trot Nixon led off the inning with a harmless groundball to Tino Martinez. Lansing swung and missed at a third strike, and Alcantara watched the third strike to end the frame. Through four innings, Mussina had thrown 45 pitches, struck out six Red Sox, and not yielded a ball hit out of the infield.

Cone responded in kind, striking out two Yankees and inducing a popup. The Red Sox tried to work Mussina in the fifth inning, hoping to catch a mistake deep in the count. Manny Ramirez fouled off three pitches, but eventually watched a third strike. Dante Bichette saw six pitches, but ended up grounding easily to third baseman Randy Velarde. Brian Daubach survived only to the fourth pitch before he headed back to the dugout after a third strike. Five perfect innings were complete for Mussina.

In the sixth, Chuck Knoblauch singled to lead off, but Cone promptly threw a double-play ball, and then fanned David Justice. Nothing was coming easy for the Yankees at the plate. But then, Mussina wasn't letting up on Boston either. Shea Hillenbrand hit a routine fly to center field on the second pitch. Lou Merloni popped a shallow fly to O'Neill in right. Catcher Joe Oliver watched Mussina's third strike, and thus became his 11th strikeout victim in six innings.

After Mussina's second perfect trip through the Boston lineup, it was apparent that something special was in the works. Between the two rivals matching up on the field and the superb pitching on both sides, the game felt much less like a relatively meaningless late-season game than like a hidden extra playoff game. Bernie Williams told reporters after the game that it was one of the best games he had ever played in—and for a player who had won four World Series rings in the last five seasons, that was saying something.

In the New York seventh, Jorge Posada grounded a double into right field, but Cone struck out pinch-hitter Nick Johnson to strand two

Yankees. Mussina began the seventh inning, and his third trip through the Boston lineup, by getting Trot Nixon to ground out easily to Martinez at first. Mike Lansing took a strike, and then lined Mussina's second pitch at Alfonso Soriano for the second out. Alcantara fouled off three straight two-strike offerings, but eventually watched Mussina split the plate for his 12th strikeout of the night.

In the New York eighth, the Yankees put two runners on base against Cone with two outs. Bernie Williams slammed a drive to center field that Nixon chased awkwardly. The ball hung up, and in the oddly designed confines of Fenway Park, Nixon found a way to chase the drive down and keep the game scoreless. Mussina later admitted that when Nixon made the play, he suddenly grew apprehensive. "It actually flashed through my mind that I'm going to go nine innings and we're not going to score and I'd get one of those asterisk jobs somewhere, because we'd play 11 innings."

Mussina began the eighth inning with a rare control struggle. He missed the plate twice to Manny Ramirez, and after a foul ball, missed again, to fall behind 3-1 in the count. Mussina challenged Ramirez, getting a foul ball and then a harmless popup to Jeter for the first out. Dante Bichette, on the other hand, swung at the first pitch, and popped a routine flyball to Williams in center field. Brian Daubach fouled two pitches away, and then watched the third pitch split the plate for strike three and the 24th consecutive out. In the other dugout, David Cone understood exactly what he was seeing. "Part of me didn't want him to do it, because I was the last to do it," Cone told writers after the game. "But part of me wanted him to do it."

What Mussina wanted immediately was a run. Tino Martinez grounded a single to open the ninth, only the fifth hit allowed by Cone. After Posada flied out, Paul O'Neill hit what looked like a double-play ball. But for the third time in the game, Cone was victimized by poor infield defense, when second baseman Lou Merloni booted the ball and it trickled into right field as Martinez found his way to third base. Martinez was replaced with pinch-runner Clay Bellinger, and when infielder Enrique Wilson bopped a double down the right field line, Bellinger scored the only run of the game. Cone was lifted, and sat in the Boston dugout to watch Mussina make his run at history.

Staked to a lead, Mussina took the mound in the bottom of the ninth with renewed purpose. Pinch-hitter Troy O'Leary worked the at-bat to a 2-2 count, and then grounded Mussina's next pitch hard toward right field. Bellinger, fresh off of scoring Mussina's only run, now took the opportunity to preserve perfection. He dove to his right, nabbed O'Leary's grounder, and shoveled a throw to Mussina, who raced over to cover the bag, a step ahead of O'Leary. One out. Mussina later admitted that when the ball was hit, he thought O'Leary had a hit. But when Bellinger robbed O'Leary, Mussina admitted, "I thought, 'Maybe this time, it's going to happen.'"

Lou Merloni was up next, and it took only four pitches for him to become Mussina's 13th strikeout of the evening. Around the ballpark, cameras and cell phones flashed, and the Fenway crowd, half wanting to see Mussina bested and half wanting to see baseball history, was electric. Manager Joe Kerrigan went to his bench for a pinch-hitter for Joe Oliver and sent up Carl Everett.

Everett had been an All-Star in 2000 and had knocked in 100-plus runs over each of the last two campaigns. But in 2001, his batting average slumped from .325 and .300 in the past two years to .255. He had gone from being a star to being a borderline everyday player—and now, a pinch-hitter. Everett was 1-for-9 in his career against Mussina, with seven strikeouts. Mussina wasted no time, firing his first pitch in the zone, with Everett fouling it away. Mussina's second offering was a swing and a miss, and he was one pitch away from baseball immortality.

Everett took a ball, and Mussina prepared for the fourth pitch. He had some previous success with high fastballs to Everett, and his 1-2 offering was a high fastball on the outside of the plate.

Everett swung at the pitch and made solid contact, sending a looping line drive into left-center field. Knoblauch in left and Williams in center both sprinted emphatically toward the ball, but it skipped a half-dozen feet in front of Knoblauch for a solid single and an end to the perfect game. Mussina smiled an ironic grin and walked off the mound, waiting for the ball. Catcher Posada and pitching coach Stottlemyre came out to console Moose, as Everett had left the field for a pinch-runner, slapping high-fives down the line of Red Sox who were excited to have broken up the perfect game.

Trot Nixon then grounded out to second base, and Mussina's almost perfect win was in the books. It was all over except the second-guessing.

"I thought it was a hit," Mussina said of Everett's knock. "I'm going to think about that pitch until I retire, but that's the pitch I threw." For his part, Everett displayed no sympathy for his opponent. "I've never been a part of a no-hitter before as an opponent," he admitted. "It was very satisfying to get the hit."

The Yankees had won another game and stretched their lead in the standings to nine games. But the mood in the clubhouse was subdued. "It was supposed to happen," manager Joe Torre said ruefully of Mussina's near-perfect game. But soon baseball would be forgotten because of things that weren't supposed to happen.

<hr />

Nine days after Mike Mussina was almost perfect, he received a morning telephone call. Like the call from his brother in 1996 telling him about Montoursville, this one would change his life. It was his wife who called, struggling to explain what would forever be inexplicable. What had happened, of course, was 9/11. An otherworldly terrorist attack changed the very fabric of the world forever. And things like a bloop base hit were placed into perspective.

Mussina, like millions of others around the nation and the world, switched on his television and was horrified. "It was like I was watching a movie or some primetime drama, but it was 9:00 in the morning," he told a reporter. Just as the nation at large tried to sort out exactly what had happened, so too did baseball players. There were few answers.

"I just stayed at the house for about three days," Mussina recalled. "No one had any idea how long we would be out; the airline industry was shut down, the city was shut down. It was a strange week."

As he had in Montoursville years before, for a second time, Mussina found himself trying to help a town—or a giant metropolis in this case—put itself back together after a horrific airplane-related tragedy. And again, solidarity of community mattered. And for New Yorkers, the routine of baseball mattered.

The Yankees did not play between September 9th and September 18th, and it was not until September 25th that they returned to Yankee Stadium. After an emotional first game back in their ballpark, the Yankees clinched their division title. Baseball might have seemed unimportant, but it was therapeutic, and not just for the players.

"Getting back on the field may have brought us—and other people— some relief from the stress, all the anguish and the emotion," says Mussina. "We got out there, did what we were supposed to be doing and got away from it for a couple of hours." And so—vicariously—did Yankee fans everywhere.

Torre admits, "Baseball was the furthest thing from our minds, but then we realized how important it was."

Suddenly, everyone was a Yankee fan, at least for that memorable 2001 postseason. The Yankees faced Billy Beane's Oakland Athletics in the ALDS, and promptly fell behind by losing the first two games of the best-of-five series. Mussina got the ball in Oakland for Game 3 against Barry Zito. Aided by a Posada home run in the fifth inning, Mussina shut out the A's by a 1–0 score, and provided the momentum that the Yankees needed to storm back and win that series.

In the ALCS, New York faced the Mariners, who had won 116 games that season. It was no contest. Mussina won Game 2, and the Yankees won the series 4–1, earning a fifth trip to the World Series in six seasons. The Yankees faced the Diamondbacks in the Series, and after a rough start in Game 1, Mussina bounced back with a solid effort in Game 5 that helped the Yanks grab a 3–2 series lead. However, no one told Arizona that New York was the team of destiny, and after they thumped the Yankees 15–2 in Game 6, the D'backs came back against the normally untouchable Rivera in Game 7 to win the Series.

It had been an insanely up-and-down ride for Mussina in his first year as a Yankee, as he had almost pitched a perfect game, almost won a World Series, and for the second time, helped a town come to grips with a tragedy bigger than baseball.

Mussina, somewhat cruelly, was given a nickname by his good friend, Yankee bullpen catcher Mike Borzello. "I tell him, 'You're Mr. Almost,'" Borzello admitted. "'You almost won a Cy Young. You almost won 20 games. You almost won a World Series—everything.'"

Borzello's nickname stuck, only because it seemed to somehow define Mussina's consistently not-quite-there accomplishments. Indeed, eight times before 2008, Mussina topped 15 wins but failed to reach 20. Six times, he was in the top five in Cy Young voting, but he never finished higher than second. And the Yankees never quite delivered another title while Mussina was on the roster. In 2003, Mussina saved the season by coming out of the bullpen in Game 7 of the ALCS and holding the Red Sox at bay. He then started a World Series game against Florida and pitched brilliantly, earning a win with seven innings of one-run ball. He was slated to pitch Game 7—except that the Yankees were eliminated in Game 6.

Mussina never won a World Series. It wasn't exactly his fault—his career 3.42 ERA in 139⅔ postseason innings is about a half-run lower than his regular season ERA. He never reached a perfect game or a no-hitter, or earned the Cy Young Award. He did garner some small measure of satisfaction in 2008, when at age 39, he finally did win 20 games in a season. In the next-to-last game of the season, playing at Fenway Park, Mussina shut out the Red Sox for six innings to earn the win. He promptly retired.

Mussina left the game of baseball with 270 wins, 2,813 career strikeouts, and a host of accomplishments that left him almost (but not quite) certain for Hall of Fame enshrinement. The easy thing to have done would have been to hang around for another year or two—almost certainly, Mussina would have reached 3,000 strikeouts, and he had a puncher's chance at 300 victories. Of course, the Yankees also won a World Series in 2009, the first year after Mussina retired.

But Mussina clearly finished his career comfortable with his own legacy. He told a journalist in 2004, "I don't think I'll look back on my career when I'm done and say, 'I didn't win a World Series, I didn't win 20 games, I didn't win a Cy Young, so it was a failure.' I'm certainly not going to look at it that way. There's just no way I can."

There is every reason to think that Mussina will, sooner or later, be recognized with the ultimate baseball honor—membership in the Baseball Hall of Fame. The only other pitcher not currently in the Hall who has 100-plus more victories than losses (which Mussina easily surpassed with his 270-153 career mark) is Roger Clemens. The only pitchers in MLB history with more victories and a better winning percentage than Mussina are Clemens, Randy Johnson, Lefty Grove, Christy Mathewson, and Grover Cleveland Alexander. In 2014, Mussina received 20.3 percent of the vote for induction, and in 2015, support increased to 24.6 percent. The 2016 voting numbers showed a further jump to 43.0 percent. As of this writing, it is a long way to the 75 percent needed to gain entry to the Hall, but Mussina seems likely to earn membership in that community.

All of that said, even if Mussina had ever been determined to see baseball as a study in statistics, as a minefield of accomplishments met or unmet, he could never see it that way in the aftermath of the tragedies that befell Montoursville in 1996 and New York City in 2001. The inherent nobility of being part of a community, of just being Mike, the guy who went to work at the ballpark and helped everybody deal with the tough times, has to weigh heavier than being Mr. Almost. Late in that 2008 season, which became Mussina's last, he took his sons on a tour of Monument Park, the tributary garden at the soon-to-become defunct Yankee Stadium. He showed them the plaques honoring the alumni of that greatest of all baseball traditions and the words—if not spoken, implied—it was all a community. Babe and Lou and Joe D., they were part of this community. Just like the folks who were hurting and confused and needing something, and who had rooted so hard in the fall of 2001. And just like the folks back in Montoursville, where they know that the guy named Mike, as of 2016 the head coach of the high school basketball team, is one of them—a very special one of them, who one night was almost perfect.

September 2, 2001
Fenway Park, Boston, MA

	1	2	3	4	5	6	7	8	9	R	H	E
NYY	0	0	0	0	0	0	0	0	1	1	6	0
BOS	0	0	0	0	0	0	0	0	0	0	1	3

W: Mussina (14-11)
L: Cone (8-4)

The End of Mussina's Perfect Game:

Bottom of Ninth Inning, Two Outs.
1-2 pitch to pinch-hitter Carl Everett.
Everett singled to left-center field.

CHAPTER 13

PERFECTLY IMPERFECT

June 2, 2010
Cleveland Indians at Detroit Tigers
Armando Galarraga

Before June 2, 2010, the matter of perfect versus "almost perfect" was more or less the responsibility of the pitcher. Sure, there were some questions about balls and strikes—almost inarguable ones in the case of Hooks Wiltse's game, and apparently eternally arguable ones in the case of Milt Pappas's no-hitter. But never before, and hopefully never again, had an umpire's clearly erroneous call obliterated a pitcher's chances at baseball perfection.

The near-miss of June 2, 2010, became the most horrific error imaginable, attributable only to human error, and specifically to the error of the umpire: in this case, American League veteran Jim Joyce. But if Armando Galarraga's battle with destiny

Armando Galarraga, who inspired everyone from the president to schoolchildren with his positive attitude in the face of a blown call that destroyed what should have been a perfect game—and that may have helped pave the way for instant replay PHOTO BY MARK CUNNINGHAM, COURTESY OF THE DETROIT TIGERS

ended short of perfection, it also was probably the most important "almost perfect" game. First, from the ashes of a baseball train wreck, a journeyman pitcher and a well-liked umpire showed courage, class, and professionalism that inspired millions. And secondly, Major League Baseball finally got serious about implementing a replay system to right the wrongs of arbitrary misjudgment. Because of Galarraga and Joyce, not only do players and umpires know how to handle the situation, but hopefully, they will never be faced with the situation anyway. But before the National Pastime was changed by the Tigers/Indians matchup on June 2, 2010, that game had to first be shaped and formed by the history of baseball.

As far back as two teams played baseball, there had to be an umpire. But as significant as the ruling arbiter of the game has always been, his role and duties have been defined slowly over the years. For the first several decades of professional baseball, a single umpire often called a game. Managing to patrol the bases, the outfield foul lines, and the strike zone at the same time would be a Herculean feat, but it was one that early umpires pursued daily. Finally, in 1912, it became standard for one umpire to work home plate and another to call the action on the bases. Still, if early umpires were pleased to have their workload lightened, they still had plenty to be concerned about.

Umpires were subjected to abuse from all corners, whether fans, managers, or players. And the attacks were not limited solely to verbal outbursts. Competitors like John McGraw and Ty Cobb didn't mind making their points with words or fists, and of course, the path to Ernie Shore's almost-perfect masterpiece was paved by Babe Ruth's attempted pummeling of an umpire.

In 1952, the American and National League each ruled that four umpires should work each league game. The four umpires were unfailingly white, as it took 19 years beyond Jackie Robinson's breakthrough for the first African-American umpire, Emmett Ashford, to break that particular color barrier. In 1970, a one-day strike by MLB umpires resulted in the recognition of the Major League Umpires Association, and improved working conditions for umpires.

But while umpires' work situation improved, they did find themselves facing a revolution of technology. Television had ceased to become a novelty, and indeed became a common part of games. Just as four umpires now patrolled the field, television cameras shot video from every angle, and caught every mistake. Soon mistakes were broadcast—in slow motion—again and again and again, for irate fans and players to digest on a daily basis. With sports news becoming a 24-hour cycle, no mistake went undetected.

The National Football League embraced instant replay quickly, and the National Basketball Association likewise adapted a system by which some calls could be subsequently reviewed and overturned for instances of clear error. Baseball was a holdout. Unfortunately, there were many significant plays that could have benefitted from some manner of replay system.

The 1975 World Series is known as one of the best championship battles of all time. It is also notable for a blatant missed call. With Game 3 of the series in the 10th inning, Reds batter Ed Armbrister bunted badly, then paused at home plate just long enough to get tangled with Red Sox catcher Carlton Fisk. Fisk, trying to make a play at second base, threw the ball into center field. The Red Sox howled in protest, but home plate umpire Larry Barnett refused to call Armbrister for interference. Three batters later, the Reds won the game, and of course, later won the series, four games to three.

Ten years later, another very competitive World Series was similarly tainted. In Game 6, with the Royals down three games to two and losing the game 1–0, the leadoff batter in the ninth inning, Jorge Orta, chopped a groundball to first base. Cardinal first baseman Jack Clark's throw to the pitcher covering the bag beat Orta comfortably, but umpire Don Denkinger, subsequently dubbed "Jessie James" by the *St. Louis Post-Dispatch*, called him safe. A few minutes later, the Royals rallied to win the game and took the Series the following night.

As time went on, other catastrophic calls surfaced. In the 1991 World Series, first base umpire Drew Coble somehow missed Twins first baseman Kent Hrbek literally pulling runner Ron Gant off first base, and extinguished a Braves rally that had a role in the ultimate outcome of the series.

In the 1996 American League Division Series, umpire Rich Garcia missed a fan interference call that turned a Derek Jeter flyball into a game-tying home run. In 2007, umpire Tim McClelland ended a wild-card play-in game by calling Rockies outfielder Matt Holliday safe with the game's winning run when Holliday actually slid past the plate without touching it.

While baseball's stolid traditionalism was a comfort to some fans, others were increasingly frustrated by the failure of the game to provide some manner of redressing mistaken calls by the umpires. In fact, some within the game were so frustrated that they took matters into their own hands.

In 1999, while working a Cardinals/Marlins game, umpire Frank Pulli's crew had a tough call to make when Florida outfielder Cliff Floyd hit a drive off the left field scoreboard. The crew initially ruled the hit a double, then reversed course and called it a home run. Pulli ducked into the Marlins dugout, consulted a television camera there, and announced that it was a double. The Marlins protested the game, and instant replay was officially banned before it had begun.

But on August 28, 2008 (yes, in midseason), MLB commissioner Bud Selig approved the use of instant replay—albeit, only to review home run calls. On September 19, 2008, a long drive by Carlos Pena of the Rays, which was initially ruled to be fan interference, was changed to a home run via replay. Umpires, managers, players, and fans were almost universally pleased. There was finally some redress for missed calls. Unfortunately, a year and a half later, they would realize that the system didn't extend far enough.

Armando Galarraga was an unlikely choice to pitch the most famous almost-perfect game ever. Galarraga was born in Cumana, Venezuela, but at an early age, his family moved to Caracas. Galarraga acknowledges baseball, at least certainly in the days of his youth, as the dominant sport of Venezuela. "Anyplace you go, you can play. If you're in the street . . . you can just play."

Indeed, as part of the great Central American baseball culture, Galarraga quickly learned to love the game. He watched other Venezuelan pitchers make the major leagues, even if they struggled to make a lasting impact. Urbano Lugo (6-7, 5.31 ERA in 162.6 major-league innings) and Omar Daal (68-78, with a 4.55 career ERA) were two of the players whom Galarraga followed.

By the age of 16, Galarraga was filling out into a powerful pitcher himself. A year earlier, he had begun playing in a baseball academy in Caracas. Galarraga went to baseball school in the morning and regular school in the afternoon. "It was a tiring routine," he wrote, "but this did not bother me because I was superhyper."

One day at a tryout, Galarraga's life was changed. The Montreal Expos scouted him, saw the potential in the young hurler, and decided to sign him. Galarraga's parents, both teachers, were unprepared for exactly what that meant. Galarraga recalls his father being worried about not being able to pay Armando's transportation to America. He has a laugh as he remembers saying, "No, Dad, I think they're going to pay for my ticket." Indeed, the Expos signed Galarraga for $3,500.

Galarraga finished his high school education at an accelerated pace, to placate his parents. He then began a baseball odyssey. Galarraga signed at 16 in late 1998, but was 25 when he finally worked his way to the major leagues in 2007. It was a confusing path for Galarraga, especially in 2002, when he pitched just three and two-thirds innings in rookie league competition before hurting his arm. After a season of uncertainty, on his fourth MRI, torn ligaments were found and Galarraga underwent Tommy John surgery. Once he healed Galarraga worked his way up the ladder. After 2005, he was traded to the Rangers, and in early 2008, he was dealt to the Detroit Tigers.

He had worked only eight and two-thirds major-league innings for Texas in 2007, but after starting 2008 at AAA, Galarraga earned promotion and pitched well for Detroit, posting a 13-7 record and a 3.73 ERA.

This was good enough for a fourth-place finish in the American League Rookie of the Year balloting.

Galarraga began 2009 well, with a 3-0 record and a 1.85 ERA in April, even winning Detroit's home opener against the Rangers, but he injured his arm and completely lost his effectiveness. At the end of the season, Galarraga was 6-10 with a 5.64 ERA, and was working irregularly out of the bullpen. In fact, he soon would not even be a major leaguer.

Galarraga began 2010 in AAA Toledo, where he was 4-2 with a 3.65 ERA in eight appearances. On May 16, 2010, he was promoted back to Detroit. The Tigers had a talented team, and Galarraga battled with lefty Dontrelle Willis for the fifth spot in the team's starting rotation. He pitched well at home in a start against Boston, and poorly at Los Angeles. On May 28th, he pitched in relief, working an inning and two-thirds against Oakland. Three days later, the Tigers traded Willis to the Arizona Diamondbacks. The next night, the new fifth starter, Armando Galarraga staked his claim to history.

⸺

The 2010 Detroit Tigers hoped for a boost from Galarraga. Veteran manager Jim Leyland reached the 2006 World Series with the team, but they had since fallen back—in 2009, they missed the division title by just a game. The Tigers were 26-25 on June 2nd, and had just lost a game to the last-place Indians. Cleveland was 19-31, and built mostly with an eye toward the future. Right fielder Shin-Soo Choo eventually hit .300 with 22 homers and 90 RBI in 2010, but on the whole, the Indians, who finished 12th in the 14-team American League in runs scored, struggled.

Detroit was led by Galarraga's friend, first baseman Miguel Cabrera, who was in the middle of a season that ended with a .328 batting average, 38 home runs, and 126 RBI. Veterans like Magglio Ordonez and Johnny Damon offered punch, and youngsters like catcher Alex Avila and left fielder Austin Jackson showed promise. Justin Verlander was a year younger than Galarraga, and won 18 games in 2010. Max Scherzer was just 25, but he added another dozen wins. Detroit, though, lacked pitching depth, as the Tigers ended up 11th in the AL in ERA, and 14th in saves.

June 2, 2010, was a fairly cool and cloudy evening. Only 17,738 were in attendance at Comerica Park in Detroit. In his two prior major-league starts in 2010, Galarraga had not worked past the sixth inning. He had never pitched a complete game in the major leagues. But then, he had never pitched a game like the one he worked on June 2, 2010.

Even before he took the mound, Galarraga had a premonition of success. "In the bullpen," he recalled, "I remember my sinker was moving. I could throw sinkers both ways [breaking inside to either left- or right-handed hitters] . . . and I remember throwing the bullpen, it looked good, and I said, 'I feel great!'"

The Indian leadoff batter, Trevor Crowe, watched two of Galarraga's sinking fastballs miss the strike zone. But Galarraga threw two strikes, and then induced a routine flyball to center field. Three more sinking fastballs led to Shin-Soo Choo grounding to Miguel Cabrera, who threw to Galarraga covering first for the out. Austin Kearns lined a first-pitch fastball to Cabrera to end the inning.

The Tigers went in order in the home first, and Galarraga went back to work. Cleveland's Travis Hafner grounded an 0-2 pitch to shortstop. Jhonny Peralta popped another 0-2 sinker to second base. Russell Branyan grounded a 1-2 sinker to second, and two innings were gone in just 19 pitches. The sinking fastball was arriving at 92–94 miles per hour, knee high and usually on the corner of the strike zone. Galarraga looked back at the game and admitted, "I was a pitcher who didn't throw that hard . . . so I always had to have good control. When it was tough for me is when I got behind in the count. When I got ahead in the count, I had some really good games. That game in particular, I threw a lot of strikes."

In his book, *Nobody's Perfect*, he was perhaps even more direct. "I am feeling very strong, very positive," Galarraga wrote. "I am feeling like I can put the ball wherever I want."

In the Detroit second inning, Miguel Cabrera put a Roberto Hernandez pitch where he wanted—in the left field bleachers for a solo homer and the only run that Galarraga required. Staked to a lead, in the third inning, Galarraga needed only two pitches to induce Mark Grudzielanek to fly out to center field. Cleveland catcher Mike Redmond grounded a 2-1 pitch to shortstop, and Indian second baseman Jason Donald, after hitting a loud line drive foul, saw Galarraga's first slider of the night and grounded out to shortstop. After 29 pitches, Galarraga had a lead and had completed one circuit of the Cleveland batting order. For a pitcher who usually relied on mixing his pitches and keeping hitters off balance, Galarraga was having an easy time of it. "The first [few] innings," he remembered, "I only threw sinkers. I didn't throw anything else . . . The sinkers were moving a lot and they were down and I was dominating the corners."

As the game moved to the fourth inning, Galarraga began to utilize other pitches, but to similar effect. Trevor Crowe fell behind in the count and grounded a slider harmlessly to Cabrera. Shin-Soo Choo made good contact with a sinking fastball, but could only fly it into Austin Jackson's glove in center field. Austin Kearns looked at a called third strike on a breaking ball, and Galarraga had completed four perfect innings in just 40 pitches.

Galarraga struggled somewhat in the fifth inning. Travis Hafner worked the only three-ball count of the game, but eventually fouled out to left field. After Jhonny Peralta tapped back to Galarraga, third baseman Russell Branyan hit a grounder back through the box. It deflected off of Galarraga's foot, but in a moment of luck, bounced to third baseman Brandon Inge, who threw out Branyan by a step and a half. Galarraga shared a grin with Inge, as he realized he had escaped trouble. "It is very lucky that the ball bounces off my foot in just this way," Galarraga wrote. "It is almost like magic."

The spell was not broken in the sixth inning. Mark Grudzielanek struck out on a breaking pitch to open the frame. Mike Redmond flied the second pitch to center, and Jason Donald lined the first pitch to right. After 58 pitches, Galarraga completed a second perfect turn through the Indian lineup, and suddenly, became aware of exactly what was on the line.

After the sixth inning, Galarraga took his spot in the dugout and watched the other players scatter to get out of his seat. He wrote of the experience, "To get twenty-seven outs in a row, it is almost impossible. You cannot think this way as a pitcher. But to get just one out, it is no problem. . . . [I] tell myself it is just one and one and one until we are finished."

Galarraga showed no signs of losing his focus in a painless seventh inning. Trevor Crowe swung at Galarraga's first pitch and topped a routine grounder to second for the first out. Shin-Soo Choo fell behind 0-2 and then picked a breaking pitch off his shoetop, flying it harmlessly to Austin Jackson in center field. On the second pitch he saw, Austin Kearns grounded a sinking fastball right to the shortstop. Six pitches in the inning, six outs to go in the game.

"The fans . . . start to go crazy after this inning," Galarraga recalled. "It is not such a big crowd, but they are making noise like a big crowd." After Detroit failed to score, Galarraga hurried back to the mound for the eighth inning.

"I am relaxed," he wrote, "but it does not feel like I can breathe. . . . There is no time for a deep breath. There is no time to stop and appreciate this moment. Everything is happening very fast."

Travis Hafner led off the inning by watching two pitches, before slapping a groundball right at shortstop Santiago for the first out. Galarraga worked to a 1-2 count on Jhonny Peralta, and then threw a diving slider, which Peralta chased for Armando's third strikeout of the night. Russell Branyan also fell behind 1-2, and grounded the ball harmlessly to second baseman Guillen to end the inning. In just 71 pitches, Armando Galarraga had retired 24 consecutive Cleveland Indians and placed himself on the threshold of baseball immortality.

"Now I leave the field and I am not thinking so much about keeping it close," Galarraga admitted. "I am not thinking about the win or the shutout. I am not even thinking about the no-hitter. I am thinking only about the perfect game, because the perfect game . . . is like the full package."

In the bottom of the eighth Magglio Ordonez singled home two runs off Hernandez, and Detroit's lead was increased to 3–0. Still, everything other than perfection was secondary to the man on the mound.

After 24 relatively easy outs, Galarraga had his closest call of the night to lead off the ninth inning. Mark Grudzielanek got a first-pitch fastball from Galarraga and drove it up the left-center field alley. "I thought it was a home run," Galarraga later recalled. "But the ball stopped." Austin Jackson in center field had good speed, and made a prompt read on the ball off of Grudzielanek's bat. He turned and ran, not unlike a wide receiver trying to catch up with a long pass, or in a more baseball-appropriate analogy, up the left-center field alley in a vague imitation of Willie Mays's basket catch in the 1954 World Series. Like Mays, Jackson did not have time to turn around, but stuck his glove out, and the ball fell safely into the glove.

On the mound, Galarraga tried to hide his reaction, but his smile snuck through. He would later write, "As soon as Austin Jackson makes this catch, I know I will pitch a perfect game. I know this in my heart, in my bones."

Galarraga proceeded to get ahead of catcher Mike Redmond by a 1-2 count. He threw Redmond a slider, which was grounded to shortstop Santiago for the second out of the inning.

Indians shortstop Jason Donald was the batter who stood between Galarraga and history. Donald was a rookie, called up by the Indians for the first time only two weeks prior. He had two hits the day before, which gave him a total of 13 major-league hits. Donald was batting .265 in his brief major-league career, and as a scrappy young player, he was hardly conceding the moment.

Galarraga's first pitch hit the outside corner for a strike. He then threw a slider off the plate, which evened the count.

On a 1-1 pitch, Galarraga threw another sinking fastball, and Donald topped it into the ground toward first base.

Miguel Cabrera had to move to his right to field the ball, which he did cleanly.

"It was not an easy groundball," remembered Galarraga, who had taken off from the mound toward first base on contact.

Donald ran hard down the line, making the play closer than it normally might be. Three years later, Donald and Galarraga played together, and Galarraga told him then, "Man, you were running fast on that play!" But in spite of Donald's speed and effort, Cabrera fielded the ball cleanly, threw accurately to Galarraga, who caught the ball and tagged first base, a step ahead of Donald's arrival. Galarraga recalls, "At that time, when I catch the ball, and I touch the base, I know it was an out." Armando Galarraga had pitched a perfect game.

Except that umpire Jim Joyce interrupted the party with one emphatic gesture, hands flying out, palms flat and down. SAFE!

Like Galarraga, Joyce had not enjoyed a quick path into the major leagues. A former college player, after his graduation, Joyce had worked as an umpire in the Midwest League, the Florida Instructional League, the Texas League, the Pacific Coast League, the Dominican League, and the International League. It took almost a decade for him to make his way to the major leagues.

Once he did, Joyce was well regarded throughout baseball. By June 2, 2010, he had worked two All-Star Games, two World Series, and 12 other postseason series. A few weeks later, ESPN polled MLB players anonymously in regard to umpires. Fifty-three percent of the players polled chose Joyce as the best umpire in baseball.

On June 2, 2010, the best umpire in baseball was working first base. And as Donald ran down the line with history in the balance, Joyce watched the play develop.

"My eyes tell me the runner beat the throw," he later writes. "Plain and simple. No doubt in my mind. So I fling my arms out to show he's safe, and it's like a hush falls over the stadium."

In the wake of the hush, the stadium remained strangely calm. Cabrera erupted first (Galarraga remembers him yelling "No f—ing way!"), and Detroit manager Jim Leyland walked onto the field to question Joyce. For his part, Galarraga refused to join in the tumult. He just stood there grinning a smile of utter and complete disbelief. The broadcasters, the fans, apparently other umpires all knew. Joyce missed the call.

On the mound again, Galarraga induced Trevor Crowe to ground to third to end the game. "[T]hen," remembered Joyce, "everything kicks up a notch. The yelling. The booing. . . . [T]he small sliver of doubt I have out on the field, it starts to grow as I make for the clubhouse."

In the clubhouse, Joyce looked at a monitor and the sliver of doubt became an explosion of sadness. In tears, distraught over the call, Joyce did the only thing he knew to do—he took the media requests and gave a candid response. "This is a history call," he said. "And I kicked the shit out of it. And there's nobody that feels worse than I do."

Joyce sought out Galarraga, and apologized to him as well. For his part, Galarraga expressed no bitterness. "He probably feels more bad than me," Galarraga said after the game. "Nobody's perfect. Everybody's human. I understand . . . I gave him a hug." Years later, Galarraga said, "I was in shock because everything happened, but I was so excited inside. . . . I was fighting for my spot [in the rotation]. I was so happy to throw a one-hitter."

As tempers subsided, Galarraga's reaction seemed to be mirrored throughout the clubhouse. Leyland, a baseball lifer himself, reflected, "It's a crying shame. Jim is a class guy. . . . [N]obody is going to feel worse than he does."

The sentiment spread throughout baseball. Yankees reliever Mariano Rivera was asked about the play and admitted, "It happened to the best umpire we have in our game. The best. And a perfect gentleman. Obviously, it was a mistake. It's a shame for both of them, the pitcher and the umpire."

What nobody could have guessed was that the pitcher and the umpire were about to turn a shame into an education in sportsmanship, in forgiveness, and in real life.

Once his night at the ballpark finally ended, Joyce, as he had planned before he became an unfortunate part of history, traveled to his mother's home in nearby Toledo, Ohio. She had not watched the game, so he shared his story and began a more or less sleepless night. The bitter fans appeared, threatening Joyce's life on his children's social media pages. Indeed, MLB provided security surveillance to both Joyce's home and his mother's home.

But as the sleepless night bled into the next day, a funny thing happened. The messages moved from hate to concern, respect, even condolence.

Joyce particularly treasured an e-mail he received from an 11-year-old spina bifida patient named Nick Hamel. The boy had been struggling in his efforts to walk, and a therapist had told him not to cry over spilled milk. Hamel asked that Mr. Joyce be told that this was just spilled milk. The e-mail led to a friendship that included Joyce giving Hamel the cap he wore the night of Galarraga's game.

The next day's Tigers/Indians game was a day game, and Jim Joyce was sleepless and emotional. But when he took the field, tears streaming down his face, a funny thing happened. The partisan Tigers crowd delivered not a chorus of profanity or boos, but they cheered Joyce. When the umpire arrived at home plate to take the lineup cards, Armando Galarraga brought the Tigers lineup to him. Joyce and Galarraga shook hands, and Joyce, after trying unsuccessfully to wipe away his tears, studied the card briefly, and delivered a firm pat on the back to Galarraga.

As for Galarraga, the spoils of near-perfection had their moments. The Tigers went to Kansas City after the next day's game, but Galarraga recalled returning home after that series and finding chocolates and flowers at his home from well-wishers. More immediately, on the day after the near-perfect game, General Motors awarded Galarraga a Corvette in a pregame ceremony. In fact, Galarraga upgraded to a Corvette ZR1, paying the difference in price between the free car and the one he wanted. "I am happy with this decision because it feels symbolic," he wrote. "It represents how I feel about the [near perfect] game. . . . It shows how you can come so very close to something so very wonderful . . . and still not be able to reach it all the way. . . . However, it shows that you can sometimes reach the rest of the way if you give something extra, something of yourself."

In the aftermath of the Galarraga game, Major League Baseball experienced a huge demand that the missed call be overturned. Joyce himself indicated that he wished the call would be overturned. Tony La Russa agreed, telling a reporter, "If I was [Commissioner] Selig, in the best interest of the game . . . I'd give him the perfect game." Support even came in from fellow almost-perfect alum Milt Pappas, who among other remarks indicated, "I can't believe that." A Michigan congressman indicated that he would introduce a resolution asking MLB to overturn the call.

But Bud Selig refused to overturn the call. He did, however, note, that he would "examine [the] umpiring system [and] the expanded use of instant replay," while also noting that any changes would have to go through the proper channels, including labor unions. The advocates of instant replay had a perfect case—a likeable umpire, a thoroughly kind and decent player, and a blown call of historic proportions. For the good of everyone, why not allow these types of errors to be corrected?

In January 2014, Major League Baseball announced that it was time for an expansion of replay. (Galarraga recalled the MLB Players Association calling him and asking his thoughts. He told them, "Yes! I agree with replay!") Replay was expanded to not only home runs and ground-rule doubles, but fan interference, fair/foul calls, trap/catch calls, hit by pitches, passing runners, tag plays and, finally, force plays. Managers were granted one, or if it was used successfully, two challenges to use in the first six innings of the game, and thereafter, challenges were brought about by the umpiring crew. While baseball's establishment was nervous about implementing the changes, the ultimate result was a success. Tigers pitcher Max Scherzer, one of the hapless baseball spectators to Armando Galarraga's near-miss took to Twitter to write, "Finally we have replay!!"

By the 2014 All-Star Game, managers had challenged 606 calls, with 52 percent of the calls being overturned. Reviews took an average of one minute and 50 seconds, and the system was mostly considered a success. Never again would a perfect game be lost because a mistaken call on the bases could not be changed. A wrong had been righted, even if it came about three and a half years too late for Galarraga and Joyce.

The changes in instant replay for 2014 had little impact on Galarraga, as he was pitching in Taiwan that season. Galarraga won just two more games for Detroit in 2010. After the season, he was traded to Arizona for two minor leaguers. Galarraga went 3-4 with a 5.91 ERA in Arizona and was sent down to AAA. He signed with Baltimore after the season, but was released early in 2012. He signed with Houston during the season and worked his way back to the majors. But after five starts in Houston, he was 0-4 with a 7.50 ERA, and that was the end of his major-league career.

Galarraga spent 2013 in the Cincinnati Reds organization. He posted a 2.98 ERA in 16 starts for AAA Louisville (where he played with Jason Donald, whose MLB career was also over after 142 big-league hits), but was never called back to the majors. After a year in Taiwan and a year in the Mexican League, he retired following the 2015 season. His career major-league record was 26-34 with a 4.78 ERA. The near-perfect game was his only major-league shutout.

Arm injuries were at the center of Galarraga's troubles. He had some elbow issues and was rarely healthy. When asked if he is comfortable with a legacy as the pitcher who was robbed of a perfect game, Galarraga admits, "I want people to know me for different things that I know I could do, but I would always get hurt."

Still, if baseball on the field got tougher for Galarraga, his popularity off the field exploded after the near-perfect game. He and Joyce presented an ESPY award for ESPN's best sports moment of 2010. The two men collaborated on *Nobody's Perfect*, which paralleled their versions of the near-perfect game they shared. As his career wound down, Galarraga channeled his passion for pitching into the Armando Galarraga Academy, where he leads children ages seven through 15 through tutoring on various baseball lessons. When Galarraga talks of using video to teach young pitchers better mechanics, the excitement in his voice is clear. Before the 2016 season, the New York Yankees signed Galarraga as a minor-league pitching instructor. Certainly, young players looking for advice on handling the up-and-down nature of baseball could learn a thing or two from Galarraga.

Jim Joyce, as of this writing, is still an active major-league umpire. He turned 60 near the end of the 2015 season, and is approaching three decades in the big leagues. MLB banned Joyce from working any games involving Galarraga after the two collaborated on *Nobody's Perfect*. Since the Galarraga game, Joyce has worked another All-Star Game, and two more postseasons, including the 2013 World Series. If Joyce had anything to make up for in the wake of the Galarraga game, he made perhaps his best call in August 2012, when he administered CPR to a Diamondbacks employee named Jayne Powers, who was having a seizure and had stopped breathing. Joyce continued with CPR until paramedics could successfully perform defibrillation on Powers. Joyce, in typical fashion, downplayed his role in saving Powers's life. "It's not a hard thing," he told reporters. "You don't need a degree. It's very simple and very easy." As in the aftermath of the Galarraga game, Joyce's crew offered to move him off of his assigned home plate duties, but he refused. Blow a call, save a life; one gets the sense that Jim Joyce recognizes that it's all part of his odyssey in baseball.

It is perhaps appropriate that the Galarraga experience is highly unlikely to ever be repeated. Due in part to the impact that the game had on the culture of baseball, never again will an umpire's error uncorrectably change a perfect game into an almost-perfect game. But more than that, it's hard to imagine a player and an umpire ever handling such a situation with more class than Galarraga and Joyce. The call has diminished in significance compared to what the call revealed about the fundamental decency and courage of a journeyman pitcher on the best day of his life, and a great umpire on perhaps the worst day of his. Mistakes happen, and nobody is truly perfect. But perhaps nobody will ever be as imperfectly perfect as Jim Joyce and Armando Galarraga.

June 2, 2010
Comerica Park, Detroit, MI

	1	2	3	4	5	6	7	8	9	R	H	E
CLE	0	0	0	0	0	0	0	0	0	0	1	1
DET	0	1	0	0	0	0	0	2	X	3	9	0

W: Galarraga (2-1)
L: Hernandez (4-4)

The End of Galarraga's Perfect Game:

Top of Ninth Inning, Two Outs.
1-1 pitch to shortstop Jason Donald.
Donald was credited with a single when he grounded out to first baseman Miguel Cabrera, whose throw to pitcher Galarraga covering the base beat Donald for the final out. Veteran umpire Jim Joyce erroneously called Donald safe, and he was thus credited with a hit.

CHAPTER 14

NEAR PERFECTION FROM THE LAND OF THE RISING SUN

April 2, 2013

Texas Rangers at Houston Astros

Yu Darvish

In the era when baseball had reached its prime, American soldiers, called into the largest war modern society has ever known, found themselves thousands of miles from home, struggling for their lives in the jungles of the South Pacific. Their enemies, the Japanese Imperial Army, knew a few things about America. "TO HELL WITH BABE RUTH!" they shouted at the Americans. Not Franklin Roosevelt, or Abraham Lincoln, or Jefferson or Washington. America, the Japanese clearly believed, was Babe Ruth, then retired for the better part of a decade. America was baseball.

But in fact, baseball had already become a worldwide game, and one of the places it had flourished particularly was Japan. Baseball was played in Japan as early as the 1870s, and by 1883, the first Japanese baseball team, the

Yu Darvish, who used a dizzying array of pitches to nearly throw a perfect game, and who has battled injuries in the ensuing seasons KEITHALLISONPHOTO.COM

Shimbashi Athletic Club Athletics, had been founded. American touring teams passed through in the late 1900s and the 1910s, including John McGraw's barnstorming squad that featured Hooks Wiltse, the first "almost perfect" MLB pitcher.

Baseball in Japan took off due to the influence of Suishu Tobita, a great Japanese manager, who at 5'3" might have been McGraw's doppelganger in the Land of the Rising Sun. Author Robert Whiting recounts Tobita's own description of making his players field groundballs "until they were half dead, motionless, and froth was coming out of their mouths." Tobita adopted a personal motto of "perfect baseball."

While most of the early Japanese players were poor competition for their American competitors, the game was changing—and quickly. In 1934, an 18-year-old pitcher named Eiji Sawamura led a team of locals against an American All-Star team. Sawamura gave the Americans all they could handle. In one particular game, he held the American team hitless until the fifth inning, and whiffed Charlie Gehringer, Babe Ruth, Lou Gehrig, and Jimmie Foxx in order. Gehrig managed a seventh-inning solo homer, and America beat Sawamura 1–0, but clearly Japanese baseball was working toward its own level of perfection.

The biggest problem that Japanese players faced was the culture shock between Eastern and Western baseball. One author noted that Sawamura turned down an offer to pitch in the major leagues, telling a magazine, "My problem is I hate America and I cannot make myself like Americans." While many Japanese apparently did hold the great Ruth in special reverence, it was nothing that World War II couldn't overcome. During the war, the Japanese changed even the name of baseball, calling the game (in translation) field ball. The good news is that whatever baseball was called, it was too deeply ingrained in Japanese culture to be destroyed by war.

That said, the major leagues did not add any Japanese players until 1964. In that year, the Nankia Hawks sent three players to spend the season in the San Francisco Giant organization. A left-handed pitcher, Masanori Murakami, impressed the Giants' staff so thoroughly that he was called up to the big leagues. After some careful negotiation,

Murakami also spent the 1965 season with the Giants. All totaled, he pitched in 54 games for the Giants, working 89⅓ innings, posting a 5-1 mark and a 3.43 ERA. The Giants wanted to keep Murakami, but he returned home after 1965. He pitched until 1982, stardom eluding him in Japan, where his career record of 103-82 was solid, but not the stuff of legend.

There were other great Japanese stars. Sadaharu Oh hit 868 home runs. Masaichi Kaneda was the Walter Johnson of Japan, winning 400 games and fanning 4,490 batters while pitching for a perennially underwhelming team. But these stars, and others like them, made their marks solely on the Asian side of the Pacific Ocean. The culture war was generally running the other direction during the 1970s, 1980s, and early 1990s, as several American players extended their careers by playing in Japan. After 1988, slugging first baseman Cecil Fielder couldn't get playing time in the big leagues. He played in 1989 for Hanshin in the Japan Central League. Fielder hit .302 with 38 home runs, and drew the interest of the Detroit Tigers. Back in America in 1990, he slugged 51 home runs and knocked in 132 runs for the Motor City team.

But the wait for a great Japanese major leaguer ended in 1995, in a phenomenon called Nomo-mania. Fourteen years prior, the Dodgers had brought up Mexican hurler Fernando Valenzuela, and watched him blow away the National League and turn Dodger baseball into world news. L.A. management recognized a second grab at the brass ring with Hideo Nomo.

Nomo had risen to prominence in Japan with the Kintetsu Buffaloes of the Pacific League. He had a sharp fastball and a tough forkball, which combined with his somewhat bizarre windup to dazzle opposing hitters. From 1990 to 1994, Nomo was 78-46, with a 3.15 ERA and 1,204 strikeouts in Japan. But how would Nomo get to the major leagues? The loophole Nomo and agent Don Nomura found dictated that if Nomo "retired," then he could sign with whomever he wished should he "return" to baseball. No sooner realized than done. And in February 1995, the Dodgers signed Nomo to a minor-league contract with a $2 million signing bonus.

After one minor-league start, Nomo arrived in the big leagues. He baffled the National League, going 13-6 with a 2.54 ERA and 236 strikeouts. He was an All-Star, the Rookie of the Year, and finished fourth in the 1995 NL Cy Young Award voting. He held the same position in Cy Young Award balloting in 1996, going 16-11 with a 3.19 ERA. Not only was Nomo good, but he was glamorous, again emphasizing the world popularity of baseball, and opening the doors for players after him.

Nomo ended up posting a 123-109 mark in the major leagues, still winning 16 games in both 2002 and 2003. He was quickly joined by other Japanese stars, like the Yankees' Hideki Matsui, the Red Sox' Daisuke Matsuzaka, and the Mariners' Ichiro Suzuki. Nomo even threw two no-hitters, becoming one of just five pitchers to throw no-hitters in both the American and National Leagues. There was little left for an encore. Except maybe a pitcher who could embody Suishu Tobita's philosophy, at least for a day, and pitch "perfect baseball."

The global nature of baseball is certainly reflected in the youth and seasoning of Yu Darvish. Darvish was born to an Iranian father and a Japanese mother who met each other at a college in Florida. Farsad and Ikuyo Darvish moved to Japan in 1982, and Yu was born four years later. As one writer noted, "Japan prides itself on homogeneity, a significant majority of its [population] with 100 percent Japanese heritage. There are the Yamato people, the indigenous ethnic majority, and there is everyone else, like Yu Darvish."

Indeed, it rapidly became apparent that Darvish, who says that he considers himself to be Japanese, was not like everyone else. Darvish's father had played soccer and competed in motocross, but Yu had no interest in the games. He loved baseball, and as he filled out to 6 feet 5 inches tall, the game loved him back. Darvish dominated high school baseball in Japan, and despite a minor scandal that erupted when a gossip magazine caught him smoking a cigarette at age 18 (smoking being illegal in Japan for those under age 20), he was drafted by the Hokkaido

Nippon-Ham Fighters. Despite early interest from America, Darvish stayed with the Fighters for seven seasons. He was 93-38 over those seasons, with a 1.99 ERA. Twice, Darvish was the MVP of Japan's Pacific League, and five times, he was chosen as an All-Star.

After 2011, Darvish decided he was ready for America. He asked the Fighters to post him to Major League Baseball. Under that process, MLB teams could submit blind posting bids for the right to negotiate with Darvish. The Texas Rangers, with a bid of $51.7 million, won the right to bid on Darvish. If they could sign Darvish, they would pay the $51.7 million to the Fighters as a transfer fee, and if Darvish did not sign, no funds would change hands and Darvish would remain a Fighter.

Darvish was represented by two agents, Arn Tellem and Don Nomura. Texas had until 4:00 p.m. CST on January 18, 2012, to sign Darvish, or they would lose the chance. At 3:57 p.m., an agreement was reached. Darvish signed a six-year, $60 million contract with the Rangers. In light of having just spent $112 million to lock up Darvish, the Rangers were confident. Manager Ron Washington said at his introductory press conference, "Baseball is universal. We just want him to come in and be Yu Darvish." As for Darvish, his goals were a bit more concrete. He told the media, "I want to become the kind of pitcher that will make people say, 'Darvish is the number-one pitcher in the world.'"

Darvish made a fine start in 2012. He went 4-0 with a 2.18 ERA in his first month, winning AL Rookie of the Month. While there were some bumps in transition, Darvish won 16 games, was chosen for the AL All-Star team, and struck out 221 batters. As 2013 approached, Darvish's goal of making people say that he was the top pitcher in the world was within reach. And what better way to do that than to deliver pitching's Holy Grail? In the second game of 2013, on April 2nd, Darvish nearly did that.

⌇

The Houston Astros were undefeated. Granted, they had played one game, which had been their first as a member of the realigned American

League West. But Houston, having lost 106 and 107 games in 2011 and 2012 in the NL Central, must have thought they had turned a corner. In the season opener, they thumped the Rangers by an 8–2 score, and thus earned intrastate bragging rights as well as their first win in the American League. The Astros didn't know it at the time, but this would be the high-water mark of their season.

The Astros were a young team, and they simply weren't very good. First baseman Chris Carter went on to lead the team in 2013 with 29 homers and 82 runs batted in. He also hit .223 and struck out 212 times. Catcher Jason Castro was probably the team's best all-around player, as he hit .276 with 18 homers. Second baseman Jose Altuve—a 2012 All-Star—showed promise, batting .283 and stealing 35 bases. But overall, Houston was next-to-last in the AL in batting average and runs scored, and finished last in the league in hits.

The pitching staff was similarly poor. Young Dallas Keuchel would one day be a star, but in 2013, he went 6-10 with a 5.15 ERA. No pitcher won more than seven games, and aging closer Jose Veras, who saved 19 games, was the team's star by default.

The Rangers, as the successors of the old Washington Senator franchise, knew a few things about poor seasons. From 1972, when the Rangers were born in Arlington, the franchise waited 24 years for a post-season series. But times had turned, and in 2010 and 2011, the Rangers had reached the World Series, although they lost both Series. The 2012 team had reached the playoffs as a wild card, and expectations were high in Texas.

Third baseman Adrian Beltre was brilliant in 2013, hitting .315 with 30 home runs. Outfielder Nelson Cruz made his second All-Star team, hitting .266 with 27 homers. The Rangers hit .263 as a team, and were second in the American League in stolen bases.

Even aside from Darvish, the starting pitching was solid. Derek Holland and Martin Perez each won 10 games in 2013. But the bullpen, with lights-out setup man Tanner Scheppers and ace closer Joe Nathan, was superb. Scheppers sported a 1.88 ERA, and Nathan topped him at 1.39 with 43 saves.

Manager Ron Washington sent Darvish to the mound in the season's second game. He was opposed by Houston's Lucas Harrell, who had posted an 11-11 record in 2012. Harrell was a tough competitor who induced groundballs at a very high rate, but he was outclassed by Darvish. It rapidly became apparent how severely he was outclassed.

Despite a two-out single, Texas didn't score in the first, and so Houston came to bat promptly. The Astros had faced Darvish in interleague play in 2012, and struggled with him, managing only two runs with 11 strikeouts in eight innings. But that would look like child's play compared with what they saw on April 2, 2013.

Altuve led off for Houston, and worked a full count. Darvish alternated between low fastballs and a cut fastball that rode in on Altuve. On the payoff pitch, he broke off a sharp curveball that left Altuve whiffing air. Ranger play-by-play television broadcaster Steve Busby aptly predicted that Darvish had the stuff to pitch a high-strikeout game. Third baseman Brett Wallace reached a 2-2 count and then chased a biting slider for the second out. First baseman Carlos Pena grounded a 3-1 pitch to deep second base, where he was easily thrown out. Darvish's pitches were moving wildly, jumping up, darting away, and Houston looked lost.

The Rangers were set down in order in the top of the second, and Darvish went back to work on Houston. Whiff-happy first baseman Chris Carter saw eight pitches, but the eighth was a late-breaking slider that sent Carter back to the dugout. Houston outfielder Rick Ankiel batted fifth. Ankiel had once been a pitching phenom for the St. Louis Cardinals. On this day, he was just another hitter chasing Darvish's offerings as he haplessly cut and missed on a 1-2 curve. Center fielder Justin Maxwell needed only three pitches to join them, watching 93-, 94-, and 96-mile-per-hour fastballs split home plate. Darvish had struck out five of the first six Astros to face him.

In the top of the third, Texas outfielder Lance Berkman singled in a run that provided Darvish with all the offensive help he would need. In the bottom of the third, Houston tried unsuccessfully to answer. Jason Castro, serving as the DH, chopped the first pitch he saw to second base for a quick out. Catcher Carlos Corporan worked the count, but tapped a 2-2 fastball back to Darvish. Shortstop Marwin Gonzalez batted ninth. The Venezuelan second-year player hit just .234 as a rookie in 2012, and was in the lineup mostly for his glove. He chased a 1-2 breaking pitch, and completed Darvish's sixth strikeout and first jaunt through the Houston batting order.

After a scoreless top of the fourth, Darvish began his second trip through the Houston lineup in style. Altuve took the pitcher to a full count, but cut over top of a diving breaking ball. Brett Wallace saw seven pitches, but also went down chasing Darvish's curveball. Pena finished the inning by following the trend, swinging through a 97-mile-per-hour fastball. Darvish had set down the first 12 Astros, nine of them by strikeout.

The Rangers stranded two runners in the fifth inning and held their 1–0 lead. Darvish had thrown 61 pitches in four innings, and in only the second game of the year, his pitch count had proven to be a more daunting foe than the Astros for four frames. Leading off the fifth, however, Chris Carter caught up with a 2-1 offering and drove it high and deep into left field. Rangers left fielder David Murphy hurried to the wall, stopped, and caught the fly on the warning track. Darvish grinned slightly at his luck. Ankiel fouled off a pitch and then lined a shot that first baseman Mitch Moreland snagged with a slight leap, a good enough play that one reporter termed it "a nice catch." Darvish, perhaps feeling that he was cutting things a bit too close, threw three pitches past Jason Maxwell, ringing up the third strike on a curveball that froze the Houston hitter. Five perfect innings were complete.

Lucas Harrell held the Texas hitters in check for his sixth and final inning of work, and brought Darvish back to finish his second tour of the Houston lineup. Jason Castro began the inning by chasing a two-strike curveball for Darvish's 11th strikeout. Carlos Corporan lined a fastball gently to first baseman Moreland, and Marwin Gonzalez grounded to

Moreland to end the inning. Darvish had pitched six perfect innings, but had thrown 82 pitches. As smooth as his pitching had been, the questions became how long could he pitch, and, of course, how long could he stay perfect?

From the standpoint of winning the game, any pressure on Darvish was lightened greatly when Ian Kinsler hit a two-run homer in the Rangers' seventh, extending the lead to 3–0. With the emphasis growing on the perfect game, Darvish began the inning with a pitch that Altuve popped up to second baseman Kinsler. Third baseman Brett Wallace had struck out swinging in his first two at-bats, and while he extended the at-bat to seven pitches, the result was the same as he chased a curveball. Carlos Pena then chopped a 1-1 pitch, Darvish's 93rd of the evening, to first baseman Moreland to end the inning.

Texas manager Ron Washington faced decision time. Darvish's longest outing of spring training had been 78 pitches. Washington and pitching coach Mike Maddux had begun checking with Darvish after each inning. How was he feeling? The answer was always that Darvish was fine. Washington decided that perfection would be the pitch count. "If he had a high pitch count, we would have had to make that decision," he acknowledged after the game. But in the meantime, so long as Darvish was perfect—and felt fine—he would continue to pitch.

Darvish felt fine in the eighth, especially after the Rangers pushed across two more runs for him. He began the bottom of the inning facing Chris Carter, whose deep flyball was perhaps the closest call Darvish had experienced all night. Carter fought through a nine-pitch at-bat, with some of the Houston crowd rising to its feet in anticipation. But again, Carter was set down—this time by a wicked slider. Ankiel took only four pitches to follow suit, watching a curveball slide past and becoming Darvish's 14th strikeout of the night amid growing cheers. Jason Maxwell grounded Darvish's first pitch to second base, and Yu was now three outs away from perfection.

The Rangers added two more runs in the top of the ninth inning, but saying that no one really cared would be an understatement. Even on the road, Darvish was greeted with a thunderous ovation when he stepped out of the dugout to pitch the bottom of the ninth inning. Jason Castro began the bottom of the ninth by taking a strike and then tapping a harmless grounder to shortstop Elvis Andrus. Andrus threw him out by two full steps, leaving two outs to go. Carlos Corporan saw no point to wait on a good pitch. He grounded Darvish's first offering gently to second base, where Ian Kinsler threw him out easily. After three pitches, Darvish found himself one out from immortality.

Marwin Gonzalez batted ninth. He had never faced Darvish, and told the media afterward, "I didn't want to be the last out. I was trying to look for a good pitch to hit and put it in play. That's all I was thinking."

Gonzalez did not wait long.

Darvish's first pitch, his 111th of the night, caught the meat of the plate. Gonzalez went with it and grounded it sharply back through the mound area.

"That was impossible to catch," Darvish told reporters after the game, and indeed, when Darvish missed a fleeting chance at the sharp grounder, shortstop Elvis Andrus's headlong dive was destined to end up short of the ball, which rolled into center field. It was a clean single, and an end to history.

On the mound, Darvish threw his hands into the air, but then broke into an ironic grin. He smiled as his infielders rushed in to console him, and manager Ron Washington walked to the mound to bring in a reliever. Two batters later, the 7–0 win was completed in front of a disappointed crowd.

After the game, Darvish, with his right shoulder wrapped in padding that made him look like a lopsided bodybuilder, professed relief, telling reporters through a translator that he thought, "I can now go back to the dugout. Even if I got the complete game today, it's not going to translate to three or five wins."

Darvish denied negative feelings. "I went that far. I'm really satisfied," he said after the game. He elaborated, "I think my teammates were more disappointed than I was."

He had been unhittable for 26 batters, and even if it wasn't perfect, the game again made Yu Darvish the talk of baseball.

⌇

In 2013, Darvish was certainly one of the best pitchers in baseball. His record was just 13-9, but his 2.83 ERA and major-league high 277 strikeouts spoke to the excellence of his pitching, which earned him second place in the American League Cy Young balloting. On August 12th, Darvish nearly had another historic meeting with the Astros, pitching seven and a third hitless innings before surrendering a home run to Carlos Corporan. He did strike out 15 Astros and won the game 2–1. In another highlight, Darvish pitched well in a winning cause on the last day of the season, drawing the Rangers into a tie for the last AL playoff spot. However, they lost a one-game playoff to the Devil Rays, 5–2, and did not advance into postseason play.

The following season was a trying one for the Rangers and for Darvish. Texas posted the worst record in the American League at 67-95, and manager Ron Washington was fired during the season. Darvish was effective, although his team's struggles left him with just a 10-7 record to accompany his 3.06 ERA and 182 strikeouts. Late in the season, Darvish experienced some elbow inflammation, and with the pennant race long over, even after the elbow checked out fine, the Rangers shut him down on August 9th and looked ahead to 2015.

With Darvish set to establish his reign as one of the best starting pitchers in baseball, his luck took a decidedly bad turn in 2015. After pitching one inning in spring training, Darvish had some tenderness in his triceps. An MRI indicated that he had a partially torn ligament in his right elbow. Darvish underwent Tommy John ligament replacement surgery with Dr. James Andrews and did not pitch again in 2015.

"I didn't think this was going to happen," Darvish told reporters when the injury was revealed. "I thought it was nothing more than elbow inflammation." Darvish could only sit and watch as the Rangers won the AL West division and then grabbed the first two games of the best-of-five Division Series with Toronto before losing the series to the Blue Jays, three games to two. Darvish remained in Texas throughout the season, rehabbing his elbow under the team's supervision.

In November 2015, Darvish returned home to Japan for a brief rest from his rehab. He and his wife became parents during the 2015 season, but if domestic life enabled Darvish to temporarily forget the cultural stakes for which he was aiming, he didn't have to go far for a reminder. In Kobe, where Darvish spent much of his childhood, The Space 11 Darvish Museum has existed since November 2013. In fact, in tribute to Darvish's uniform number of 11, the museum opened on November 11 at 11:11 a.m. Inside the museum are Darvish's glove and uniform from a no-hitter he pitched in 2004 during Japan's national high school tournament, and a computerized program giving tourists the chance to "virtually" face all of his variety of pitches.

Darvish was 29 years old on Opening Day of the 2016 season. If he can continue to pitch as he did before his surgery, his résumé of 93 Japanese League wins and 39 major-league wins is a promising start to a career that could surpass Nomo's as the best ever for a Japanese pitcher in the major leagues. Darvish has already totaled 1,930 strikeouts between Japan and American baseball, and even if his totals won't quite equal those of Rangers legend Nolan Ryan, his pitching could still be the stuff of history. On May 28, 2016, Darvish made his first start back in the big leagues, and promptly struck out seven hitters in five innings for a victory.

In what he hopes is mid-career, Darvish is still striving—trying to lead the Rangers to that elusive championship, trying to put together a career to make himself known, as he had hoped, not just as the best Japanese pitcher in the American version of the game, but as the best pitcher in the world. Even if he ended up missing perfection on an April night in 2013, over the long haul, being the best in the world and perhaps one of the best ever would be a pretty fair consolation prize.

April 2, 2013
Minute Maid Park, Houston, TX

	1	2	3	4	5	6	7	8	9	R	H	E
TEX	0	0	1	0	0	0	2	2	2	7	12	0
HOU	0	0	0	0	0	0	0	0	0	0	2	0

W: Darvish (1-0)
L: Harrell (0-1)

The End of Darvish's Perfect Game:

Bottom of Ninth Inning, Two Outs.
First pitch to shortstop Marwin Gonzalez.
Gonzalez singled to center field.

CHAPTER 15

DOWN TO A DREAM

September 6, 2013
Arizona Diamondbacks at San Francisco Giants
Yusmeiro Petit

It was the spring of 2011, and no major-league team wanted Yusmeiro Petit. At age 26, the native of Venezuela was a veteran of four partial big-league seasons. He had paid his baseball dues, working his way up the professional ladder for five seasons before reaching the majors. But once he had arrived, things had not gone smoothly. From 2006 to 2009, he compiled just a 10-20 record, with a humbling 5.57 ERA. He had been traded twice, and after a mediocre 2010 campaign in AAA in the Seattle organization, the path to baseball success not only was rocky, it was looking nonexistent.

Yusmeiro Petit, who made his way back from the Mexican League to a near-perfect game and World Series glory NATIONAL BASEBALL HALL OF FAME

Petit was living in Miami, and as the 2011 season began, found himself still sitting at home, awaiting another chance to prove himself on baseball's biggest stage. When the call came, it wasn't the one Petit expected. It wasn't one of the 30 MLB teams, or even an eager minor-league squad. It was Oaxaca. In the Mexican League.

Yusmeiro Petit found himself spending 2011 as a Guerrero de Oaxaca. It was a long way from the first-class lifestyle of major leaguers to living in a $115 per month retirement hotel in Oaxaca. After the difficult year in 2010 and reluctance from the Mariners to give him a shot at the big-league roster, Petit admitted, "I didn't have an answer for anybody."

He continued, "I had to make an adjustment, go to Mexico, to Oaxaca. They gave me a chance, gave me a job for four months. I appreciated that because there wasn't anybody believing in me for the moment."

As for the mental issues apparent in making the move to a decidedly lower level of baseball, Petit recalled, "It's hard. You have to keep in your mind that you can do the job, working hard to come back to the United States." After the season, Petit did not return to America, but went on to his homeland of Venezuela to play in winter ball. An outsider might wonder if the trip home was the closing of a circle of a baseball career. But doubt about his baseball future wasn't a novel experience for Petit, and just as he had worked through the questions about his career path as a teenager, he was preparing an even more improbable rise to baseball glory. "There are challenges put in front of you by God to see how mentally strong you are and how you're going to react," said Petit.

Petit grew up in Maracaibo, the Venezuelan town that was the home of Luis Aparicio, the slick-fielding shortstop who is the nation's first member of the Baseball Hall of Fame. A large teddy bear of a man, Petit seems unlikely to have identified with the great but pint-sized Aparicio. When Yusmeiro was six, another local product, Wilson Alvarez, threw a no-hitter with the Chicago White Sox. Like Petit, Alvarez was a big-built pitcher with a strong arm. Petit came from a baseball-loving family, but he explains that none of his family members played professionally. As the child of an agricultural surveyor and a teacher, Petit was not necessarily expected to become the next Aparicio or Alvarez. Indeed, at the age of 16, his dreams and his reality reached a point where the two might have diverged.

"When I was 16, I had to make the next step for university," recalled Petit. "I talked to my mom, and she said, 'You have to go to the university.' My dad, he asked me, 'What do you want to do?' I want to play baseball. . . . I said to my dad, 'Give me one year for signing. If I don't sign for one year, I'll go to university and be a student for a professional career.'"

Petit's request met his parents' approval, and he dedicated the next year to showing the professional baseball scouts around Venezuela just what he could do.

"My dad gave me a chance and I went to the Minnesota Academy in Venezuela, and I stayed for four months, working hard every day," said Petit. "After that, they don't sign me. I went to the other academy, and then the Mets gave me a chance."

The first time that Petit's baseball dreams were at the crossroads, the Mets came to the rescue, signing him for $20,000 a week before his 17th birthday. Bouncing up the minor-league trail from Kingsport, Tennessee, to Port St. Lucie, Florida, to Binghamton, New York, and Norfolk, Virginia, was just part of the experience for Petit.

Now, spending your late teens in the lower minors to make your way to the big leagues at 21 is one experience. What about pitching at the edge of the baseball world as 30 approached?

Petit pitched, and dreamed, and knew that he could still help a major-league team, if only he could find a team that he could convince of his abilities.

It was in Venezuela that Petit got his break in late 2011. Pitching for the Bravos de Margaritas, Petit showed command of his pitches, and an ability to keep hitters off-balance. The Bravos happened to have two coaches—Hensley Meulens and Jose Alguacil—who also were employed by the San Francisco Giants. Both were impressed by Petit and both happened to mention to their superiors in the Giants organization that Yusmeiro Petit might just be a pitcher on whom they should take a chance.

Meulens called Petit's story "unbelievable" in 2014. He related, "He never thought he was going to get another chance—he was thinking about going back to Mexico [in 2012]. That's so far away from the major leagues."

As far away as Petit was from the major leagues, could he have even dreamed of perfection? Could he have dreamed of being the most perfect pitcher the game of baseball had ever seen? If so, it would only be because Yusmeiro Petit had learned to dream big dreams.

～

Fresh from the winter ball recommendations of Meulens and Alguacil, the Giants did indeed give Petit a shot in 2012—a shot in AAA Fresno. For his part, Petit showed signs of progress. He developed his curveball with Giants pitching coach Dave Righetti, and put together a solid year in Fresno, going 7-7 with a 3.46 ERA in 28 starts. In fact, Petit's season was impressive enough that in many organizations, he would have earned a quick promotion to the big leagues. But the pitching-rich Giants had solid veterans like Matt Cain, Barry Zito, and Ryan Vogelsong, as well as talented young lefty Madison Bumgarner. Petit was promoted to the big leagues in September and made one start for the Giants, allowing two earned runs in four and two-thirds innings and leaving the game with no decision. The Giants fared well, winning their division by eight games and running through the playoffs, eventually sweeping the Detroit Tigers to win the World Series. Petit had been very solid in 2012, but not quite good enough to stick with the parent club.

He went immediately into winter ball, pitching a third consecutive season with the Bravos de Margarita. Petit began 2013 in Fresno again, and pitched solidly. In July, he was called up by the Giants briefly, pitching five and a third innings of relief against Cincinnati and striking out seven. Five days later, it was back to Fresno. Petit was close to sticking in the big leagues and pitched accordingly. He made three starts back in Fresno, pitching 19 innings and allowing four runs. In the last start, Petit pitched six innings of one-hit ball with eight strikeouts. San Francisco noticed.

On August 23, 2013, Petit was recalled to the big leagues. He started on August 27th against Colorado and won, holding the Rockies to two runs in six innings. On September 1st, he beat his old team, the Diamondbacks, again allowing just two runs in six innings. Petit's next turn to pitch came again on September 6th, this time at home, but again versus Arizona. For a man who had pitched 22 major-league innings since 2009, a third consecutive win was a feasible goal—as was a solid outing, one to hopefully help Petit stick with the Giants. Instead, Yusmeiro Petit was almost perfect.

⸺

After a 2012 season in which virtually everything had gone right, 2013 was a struggle for the Giants. Bumgarner continued to pitch like an ace, but the clock was running out on some of the San Francisco veterans— Zito posted a 5.74 ERA and Vogelsong almost matched him with a 5.73 mark. The offense was relatively toothless as well, aside from Hunter Pence, who would finish the year with 27 home runs and 99 RBIs. By September 6th, the team was 62-78, dead last in the NL West.

Arizona was one of the teams ahead of the Giants in the division standings. The Diamondbacks were a solid team, led by slugging first baseman Paul Goldschmidt, who hit .302 with 36 home runs and 125 RBI in 2013. The Diamondbacks had a young pitching staff, which was talented enough to keep them competitive, but inexperienced enough that they never seriously challenged the Dodgers for the division crown. They were 71-68 on September 6th, good for second in the West, and still within the realm of chance for the NL wild-card playoff spot. Talented young lefty Patrick Corbin, who led the team with 14 wins and made the 2013 NL All-Star team, was ready to oppose Petit.

⸺

September 6, 2013, was a beautiful night for baseball in San Francisco. Temperatures lingered in the low 70s and the sun was still out shortly after 7:00 p.m., when Petit took the mound to begin the game. Wind is always an issue in San Francisco, but AT&T Park was built much more carefully than its predecessor, Candlestick Park, where Giants pitcher Stu Miller was infamously blown off the pitching mound on a particularly brisk day. A steady breeze blew out to right field, but it was not offensive. Despite the Giants' poor season, 41,180 enjoyed a comfortable evening at the ballpark.

The Diamondbacks had won the series opener the previous day, 4–2, and essentially used their normal lineup. Shortstop Chris Owings was tabbed for his first major-league start, but Petit was otherwise given no advantage. He would need none.

"I had good stuff," Petit recalled later. "That day, I remember, everything was good. I could throw whatever I wanted."

Arizona center fielder A. J. Pollock opened the game by grounding Petit's second pitch sharply, but right at Giants second baseman Marco Scutaro, who threw him out easily. Petit then blew a two-strike fastball past Adam Eaton. Goldschmidt ripped Petit's first off-speed pitch of the night to deep short. Shortstop Joaquin Arias went to his knees to field the shot, pivoted, and fired to first, nailing Goldschmidt by a step. Petit appreciatively pounded his mitt in applause as he walked back to the dugout with the first inning behind him.

The Giants were retired in order, and Petit quickly returned to the mound for the second frame. He dispatched Martin Prado on a foul popup to first base. Petit had fanned 10 Diamondbacks in his previous start, and he notched his second strikeout of this game on a nasty breaking ball to Aaron Hill. Petit's fastball was arriving at 88–90 miles per hour, but it was consistently brushing the bottom edge and/or the outside corner of umpire Phil Cuzzi's strike zone. After a particularly sparkling fastball to Arizona catcher Miguel Montero, Giants broadcaster Duane Kuiper admiringly exclaimed, "He is throwing darts!" Montero flied out easily to left field, and after two nine-pitch innings, Petit was cruising.

In the bottom of the second, a trio of singles and an error by shortstop Owings allowed the Giants to plate the single run that would prove to be all the support that Petit required. Buoyed by the lead, Petit worked another strong inning. Owings flied out to left field. Gerardo Parra tapped an 0-2 pitch to first for an easy out. Corbin looked hopeless against his fellow pitcher, requiring only four pitches for an inning-ending strikeout, and completing Petit's first run through the Arizona lineup.

The Giants went down in order in the bottom of the third inning, and Petit prepared for the top of the order in the Arizona fourth. In the first trip through the order, Petit had relied heavily on the fastball. He began the second run throwing two breaking pitches to Pollock, who grounded to Arias. Petit started Adam Eaton with a curve, and actually fell behind on a 2-0 count before he induced another grounder to Arias. With two out, the ever-dangerous Goldschmidt (who was second in the NL in home runs and first in RBIs) stepped up to hit. Petit went off speed for strike one, and then blew two fastballs past Goldschmidt to end the inning. After four innings and 37 pitches, Petit was perfect. Catcher Hector Sanchez singled home another run in the second, and Petit was staked to a 2–0 advantage.

Arizona cleanup hitter Martin Prado took a strike and then popped up to shortstop. Aaron Hill had struck out in his first at-bat, and he repeated the feat on a 2-2 fastball that arrived knee-high and on the outside corner of the plate. Miguel Montero finished the frame with a harmless bat-shattering grounder to Scutaro at second base. Not only wasn't Arizona hitting Petit, they hadn't really come close in five innings.

After an uneventful Giant fifth inning, Petit prepared to complete his second turn through the Arizona lineup. Outfielder Juan Perez entered the game in left field for Brett Pill. Perez, a frequent late-inning defensive substitute, would quickly assume a key role in the game. First, shortstop Owings opened the inning by tapping back to Petit on his third pitch. Gerardo Parra worked a deep count, but grounded out to shortstop Arias. Patrick Corbin cut and missed at two off-speed offerings, but then, the .133 hitting pitcher nearly ruined the game. Petit's 59th pitch was a fastball that caught more of the plate than most on this night. Corbin, swinging left-handed, went with the pitch and drove it sharply into short left field. The newly inserted Perez was playing shallow, but the ball was hit hard and on a low line. He sprinted for it, dove, and rolled over, with the line drive securely nestled in his glove. The crowd roared and Petit pointed appreciatively at Perez. The second jaunt through the Diamondbacks was perfect.

Petit told a reporter after the game, "I realized what was going on when Juan Perez made that catch in the sixth inning. From then on, I just tried to concentrate on every pitch."

After an uneventful bottom of the sixth, Petit was dominant in the seventh inning. He needed only six pitches—two to each batter—to dispose of the top third of the Arizona lineup. A. J. Pollock watched a breaking-ball strike and then flied out to Angel Pagan in center field. Adam Eaton took a ball and then grounded a fastball right at first baseman Brandon Belt. Paul Goldschmidt watched a fastball on the outside corner and then tapped a breaking ball to Belt as well. With just 65 pitches, Petit had worked seven perfect innings.

The Giants went down in order in the home half of the seventh, and by now, the Giants bench pointedly kept baseball etiquette by allowing Petit distance and peace. The pressure was mounting in AT&T Park, as the crowd was producing an audible, constant buzz in nervous support of Petit. "It pumped me up," Petit recalled. "It's like that in Venezuela, every pitch, every out, every inning, it's loud. I like the emotion."

Petit pitched as if he were right at home as he opened the frame against Martin Prado, who chased a nasty 1-2 breaking ball in the dirt for Petit's sixth strikeout. Petit quickly threw two strikes to Aaron Hill, and induced him to pop a high fastball up to second baseman Scutaro. After Petit worked to a 1-2 count on catcher Miguel Montero, he faltered briefly. Only four batters had even gotten to a two-ball count on Petit, and he had not yet reached a three-ball count. A curve in the dirt evened the at-bat. Montero foul-tipped a fastball, and Petit then missed low, bringing the count full. Montero fouled off another fastball. On his eighth pitch, Petit threw another fastball on the outer edge of the plate. Montero swung and dribbled a grounder to first. Belt fielded the ball, and beat Montero to the bag by two steps. Eight perfect innings were complete.

Hunter Pence homered in the bottom of the eighth, and the Giants' lead extended to three runs. But the San Francisco crowd was focused on Petit's pursuit of perfection. The previous year, Giant Matt Cain had pitched a perfect game at home. Earlier in the 2013 season, Giant Tim Lincecum added a no-hitter in San Diego. Yusmeiro Petit settled in for his own shot at history. The Giants television crew had spotted his wife in the stands in the eighth inning, and her nervous vigil now paralleled her husband's.

Chris Owings, in his first major-league start, might have been the only player more nervous than Petit. He swung through a curveball, then chased another breaking ball, and finally whiffed on a nasty curve on the outside corner, Petit's 84th pitch of the night yielding his seventh strike-out. The television cameras captured Mrs. Petit nervously covering her mouth with her hands, as Yusmeiro was now two outs from perfection.

Gerardo Parra followed. Petit aimed for the outside corner, and placed two fastballs there. Phil Cuzzi's strike zone, relatively ample all night, suddenly tightened. The first ball drew boos from the crowd, and the second pitch was perhaps a bit off the plate. Still, in the relatively unusual position of pitching from behind in the count, Petit delivered another outside fastball. This one cut across the plate, and Parra swung, grounding the ball solidly but safely to Marco Scutaro at second base. Two outs.

Patrick Corbin's spot in the order was due, but Arizona manager Kirk Gibson called for pinch-hitter Eric Chavez. A California native, Chavez was a star in Oakland in the early 2000s. He hit 30 homers twice in a season as an Athletic, and knocked in 100 RBI four times. At age 35, Chavez was a part-time third baseman for Arizona. He was less than a season from the end of his career, but was hitting .286 with nine homers and 42 RBI. He had never faced Petit in a major-league game.

Petit threw a nasty breaking pitch that Chavez watched for a ball. An outside fastball just missed the corner of the plate, and for the second consecutive batter, Petit was behind by a 2-0 count. He changed nothing. The 2-0 pitch was another fastball, slightly harder, slightly farther in, drawing a strike call from Phil Cuzzi as the crowd roared. The next pitch hit the same spot. All night long, Petit's command of the corner of the plate was superb, and Cuzzi gave him the close pitch. Strike two. Petit followed with a filthy slider, over the plate, but dipping low in the strike zone. Chavez watched it drop and didn't swing. Ball three.

Petit went behind the pitching rubber to collect himself. He later remembered, "When I got to 3-2, I thought, 'I'll win or I'll lose. I want to make my pitch.'. . . Even if he walked, I would get a no-hitter. But I didn't want something nice, something good, I wanted something perfect."

Petit threw another fastball aimed knee-high at the outside corner. "I didn't throw a bad pitch," he recalled. "It was a good pitch."

Chavez, though, was sitting on it. He reached out and lined it hard to right field. The ballpark held its breath, and Petit first bent into a squat, and then stood at attention to watch with the other 41,180 spectators as Giant right fielder Hunter Pence sprinted toward the ball. "It felt like . . . one of those dreams where you can't run fast enough," Pence told reporters after the game. He extended into a dive, reaching and finding the ball . . . just as it bounced off of the grass in front of him. Petit threw his arms into the air, and Chavez had a single. Two years later, asked what his reaction was, Petit recalled thinking, "Wow! That's too close!"

Petit's wife had been escorted by security to the area behind home plate. They quickly ducked into the tunnel as the game now continued. Yusmeiro worked quickly, throwing another fastball on the outside corner to A. J. Pollock, and then one last pitch yielded a grounder to third baseman Joaquin Arias, which closed the game.

On the mound, Petit did not betray frustration. He raised his arms in the air in triumph, his index finger pointing to the sky as his teammates filed past, some congratulating, some consoling, some just pulling him into a quick hug.

Temporary sadness aside, Petit had proven himself—again—as a major-league pitcher. After the game, Giants manager Bruce Bochy commented, "He's kind of sent a message this is where he belongs and this is where he should be pitching." The dream that had been on life support in the Mexican League was alive and well. In fact, near-perfection was only the beginning.

Petit finished 2013 with a 4-1 mark and a 3.56 ERA in 48 major-league innings. In 2014, there would be no trips to Fresno. That said, on a loaded Giant team, Petit had a different role every day. He started 12 games and pitched in 27 more in relief. Sometimes he pitched an inning or two, sometimes a longer stint. For the year, he posted a 5-5 mark and a 3.69 ERA in 117 innings. He also made history.

How perfect can a pitcher be? Of course, Harvey Haddix managed 12 innings before cracking in his battle with history. No pitcher has ever seriously flirted with consecutive perfect games. The closest anyone has come was a 2009 run by Mark Buehrle, in which he pitched a perfect game and then retired the first 17 batters he faced in his next start. When added to the out that he had drawn in his last start before the perfect game, it added up to 45 consecutive batters retired—15 innings, a game and two-thirds.

That was the record. Until 2014, when a swingman three years removed from the Mexican League rewrote the record book. The streak began inauspiciously. In an ineffective start against the Phillies on July 22nd, Petit gave up five runs in five innings, getting no decision in a comeback win by the Giants. The last batter he faced that day, Grady Sizemore, tapped back to Petit to end the fifth inning.

Four days later, on July 26th, Petit pitched the last two innings of a 5–0 loss to the Dodgers, and set down all six batters he faced. Seven consecutive outs.

Two days later, on July 28th, he worked two innings in a 5–0 loss to the Pirates. Again, six batters faced Petit, and all six made outs. Thirteen consecutive outs.

On August 7th, Petit worked an inning in a 3-1 loss to the Brewers, and again retired the side in order. Sixteen consecutive outs.

Petit's next outing was August 10th in Kansas City. He pitched an inning against the Royals, and picked up three more outs, running his streak to 19 in a row.

Petit didn't pitch again until August 21st, when he was called on to work two innings to help complete a rain-suspended game with the

Cubs that had begun two days prior. He promptly whiffed five of six Cubs batters and continued his perfect streak, which at 25 outs in a row, was approaching a full perfect game.

On August 23rd, the Nationals ripped Tim Lincecum for six runs by the third inning. Petit took over in relief and pitched four and a third perfect frames, fanning five more hitters and running his streak to 38 consecutive outs. Petit said in 2015 that he became aware of the record from the media after the game with the Nationals.

Five days later, on August 28th, Petit started in place of Lincecum, and had his shot at baseball history. With his wife again in the stands, he began the game seven outs shy of Buehrle's record, and edged closer when he sat down the Rockies in order in the first inning. In the second inning, Petit induced a flyout and then struck out the next two batters. He was one out shy of the record.

Catcher Jackson Williams led off the third inning and struck out swinging. Shortstop Charlie Culberson followed, and when he also fanned, Petit had retired 46 consecutive batters and established a new major-league record. The next batter doubled, but Petit allowed just one run in six innings for his fourth win of the season.

Petit's cap was collected by the Baseball Hall of Fame. When he was asked a year later how he wanted to be remembered in baseball, he did not hesitate in mentioning his historic record. "It was hard!" he emphasized. "Facing 46 batters and not giving up a hit or a walk, you have to be perfect in your command."

And what does it mean to be in the MLB record book, with Young, Ryan, Koufax, and all the others? "It's pretty cool," Petit admitted.

What does a pitcher do for an encore to being the most perfect pitcher ever? He helps his team win a championship, of course. Petit picked up a win in Game 2 of the NLDS, working six scoreless innings of the Giants' 18-inning triumph. When San Francisco advanced to the NLCS, Petit earned another win, pitching three scoreless innings in Game 4 of that series. He added a win in Game 4 of the World Series, with three more scoreless innings, and even managed a base hit in the game. When the Giants won the Series in seven games, Petit could be forgiven if he wondered what could possibly be left.

"That's my dream," said Petit of the Series run. "When you've been pitching in Mexico, in Oaxaca, to go three years later and maybe be the difference in winning a championship, that was my dream."

Despite his World Series triumph, Petit's ultimate career trajectory was somewhat blocked by the abundance of pitching talent in San Francisco. He started just once in 2015, but pitched in 42 games, going 1-1 with a 3.67 ERA. He earned $2.1 million in 2015, a far cry from Oaxaca and living in a room with a daily rent slightly cheaper than a hamburger value meal. After the season, Petit signed as a free agent with the Washington Nationals, where as of this writing, he was again an effective bullpen component of an NL pennant competitor.

For Petit, it has been a historic run, with an almost-perfect game leading up to a record of perfection and a key role in a World Series title. But before the run came the dream. Not just any pitcher could've worked his way from Oaxaca to history. Only one who was brave enough to make the dream a reality.

September 6, 2013
AT&T Park, San Francisco, CA

	1	2	3	4	5	6	7	8	9	R	H	E
ARZ	0	0	0	0	0	0	0	0	0	0	1	1
SF	0	1	0	1	0	0	0	1	X	3	8	0

W: Petit (3-0)
L: Corbin (13-6)

The End of Petit's Perfect Game:

Top of Ninth Inning, Two Outs.
3-2 pitch to pinch-hitter Eric Chavez.
Chavez singled to right field, just in front of a diving Hunter Pence.

CHAPTER 16

THE ILLUSION OF CONTROL

June 20, 2015

Pittsburgh Pirates at Washington Nationals

Max Scherzer

It is somehow appropriate that Max Scherzer has two different-colored eyes. The phenomenon known as heterochromia iridum shows up readily when the tall right-hander comes into view. Scherzer's right eye is bright blue and his left eye is dark brown. The condition is unusual, but peculiarly appropriate for the pitcher who was sent to the minor leagues to clear the way for one almost-perfect game, only to pitch his own near-gem five years later. A bright side and a dark side are a natural fit for the pitcher who had one of the most remarkable seasons ever, but had it for a highly

Max Scherzer, showing the form that led to a near-perfect game and two no-hitters in 2015, as well as a 20-strikeout outing in 2016 COURTESY OF THE WASHINGTON NATIONALS BASEBALL CLUB

regarded team that was perhaps the biggest disappointment in baseball. If anyone is prepared to acknowledge multiple ways of seeing the same world, it would have to be the high-priced ace who watched his childhood baseball dreams come true, but has suffered through the pain of living out those dreams without the companion who shared them with him. Forget two different-colored eyes; for Max Scherzer, the ebb and flow of great success and heartbreaking disappointment are so intertwined that it could seem as if he has two different lives, joined together only by what happens on the pitching mound. And even on the mound, Scherzer had to learn— with a little help from his brother—just how much he couldn't control.

⁓

Max Scherzer was born on July 27, 1984, in St. Louis and grew up in the suburban area of the city. From an early age, Max and his brother, Alex, who was three years younger, were inseparable. Max Scherzer has admitted knowing in the third grade that he would be a professional baseball player, but Alex Scherzer nearly matched Max's athletic skills with his understanding of numbers and statistics. Max might have played baseball, but Alex understood the game in a way that presaged the sabermetric Moneyball culture that would soon flourish.

Max and Alex were the only children of Brad and Jan Scherzer. Their father called them "classic, All-American kids," and the friendship remained as Max began climbing the ladder of professional baseball. Scherzer played his high school baseball at local Parkway Central High, and the Cardinals gave him the chance to fulfill his hometown hero dreams when they chose him in the 43rd round of the 2003 MLB Draft. Scherzer passed on the pros, choosing his parents' alma mater, the nearby University of Missouri, for his collegiate baseball career. As a sophomore, Scherzer was the Big 12 pitcher of the year with a 9-4 mark and a 1.86 ERA. After his junior season, he reentered the MLB Draft and was chosen 11th overall by the Arizona Diamondbacks.

After protracted negotiations involving Scherzer's agent, the eternally polarizing Scott Boras, Arizona signed the Missourian. He was in the majors by 2008, but was only so-so for the Diamondbacks. He was 9-15 in a season and a half for Arizona, although his relatively low ERA and high strikeout numbers suggested the potential for success. They certainly did to Alex Scherzer.

By 2009, Alex was finishing up his economics degree at Missouri. He followed Max's career closely, and loved to argue with Max on the intricacies of the game. Alex taught Max about some of the finest new statistical tools—a way to impose order on the chaos of baseball—but ironically, that lesson came with the knowledge that sometimes, there was no control. In one 2009 interview, Max admitted to a journalist that he and Alex had argued for months after Alex brought up the concept that the pitcher has no control once the batter hits the ball. "It took about a year of arguing with him for me to realize that actually is the correct way to think," admitted Max. Accordingly, with Alex's tutelage, Max was studying BABIP (Batting Average on Balls in Play), tERA (true ERA), and WAR (Wins Above Replacement) numbers. "I'm well aware that the numbers aren't everything," he said in 2009. "They just explain a good portion of what happens."

After the 2009 season, Arizona traded Max to the Detroit Tigers in a three-team trade. In 2010, Max began the year pitching terribly in Detroit. In eight starts, he was 1-4 with a 7.29 ERA. When Detroit sent him to AAA Toledo, rotation replacement Armando Galarraga pitched a near-perfect game. Scherzer's hard work was getting him nowhere, and in the toughest times, when doubts piled up, it was Alex who would text him and encourage him to keep plugging.

On the surface, all was well with Alex Scherzer. He earned his economics degree from Missouri and considered law school before deciding to complete an MBA. However, in the winter of 2009, he confided in his mother. He had been depressed, and had even considered suicide. Jan talked Alex into seeing a psychiatrist, and he was prescribed an antidepressant. As he returned to school and his usual self, his family hoped that this was just a tiny blip that would soon be forgotten. In fact, the matter seemed so quickly resolved that no one told Max.

As for Max, his poor pitching similarly seemed an aberration. After Detroit recalled him from the minors on May 30th, he posted an 11-7 mark with a 2.46 ERA for the rest of the 2010 season. The 2011 season was up and down, as a 15-9 record belied a career-high 4.43 ERA. Alex reassured Max, telling him by text, "If there's anything I've taught you, it's that #1 shit happens, #2 the non-scientific meaning is that you've now banked your juju for the playoffs." Alex was right, as Max won a game against the Yankees in the AL Division Series, before the Tigers fell to the Rangers in the ALCS.

Things were looking up for the Scherzer family in 2012. Max was now earning a cool $3.75 million in Detroit and was rapidly developing into one of the better young pitchers in baseball. Alex was working for Morgan Stanley as an assistant financial analyst, after he had amazed his coworkers by veritably sprinting through the firm's training program. Max had some struggles early in the season, but threw eight shutout innings on June 17th to move to 6-4 on the year. But from a quick high, Max was plunged into a subterranean low. Four days later, he had a call from his father. To the shock and horror of the entire Scherzer family, Alex was suddenly dead. He had hanged himself in the family's basement.

Two days later, with his remaining family at the park to support him, Max pitched against the Pittsburgh Pirates. His focus was nonexistent, and he felt more exhausted than he ever had on the field. He pitched six innings, allowing three runs, and striking out seven, and then sobbed in the field crew's room when he was pulled from the game. His teammates, his manager, and all of baseball were astounded at the dedication and competitive spirit Max had shown—and at the love for his brother, which tore at him. Tiger catcher Alex Avila told reporters, "It's a situation where I don't think anyone can understand it unless you've gone through it."

Scherzer dealt with his grief in many ways. He gave a statement to the press a few days later in Texas. He refused to delete Alex's old texts from his cell phone. He wrote a letter to Mark McGwire, a childhood hero of the Scherzer brothers, and asked for one of McGwire's bats to remember his brother. Not only did McGwire send the bat, but he admitted that he was so touched by the letter that he planned to save it forever. But mostly, Max played baseball. As one writer noted, "A happy amnesia flowed over him when he was on the mound. Game after game, life got a little simpler. Ball, hitter, catcher's mitt."

From tragedy, Scherzer found the strength to become the pitcher that his brother had always insisted that he could be. He finished 2012 with a 16-7 mark, and his ERA fell from 5.17 at the time of Alex's death to 3.74 at the end of the season. He won a game in the ALCS against the Yankees, and pitched well in a start in the World Series, although the Tigers were swept.

But if Scherzer had finished 2012 pitching well, he was absolutely untouchable in 2013. He went 21-3 with a 2.90 ERA and 240 strikeouts. He started the All-Star Game and won the American League's Cy Young Award. He struck out another 34 batters in 22⅓ postseason innings, although the Tigers lost in the ALCS. As an encore, he went 18-5 in 2014, again leading the AL in wins, making the All-Star team, and fanning 252 batters. The Tigers again faltered in the postseason, losing the ALDS.

As a free agent after the 2014 season, Scherzer was in position to find out just how highly regarded he was. He had turned down an offer from Detroit of $144 million for six seasons, and in January 2015, he signed with the Washington Nationals in a seven-year, $210 million deal. After working their way back to competitive status and winning the NL East in 2014, Washington added Scherzer to a starting rotation including Stephen Strasburg, Jordan Zimmerman, and Doug Fister. The Nationals had a solid offense, which centered on young star outfielder Bryce Harper, who would become the NL MVP at the ripe age of 22 in 2015. Suddenly, the Nationals were an odds-on pick for a World Series title, and Scherzer was positioned to be one of the most successful pitchers in baseball.

On June 20th, the Nationals stood at just 35-33. It was good for first in a very weak NL East, but there were rumblings that veteran manager Matt Williams was losing control of his team. Scherzer was pitching exceptionally well, although his crumbling team struggled to support him. He was 7-5 on June 20th, despite having just a 1.93 ERA. Even in his five losses, Scherzer was sporting a 2.88 ERA. Five times in his first 13 starts, he had fanned more than 10 batters, and in his last start, at Milwaukee, he whiffed 16 batters, and had been perfect for six innings. He allowed a single to lead off the seventh, and a walk in the eighth inning, and otherwise shut the Brewers down completely. So the Pittsburgh Pirates were prepared for the possibility that the game would not be a picnic.

The Pirates themselves were not exactly chopped liver. Pittsburgh ended up with 98 wins in 2015, and was led by all-everything outfielder Andrew McCutchen. Slugging first baseman Pedro Alvarez was always a threat, and a pitching staff headlined by ace Gerrit Cole and tricky lefty Francisco Liriano gave Pittsburgh one of the best teams in the league. At 39-28, Pittsburgh trailed only the St. Louis Cardinals for the best record in the NL on June 20th. On a 90-degree-plus afternoon in the nation's capital, the Pirates faced Max Scherzer, hot off perhaps the best pitching performance of his career—the best until that particular afternoon anyway.

Pirate second baseman Josh Harrison began the game by swinging at Scherzer's first pitch—a 92-mile-per-hour fastball—and popping it up harmlessly to second base. Outfielder Starling Marte then looked at two fastballs before punching a 1-1 pitch into right field. The ball carried well off the bat, but Bryce Harper caught the ball a step shy of the outfield wall. The eternally dangerous McCutchen batted third. McCutchen had hit the three-run homer that beat Scherzer in his first outing after his brother's death, but on June 20th, he harmlessly chopped a second-pitch fastball to shortstop Ian Desmond to end a six-pitch first inning. The Nationals went down to Liriano in only eight pitches, and Scherzer promptly returned to the mound for the second inning.

Pirate Jung Ho Kang took a strike and then flied Scherzer's first breaking pitch out to Harper in right field for a routine out. Catcher Francisco Cervelli similarly flied to center field. Pedro Alvarez lofted a 1-2 flyball to left fielder Michael Taylor, who barely moved before he ended the inning with an effortless catch. As Nats' broadcasters Bob Carpenter and F. P. Santangelo noted, after Scherzer's 16 strikeouts in his last start, the Pirates were not exactly waiting around at the plate. "They were a very aggressive team," noted Max after the game. "I could tell their gameplan, and I was going to force their hand."

Scherzer opened the third inning by getting Gregory Polanco to chase a high fastball for strike three. Pittsburgh outfielder Jordy Mercer hit a first pitch fastball hard and high to left field. "I almost gave up a home run to Mercer," recalled Scherzer after the game. As with Marte's flyball in the first inning, the ball carried farther and farther, and Michael Taylor had to leap to make the grab in left field. Had Taylor missed the ball, it would've been at least a double, and maybe a home run. But Scherzer appreciatively smacked his fist in his glove after the grab, and then blew Liriano away in four pitches for his second strikeout of the day. After 26 pitches, Scherzer had completed his first perfect circuit through the Pittsburgh lineup. He would only get better.

After Liriano set down the Nationals in the third inning (despite a sharp single from Scherzer himself, who was hitting .250 in his first year in the National League), Max Scherzer began his second journey through the Washington lineup with the type of inning pitchers dream of. "Once I got through the lineup the first time," Max commented after the game, "I knew I could then start going to the rest of my arsenal, and really figure out what adjustments we needed to make to get outs." Josh Harrison saw a couple of sliders and then fanned on a 95-mile-per-hour fastball. After Sterling Marte fouled off Scherzer's first two pitches, he battled through six more pitches, working to a full count, and becoming Scherzer's first opponent to take three balls. The third of those was a 97-mile-per-hour heater, knee high and on the outside corner.

When home plate umpire Mike Muchlinski called it a ball, the pitch itself seemed to suggest the impossibility of perfection. Two pitches later, Scherzer froze Marte with a perfect slider for strike three. Andrew McCutchen spun away from an inside slider that nearly clipped him, and three pitches later, swung through a high fastball as Scherzer struck out the side.

In the Washington half of the fourth inning, Bryce Harper turned on a Liriano offering and blasted his 23rd home run of the season, a moon shot that easily cleared the center field wall and traveled a solid 420 or so feet.

The fifth inning opened with an excuse-me swing from Jung Ho Kang, which produced a meager groundball to second base on Scherzer's first pitch of the frame. Francisco Cervelli worked a 2-1 count, but then was jammed with a fastball that he popped up to short right field for the second out. Alvarez was not normally a particularly patient hitter, but he worked a full count off Scherzer. With Washington aligned in a shift with only one player on the left side of the infield, Alvarez grounded the payoff pitch to short right field, where the second baseman was positioned. Alvarez was thrown out easily on Max's 55th pitch of the game. Five perfect innings were complete.

The Nationals were set down in order by Liriano, and Scherzer returned to the mound to complete his second trip through the National lineup. His control was spotless as he threw only one ball in the sixth inning. Gregory Polanco saw three pitches and, after whiffing on an off-speed offering, returned to the dugout as Max's sixth strikeout victim. Jordy Mercer hit a loud line drive that was solidly foul, and then popped out to second base. Liriano worked a seven-pitch at-bat, with the crowd beginning to sense Scherzer's incredible momentum and applauding accordingly. TV broadcasters Carpenter and Santangelo termed it the best at-bat on the day for a Pirate hitter, but a breaking pitch fanned Liriano, and ended the second trip through the Pittsburgh lineup.

In the home sixth inning, Scherzer grounded out, but then hurried into the clubhouse. He enjoyed a lengthy break, as Denard Span reached first on a third-strike wild pitch, and was then doubled home by Anthony Rendon. Bryce Harper then singled in Rendon, and two batters later, first baseman Tyler Moore knocked in two more runs with a single. Eight Nationals came to bat, four runs scored, and Liriano was knocked out of the game. Scherzer enjoyed a roughly 20-minute break, and a five-run lead. After the game, Scherzer credited the break for a significant role in his performance. "It was pretty exhausting out there," he admitted. "It was nice and hot and humid. Going through the first six innings was pretty tiring and exhausting.... And then the offense showed up there in the sixth inning.... I just felt like that helped give me a break, some time to recuperate, to sit in the clubhouse in some air-conditioning." Scherzer was following no-hit protocol, avoiding teammates and incidental conversation, opting for a drink of water and for a frequent change of jersey. He certainly had time for both in the sixth inning. "Once I got rest," he said after the game, "I knew I could come with everything I've got."

In the seventh frame, Scherzer pitched like a man refreshed as he faced the top of the Pirate order. Josh Harrison fell behind, and looped a two-strike breaking pitch into left field for an easy out. After Sterling Marte missed 96- and 97-mile-per-hour fastballs, he chased a sharp slider for a third strike. Scherzer's fastball had new life, and he bounced off the mound, hurrying to get the ball back and make his next pitch. At one point, F. P. Santangelo admitted to the television audience, "I'm not even watching the pitches. I'm watching the pitcher after the pitches." After Max's first pitch to McCutchen missed the plate, he blew two fastballs through the zone, and whiffed the Pirate slugger on another breaking ball as the crowd stood and roared. Seven perfect innings in only 78 pitches, and Scherzer looked like a hunter who was stalking a perfect game.

Washington added another run in the bottom of the seventh inning, but the story by now was Scherzer. Jung Ho Kang fouled off several pitches, working a nine-pitch at-bat, before he flied out harmlessly to Taylor in short left field. Francisco Cervelli watched a 97-mile-per-hour fastball, nudged a slider foul, and then whiffed at another off-speed offering, notching Scherzer's 10th strikeout of the day. Pedro Alvarez watched a fastball for a strike and then grounded an off-speed offering into short right field. On another day, it might have been heartbreak, but the Nationals had the shift on for Alvarez. "When it was off the bat, I thought it was just a routine out," recalled Scherzer. "Then I looked up and saw how the shift was played, and I realized there was going to be some time to get it. I know in that shift, even when you play that deep, you have time." Even after third baseman Anthony Rendon, playing what would normally be the second base spot, missed the groundball on his dive, second sacker Danny Espinosa fielded the ball from his position in short right field and nipped Alvarez by a step at first base to end the inning. Scherzer pumped his fist excitedly at the play, and then headed back to the clubhouse, 92 pitches into an effort at history.

After the Nationals went down in order, Scherzer hurried back to the mound. Gregory Polanco led off for Pittsburgh. He swung and missed at a fastball, and then popped the second pitch toward the Pirate dugout. Third baseman Rendon sprinted over and grabbed the looping popup, catching himself on the dugout, but not falling in or losing the ball. One out.

Jordy Mercer went for Scherzer's first pitch, but the 96-mile-per-hour fastball cut in on his hands, and became a routine fly to Denard Span in center field. Two outs in only three pitches. Down to their last out, the Pirates sent journeyman outfielder Jose Tabata to bat for the pitcher.

Tabata had once been a prime outfield prospect, earning over 400 at-bats and placing eighth in the Rookie of the Year voting at age 21 in 2010. But in each season, Tabata had earned fewer at-bats. He had spent most of 2015 in AAA, and was just 10-for-32 for the season in the big leagues. He had faced Scherzer nine times before. Among the various outcomes, twice he hit singles, three times he struck out, and once, he had been hit by a pitch. Now, he was the last batter between Scherzer and baseball perfection. "I felt great," Scherzer later indicated. "My arm felt great. I knew I could come with my best fastball."

Tabata came to bat ready to hack, and he fouled Scherzer's 96-mile-per-hour fastball off to the right side for strike one. When Tabata fouled an off-speed pitch back behind the plate, he was behind two strikes, and the Washington crowd roared.

Tabata watched a breaking ball dip low for ball one.

A 97-mile-per-hour fastball then sailed high for ball two.

On an off-speed pitch, Tabata checked his swing but rolled a soft grounder up the first base line—that rolled foul by 2 or 3 feet as the crowd groaned. Tabata then fouled another fastball away on the right side. Another fastball yielded another foul ball into the first base side stands. "He was really battling me," Scherzer told reporters after the game. "I was putting some good fastballs up there in the zone, and he was fouling them off."

Scherzer readied for the slider he had thrown all day with success. "I know the slider is the right pitch," Scherzer said after the game. "I could have gone changeup as well, but . . . I just didn't finish the pitch." Most of the time that day, the slider cut inside on a right-handed batter's hands. Once it had brushed back McCutchen, but mostly it had split the plate.

The pitch froze Tabata, but it cut in, bumping his left elbow. "He tried to throw me a slider inside. . . . I stayed right there and it got me," Tabata told the media after the game.

The perfect game was gone. "That's just the worst way to lose a perfect game," opined F. P. Santangelo. "Are you kidding me?"

Santangelo immediately brought up a relevant but controversial baseball rule—6.08(b)(2)—which provides that a batter is entitled to first base when he is hit unless he "makes no attempt to avoid being touched by the ball."

"Did he make an effort to get out of the way?" Santangelo asked. As the replay ran through, he commented, "NO, he leaned into it."

"It's a call they never make," admitted play-by-play man Bob Carpenter. But if Carpenter was entirely accurate, he would say it is a call they *almost* never make. In 1968, the Dodgers' Don Drysdale kept his scoreless inning streak alive when he hit a batter with the bases loaded—only to have umpire Harry Wendelstedt rule that per 6.08(b)(2), the batter had not tried to get out of the way, and he was thus ordered back to the plate. Drysdale worked out of trouble, and kept his streak going. Scherzer was not so fortunate, as umpire Mike Muchlinski was not inclined to move into Drysdale territory.

For his part, Tabata denied any culpability. "That's my job," he said after the game. "I got to get on base whatever the situation." The following day, after being booed heavily by the Nationals' fans, he clarified, "[R]eally, it wasn't my intention to get hit in that moment." Tabata went on to collect just one more hit as a Pirate, and then was traded to the Dodgers, and played out the season in the minor leagues.

After the game, Scherzer told the media it was "pretty easy" to refocus after hitting Tabata, purporting that it "took about two seconds." He further indicated, "You focus on what you can do next. You go on to the next hitter . . . and do everything you can do."

Unfortunately for Josh Harrison, Scherzer easily settled back into everything he could do. Harrison fouled off two fastballs, but then flied Scherzer's 106th pitch of the day into left field. The ball was hit well, but Michael Taylor ran it down easily shy of the left field wall, and Max Scherzer had missed perfection, but settled for the consolation prize of pitching the second no-hitter in Washington Nationals history. He exchanged a ritual handshake with catcher Wilson Ramos, and then was mugged on the mound by his excited teammates. As his teammates playfully roughed him up, minutes before they would pour Gatorade and chocolate syrup on him as he underwent the ritual postgame TV interviews, F. P. Santangelo asked, "What else can you give us, Max Scherzer?"

What else, indeed. "My last two starts, this is some of the best baseball I've thrown," Scherzer admitted to the media after the game. He credited his teammates effusively, citing specific plays and calling it a "great team win." When asked about how a no-hitter ranked in his list of possible baseball accomplishments, he considered briefly and said, "It's definitely at the top." When asked for his feelings after the last out, he laughed, "Cloud nine. There's nothing better than celebrating with your teammates. . . . It's a great feeling." Even getting covered with six bottles of chocolate syrup ("That's awesome," Scherzer cracked, when asked about having the first chocolate-sauced jersey to be sent to Cooperstown) added something to an unforgettable day.

June 20th was the day before Father's Day, and Brad Scherzer, along with Jan, had been in town to enjoy the game. It was Max's second Washington appearance that his parents had watched, and on the day before Father's Day, Brad Scherzer picked up a memory to last a lifetime.

Unfortunately for the Scherzer family, the rest of the season was memorable for less positive reasons. Washington gradually fell out of the pennant race. Embattled manager Matt Williams seemed to have a knack for making questionable strategy decisions that blew up in his face. Many of the Nats underachieved horrifically, and the team's bullpen offset much of the excellent work that the starting rotation managed. Max Scherzer was victimized heavily in this fallout. Scherzer finished the 2015 season sixth among all National League players (including hitters as well as pitchers) in WAR. He ended up eighth in ERA and second in strikeouts. And yet he went into his last start of the year with just a 13-12 record, needing to avoid a loss to post a winning season.

But in that last start, with the team labeled as the biggest disappointment in baseball playing a meaningless game against the Mets team that had won their division and went on to win the NL pennant, Scherzer pitched another statement game. The statement was that, despite what some of the numbers would reflect, Max Scherzer in 2015 was as dominant as any pitcher could possibly be. In his previous start, Scherzer took a no-hitter into the eighth inning before it was broken up. But in his last start of the year, on October 3, 2015, Scherzer fanned 17 Mets, and was even more dominating than he had been in June against Pittsburgh. The only Met to reach base all evening was Mets catcher Kevin Plawecki, whose sixth inning groundball was fielded cleanly by Washington third baseman Yunel Escobar, but Escobar bounced his throw in the dirt in front of the Nats' first baseman for an error. There were no walks, no hit batters, and certainly no base hits. From the last out of the sixth inning until the next-to-last out of the game, Scherzer fanned nine Mets in a row. Curtis Granderson, the Mets' last batter, broke the string with a weak popup that Escobar easily nabbed at third base. For the second time in the season, Scherzer had pitched a no-hitter.

Max Scherzer became only the fifth pitcher in MLB history to throw two no-hitters in a single season, and the first since Nolan Ryan in 1973, a dozen years before Scherzer was born. Even in a disappointing and difficult season, Scherzer had made his mark on baseball history.

Heartbreak and adversity marred Scherzer's season, but as long as he had another batter to battle, Scherzer found a way to come up aces.

Scherzer's remarkable 2015 season was one which, in so many ways, defied the odds. If anyone would have appreciated his brother's brilliant pitching, and perhaps gently needled him about missing two perfect games in a season by an eyelash, it probably would have been Alex Scherzer. If only Max Scherzer's best friend, his childhood companion, the boy who was always quick to remind him that all he could do himself was pitch and that the game behind him would take care of itself, could have been there to share the roller-coaster moments of 2015. *That* would have been perfect.

Early in the 2016 season, Scherzer again found himself making baseball history. On May 11th, against his old team, the Tigers, Scherzer tied the MLB nine-inning strikeout record by fanning 20 Detroit hitters. Once again, Scherzer celebrated with his teammates but could not share the moment with his best friend and fan.

But there's that lesson again. Max and Alex argued it for a year, and Max seems to have the idea ingrained by now. The pitcher can only control the game so far. Once it's beyond his grasp, the game belongs to the fielders, to the umpires, and to the forces that determine fair or foul, safe or out, error or catch. Alex Scherzer was right.

June 20, 2015
Nationals Park, Washington, DC

	1	2	3	4	5	6	7	8	9	R	H	E
PIT	0	0	0	0	0	0	0	0	0	0	0	0
WAS	0	1	0	1	0	4	1	0	X	6	8	0

W: Scherzer (8-5)
L: Liriano (4-6)

The End of Scherzer's Perfect Game:

Top of Ninth Inning, Two Outs.
2-2 pitch to pinch-hitter Jose Tabata.
Scherzer hit Tabata with a pitch, before getting out the next batter to complete a no-hitter.

AFTERWORD

I was in a hotel in Georgia when the message from my friend Ricky buzzed through on my cell phone. "Better add Max Scherzer to your interview list." Yes, this book was originally going to consider 15 almost-perfect pitchers. I was good with that, and the work on the book having begun, had gone to Atlanta with my family, where we were preparing to take my small children to their first major-league game. And instead, history happened, Scherzer just missed perfection on the way to his first no-hitter, and the book gained a chapter—and a great story.

I can't lie—I was initially annoyed by having to add to the book. But as my family and I headed down to Turner Field, a stadium soon doomed to nonexistence, it occurred to me how wonderfully fitting it was for another near-perfect game to occur just as my family was readying to head to the ballpark. Because perfection can happen at any time, at any place, to any pitcher. Isn't that part of why we keep coming back to the ballpark?

And moreover, isn't it why we keep getting up in the morning? Even in the midst of the most humdrum existence, there exists that possibility that maybe the day comes when all of the breaks come our way, when the road bends under our feet, the sun shines at the right angle, and we do something truly memorable. As the great Jim Bouton asked in *Ball Four*, isn't an optimist really a hero?

If so, the optimist is the most heroic when circumstances go bad, and when the perfect day (or perfect game) veers away at the last second. They pick themselves up, dust themselves off, and pursue the next best thing. Near-perfection has been a step in the path to no-hitters, to championships, to even a Hall of Fame career. May our own near-misses serve to fuel us on our paths to even bigger and better things.

See you at the ballpark.

ACKNOWLEDGMENTS

As an author, there are a million reasons why I'm lucky. One is that while this is the fifth book I've had a hand in writing, on the other four, there has been someone else to share the work. If I didn't appreciate them before, I certainly do now. Thanks to my good friend and three-time coauthor, Ryan Clark, whose incredible talents are even more noticeable when I can't rely on them. And best wishes to Alan Sullivan, whose thorough research skills would've made my life easier on this book!

If cowriting a book took a village, writing one solo took a nation—which means I've got a nation of people to thank, without any or all of whom this absolutely would not have been possible.

First and always foremost is my wife, Julie, of whom I could say all of those cheesy clichés that people are supposed to say about their spouses—and all of the ones that authors say about their first and best proofreader. Suffice it to say that she is my best friend, that she makes my heart beat faster than a line drive up the middle, and that the day I married her was probably the day that I had my closest brush with any type of perfection in anything I have done.

Thanks always to my kids, Natalie and Ryan, who always remind me that writing, kind of like baseball, isn't the whole world. That said, I hope that their favorite teams, the Giants (Natalie) and the Blue Jays (Ryan) give them good reasons to remember what a great game it is that tries to periodically snow their dad under with "work."

A very sincere thanks to the almost-perfect pitchers who took time out of their lives to help me out by looking back on some very bittersweet memories. Brian Holman, Milt Pappas, Ron Robinson, Yusmeiro Petit, Armando Galarraga, and Dave Stieb were all incredibly entertaining, and I appreciated the clarity and sharpness of their memories of games gone by.

Much gratitude is also due to the folks who helped me track down those pitchers. Rachel Levitsky of the MLBPAA is an absolute rock star, and it wouldn't surprise me if she ended up being the first female commissioner of MLB. Tim Hevly of the Seattle Mariners, Erwin Higueros and Liam Connolly of the San Francisco Giants, and Chris Tunno of the St. Louis Cardinals were incredibly helpful. Aileen Villarreal and Megan Filipowki from the Detroit Tigers, Christopher Browne from the Washington Nationals, and Sue Mallabon from the Toronto Blue Jays chipped in with some excellent photos that were thoroughly appreciated. Also, I appreciated Bob Beghtol of the Chicago White Sox, who was trying to connect me with Billy Pierce before Mr. Pierce unfortunately passed away.

Of the five near-perfect pitchers who were deceased when I began writing, I was blessed to listen to lengthy interviews with two and discover an unpublished autobiography from a third. How was I so lucky? Mostly because I called on the good folks at the Giamatti Research Center at the National Baseball Hall of Fame in Cooperstown, New York. Manager Matt Rothenberg was incredibly supportive and encouraging, and pointed me in some useful directions. Big thanks also to the rest of the staff from my visit—Cassidy Lent, Gretyl Macalaster and Adam Lathrop. Those folks are big leaguers in the world of baseball knowledge, and this book was greatly improved by their able assistance.

Another team of important players helped to get this book off the ground, and they are all incredibly important. Thanks to the Howard Morhaim Literary Agency and to the incredibly thoughtful and talented Paul Lamb, on whom I could not wish more success and happiness in whichever literary arena he ends up traveling. Paul was like a veteran catcher who always knew what my next pitch needed to be, and if this book came out okay, it was only because he drew it out of me. Keith Wallman smoothly handled the arduous task of editing this manuscript, and deserves a large heap of any credit and none of any blame that may apply. He and the folks at Lyons Press (copy editor Joshua Rosenberg and production editor Meredith Dias, to mention a couple of particular stars) have been unfailingly pleasant to work with, and I thank them for giving me an opportunity.

I am endlessly grateful for the literate and professional work of prior authors and journalists on the topics covered in this book. When you can follow behind writers like Bill James, Rob Neyer, Leigh Montville, Frank Deford, various members of SABR, and some of the finest newspaper columnists of the last century or so, it's like being handed the ball in the ninth inning with a three-run lead and nobody on base. I hope I closed it out well, but if not, don't blame the starters! Appreciation is also due to the folks behind www.baseball-research.com and YouTube, without whom this book would've taken much longer to write, and probably been much less accurate.

Thanks to my good friend and law partner Joe Loney for his friendship and support in my endeavor of wearing two hats while I wrote this book. Likewise, appreciation is due to the rest of our team at Cole, Loney & Pogue, PLLC, especially Billy, if he ever reads this. Thanks to Mom and Teresa for love and encouragement. Best wishes to my friends at Woodburn Baptist Church, including and especially pastors Tim Harris and Rod Ellis, who help me understand and accept my human imperfection every day against the real and continuous perfection of God. Thanks to my friend Buster Mullins and to my father, for helping me get to my first big-league game.

And finally, thanks to the men and women who made the great game of baseball what it is today. I hope that the things I have written here about the game and some of the men who played it in no way detract from its majesty, its timelessness, and its beauty. Baseball isn't perfect, and that might be one of the best things about it.

SOURCES

CHAPTER 1: "THERE'LL SURE BE RAIN, FOR YOU HEARD THE THUNDER"

2. Background of McGraw drawn from Jensen, 39–43.

2. "McGraw's favorite trick": Deford, 28. Description of dirty play drawn from Ibid.

2. McGraw sharpening his spikes: Ibid.

2–3. "ballplayers developed an exaggerated reputation": James, 56.

3. "abandon my profession entirely": Deford, 28.

3. "There are tales that umpires": Deford, 36–37.

4. Wiltse's salary at Troy: Schecter, 53.

4. Wiltse's hitting and fielding skills: *Baseball Magazine*, November 1908.

4. Wiltse's delivery and use of curveball: James and Neyer, 429–30.

5. "the Doc Gooden of the Deadball Era": Enders, 203.

6. "[Y]oung women came to the game": *New York Evening Telegraph*, July 4, 1908.

7. Perfect game not in use—otherwise indicated to have been first used in 1909: Dickson, 630.

7. "As the fans realized": *Sporting Life*, July 11, 1908.

7. "[F]rom the sixth on": *New York Times*, July 5, 1908.

8. "sharp breaking . . . which came up": *New York American*, July 5, 1908.

8. "Wiltse and Bresnahan thought they had him": *Sporting Life*, July 11, 1908.

8. "Rigler thus robbed the pitcher": *New York Evening Telegraph*, July 4, 1908.

9. "Wiltse is the first left-hander": *Sporting Life*, July 11, 1908.

9. Wiltse's game compared to Cy Young's: *New York Herald*, July 5, 1908.

9. "I missed being the only pitcher": Document titled "Memory Lane" written by Wiltse circa 1944 and contained within the Hall of Fame Library's Wiltse file.

10. Rigler as originator of calling strike with arm: Cicotello, 25.

10. "Every time I saw Charlie Rigler": *Mid York Weekly*, approx. July or August 1953, contained within Hall of Fame Library's Wiltse file.

11. Information on Wiltse as first-base coach: Ibid.

11. Three different players claiming to be first-base coach at time of Merkle Boner: Deford, 141, also discussed in detail within private correspondence within Hall of Fame Library's Wiltse file. Murphy appears to suggest that McGinnity was the coach, 191, 196.

12. McGraw's opposition to the rabbit ball is well documented. See Jensen, 41, for instance.

12. "There has been only one manager": Jensen, 39.

12. "He gripped the imagination": Frierson, 33.

12. Mathewson's dealings with Hal Chase and subsequent war service: Frierson, 35–36.

12. McGraw talking Fuchs into hiring Mathewson: Frierson, 36.

14. Information on Wiltse's post-baseball career discussed within Hall of Fame Library's Wiltse file, also Schecter, 54.

CHAPTER 2: IN RELIEF OF THE BABE

16. Shore's background and familiar history, including quote that tobacco "just kills your back" from Leeke, http://sabr.org/bioproj/person/6073c617.

16. "If my fastball was breaking": *The State*, November 1988.

16–17. Details of the sale of Ruth summarized from Montville, 40, and Leeke.

17: Ruth's hobbies information from Wood, 457.

17: Ruth not knowing his age from Bryson, 108 and Montville, 8.

17: Information on Ruth's spring training from Bryson, 110.

17: Ruth stated as sharing Shore's toothbrush at Bryson, 110. Shore indicated that it was actually his shaving brush per Leeke.

17. Shore "didn't like a roommate": Montville, 53.

18. Shore accused of doctoring the ball at Leeke.

18–19. "Ernie Shore and Carl Mays": *Pittsburgh Press*, Unknown date 1917 (within Baseball Hall of Fame Library's Shore file).

20. "open your eyes": Creamer, 139.

20. "If you'd go to bed at night": Ruth and Considine, 42.

20. "Why don't you open": Creamer, 139.

20. "Get back out there and pitch": Ibid.

20. "Shut up, you lout": Ruth and Considine, 42.

20. Ruth threatening to hit Owens in the nose is from Creamer, 139. Ruth threatening to hit him in the jaw is from Ruth and Considine, 42.

20. "I hauled off and hit him, but good": Ruth and Considine, 42.

20. "He missed with a right": Creamer, 139, and the account of the melee is from the same source. The contrasting report is from the *Boston Globe*, June 24, 1917, and is corroborated by the *Washington Evening Star*, June 24, 1917, which confuses the issue by having the punch graze Owens's jaw. The *Washington Post*, June 24, 1917 agrees on the punch landing behind the ear, but does not mention two punches thrown.

20. "Hold them until I can get": *New York Herald Tribune*, January 22, 1961.

20. Shore's account of five warmup pitches appears in *New York Herald Tribune*, January 22, 1961, also *Sports Ilustrated*, July 2, 1962, among others.

20. "a brief warmup": *Boston Globe*, June 24, 1917.

20. "a delay of nearly ten minutes": *Washington Evening Star*, June 24, 1917.

21. "only a sensational play": *Washington Post*, June 24, 1917.

21. "Barry asked me": *Sports Illustrated*, July 2, 1962.

21. "a wicked overhand fastball": Ibid.

21. "I don't think I could have": *Sunday Eagle-Tribune* (Lawrence, MA), August 20, 1995.

22. "Henry drove out": *Washington Post*, June 24, 1917.

22. "came in like lightning": *Boston Globe*, June 24, 1917.

22. "lined . . . on the nose": *Sunday Eagle-Tribune* (Lawrence, MA), August 20, 1995.

22. "was a very sore loser": Ibid.

22. Shore's account of the last batter from *Sunday Eagle-Tribune* (Lawrence, MA), August 20, 1995 and *Sports Illustrated*, July 2, 1962.

22. "a grand play": *Boston Globe*, June 24, 1917.

22. "lifted to Barry": *Washington Post*, June 24, 1917.

22. "Ernie Shore is credited": quote is taken from both Leeke and *Brooklyn Daily Eagle*, unknown date (perhaps 1918), located within Hall of Fame Library's Shore file.

23. Players avoiding military documented in at least the case of the Chicago White Sox in Pomrenke, 13–14.

23. Shore's military rank was indicated to be unique among MLB players in *New York Herald Tribune*, January 22, 1961, and at Leeke.

23. "the first of the blockbuster deals": Leeke.

24. Causes of the offensive explosion are discussed, among other places, at Pomrenke, 578.

25. "tried selling cars and insurance": *The State*, November 1988.

25. "they came back faster": *New York Herald Tribune*, January 22, 1961.

25. Shore's debt of $20,000, the identity of the R. J. Reynolds officials (John C. Whitaker and Edward Lasater) and the accounts of his campaigning are from the *Winston-Salem Journal*, June 30, 2008.

25. "I don't mind telling you that I needed the job": *New York Herald Tribune*, January 22, 1961.

25–26. Information on the growth of the Forsyth County Sheriff's Department under Shore taken from *The State*, November 1988.

26. "He was widely known": *Winston-Salem Journal*, June 30, 2008.

26. Ruth's disappointment at not managing is discussed in depth in Montville, for instance, at 322–25, and 348–49.

26. Account of stadium fund-raising and naming issues from *Winston-Salem Journal*, April 23, 2009.

26. "That's just the way it goes": Ibid.

CHAPTER 3: "150 POUNDS OF SHEER GUTS"

29. "[J]ust look at him": Neyer (*Neyer/James*), 94.

30. "I'll never forget": Auker, 123.

30. "Every time I see": Auker, 124.

30. "It's kind of sad": *Wilson Post*, May 11, 2011.

30. "I kind of like": Ibid.

30–31. Bridges's early life information comes from the *Wilson Post*, May 4, 2011, and from Neyer (*Detroit*), 62.

30. "throwing baseballs ever since": *Wilson Post*, May 4, 2011.

31. "I would rather pitch": Ibid.

31. Information on Bridges's degree status differs. Neyer (*Neyer/James*), 92, seems to insist that Bridges did not graduate, but numerous obituaries refer to him as a graduate of UT—for instance, *The Sporting News*, April 20, 1968 and *New York Times*, April 20, 1968. That said, one contemporary but undated article in the Hall of Fame's Bridges file carefully references Bridges matriculating for an A.B. degree, but instead transferring to business school where he "spent the last two years of his college life"—which seems to be a passive way of suggesting that Bridges did not graduate.

31. The story of Bridges's debut and the "I'll be ready" quote are from Neyer (*Detroit*) 72–73.

31. "Tommy Bridges should become": *Detroit News*, May 22, 1931.

31. "If Bridges tried": Ibid.

32. "Tommy had an overhand curve": *Wilson Post*, May 4, 2011.

32. The story of Bridges's advice from Bucky Harris on the use of the curveball comes from Neyer (*Neyer/James*), 92–93.

34. General information on the game, and specifically Bridges's control, from *Washington Post*, August 6, 1932 and *The Sporting News*, August 11, 1932. The information on defensive plays comes from the same sources, as well as *Chicago Daily Tribune*, August 6, 1932. *The Sporting News* references difficult plays by second baseman Gehringer and right fielder Earl Webb. The *Post* references one ball out of the infield being a difficult chance, which was apparently the ball Webb caught. The *Tribune* refers to only one hard chance for a fielder.

34. "His curve was breaking": *The Sporting News*, August 11, 1932.

35. "pinch-hitter extraordinary": *Washington Post*, August 6, 1932.

35–36. The account of the end of the perfect game is fraught with its own inconsistency. The pitch which Harris hit is generally presumed to be a fastball, per Neyer (*Neyer/James*), 93 and Anderson, 153. That said, Bridges's obituary in the *New York Times*, April 20, 1968, calls the pitch a curveball. Neyer's account also has the ball going over the head of shortstop Billy Rogell. While Rogell was the everyday shortstop, he didn't play on August 5th, and in fact, didn't play between August 1 and August 6.

35. "sat in tense silence": *Chicago Daily Tribune*, August 6, 1932.

35. "probably the most unpopular man": *Washington Post*, August 6, 1932.

35. "There was much criticism": *The Sporting News*, August 11, 1932.

35. "I could have murdered him": Anderson, 153.

35. "It's no use": Ibid.

35. "I tried hard": Ibid.

36. Johnson's locker room congratulation: Ibid.

36. "I would have done the same thing": *The Sporting News*, April 20, 1968.

37. Information on 1933 near-misses from Anderson, 157.

37. Praise for Bridges's curveball is well cited, including Neyer (*Neyer/James*), 94 and Thorn and Holway, 12 and 152. Indeed, Bridges's curveball was so good that many believed he threw a spitball—see Neyer (*Neyer/James*), 95 and Anderson, 157–58.

37. Information on Game 6 of the 1935 Series, including "I heard the roar of the crowd": Neyer (*Neyer/James*), 94.

37. Information on Bridges's wartime service and Vicki Lowe's impressions from the *Wilson Post*, May 4, 2011 and May 11, 2011.

38. Information on Bridges's minor-league career, including Charlie Silvera's comments, from Neyer (*Neyer/James*), 96–97.

38. Dave Harris's police career noted at Anderson, 157.

38–39. Bridges's marital troubles are documented in the *Wilson Post*, May 11, 2011, and Neyer (*Detroit*), 72.

39. "One day, as I was crossing": Neyer (*Detroit*), 72.

39. "He never showed up": Ibid.

39. Auker's story of the loan and alcoholic binge documented at Auker, 125.

39. Accounts of Bridges and his family from the *Wilson Post*, May 11, 2011.

39. "I remember your mama": Ibid.

39. "just to have time": Ibid.

39–40. "It seems that a lot of people": Ibid.

CHAPTER 4: BILLY THE KID . . . "WHAT MORE DO YOU WANT?"

41. The story of Paul Richards failing to see Pierce in his father's pharmacy is recounted by Neyer (*Neyer/James*), 103.

42. "I've experienced a lot of good things": *Detroit Free Press*, July 31, 2015.

42. Pierce's background drawn largely from Neyer (*Neyer/James*), 103 and Liptak, www.baseball-almanac.com/players/billy_pierce_interview.shtml, June 2005.

42. "When I was 10", and information on Tommy Bridges from Francis, http://baseballhall.org/hall-of-fame/golden-era/pierce-billy.

42. "for two or three years" from Liptak.

43. "[I]t was a jolt": Vanderberg, 139.

43. "I was disappointed": Thomas Liley, Billy Pierce Oral History interview, 2/24/1992.

43. "Coming over here": Ibid.

44. Pierce's reliance on fastball and DiMaggio's admiration for same from Neyer (*Neyer/James*), 104.

44. "I worked a little with him": Ibid.

44. "Developing the slider", and information on same from Neyer (*Neyer/James*), 104.

48. Account of the game from Retrosheet website, Bigham, http://sabr.org/gamesproj/game/june-27-1958-billy-pierces-near-perfect-game, and *Chicago Daily Tribune*, June 28, 1958. Aparicio's "spectacular defense" noted in the latter.

48. The story of Fox and "Here's your run" are from Lindberg, 266.

48–49. Boone being pulled off the bag comes from *Chicago Daily Tribune*, June 28, 1958, although in all fairness, the exact quote is that "Earl Torgeson made a contortionist's stretch to snare a wide seventh inning throw by Goodman to get Roy Sievers." Torgeson was a first baseman for the White Sox, but he didn't play in the game, so the columnist clearly meant Ray Boone.

49. "were given further reason": *Chicago Daily Tribune*, June 28, 1958.

49. "The book on Fitz Gerald": Neyer (*Neyer/James*), 104.

49. The curve "was a good one": *New York World Telegram & Sun*, June 28, 1958.

49–50. "knee high curve ball": *Chicago Daily Tribune*, June 28, 1958.

50. Account of the double from various sources, including the *Chicago Daily Tribune*, June 28, 1958, and the *New York World Telegram & Sun*, June 28, 1958 and *The Sporting News*, July 9, 1958. Some reports, including Liptak, indicate that the ball may have been fair by as much as 5 feet, but all three of the above consistently indicate that the distance was about a foot.

50. Fox approaching the mound is from Liptak.

50. The "winner and a gentleman" tag is from the *San Francisco Chronicle*, October 10, 1964.

50. "I'll never get any closer than that": *New York World Telegram & Sun*, June 28, 1958.

50. "Give Luis plenty of credit,": *The Sporting News*, July 9, 1958.

50. Pierce "couldn't have been any more perfect": *New York World Telegram & Sun*, June 28, 1958.

50. "I didn't feel that badly": Vanderberg, 142.

51. "I am not surprised": Neyer (*Neyer/James*).

51. Pierce discussed his Game 6 win and called it his biggest thrill in baseball in the *New York Times*, October 16, 1962. That said, he called closing out the third game against the Dodgers his biggest thrill in the *San Francisco Chronicle*, October 5, 1964.

52. "I've gotten more out of baseball": *San Francisco Chronicle*, October 10, 1964.

53. Information on Pierce's post-baseball career largely from *Sports Illustrated*, March 19, 2001.

53. "the Nellie Fox society": Neyer (*Neyer/James*), 107.

54. "It would be a tremendous thrill": Liptak.

CHAPTER 5: THE GREATEST PITCHING MASTERPIECE IN BASEBALL HISTORY

58. Haddix's shooting incident detailed in *Sports Illustrated*, June 1, 2009. That said, he continued to hunt—he shot a 900-pound bison in 1964, per Freedman, 28–29.

58. Haddix's nickname and his minor-league career discussed in Miller, 298–300.

58. Haddix's injury and loss of effectiveness recounted at Freedman, 11 and Miller, 302.

58. "I had no spring": Walter Langford Oral History interview, July 3, 1987.

59. "I figured I'd have some fun": *Kansas City Star*, May 1, 1984.

59. Haddix's pitch selection per *Sports Illustrated*, June 1, 2009. Game account per Ibid. and Freedman.

60. Haddix's thoughts on the loss of Clemente for the game (and Dick Groat) per Langford interview.

60. Account of Schofield's play to open the game per *Sports Illustrated*, June 1, 2009. It is worth noting that multiple other accounts treat the play as routine. Indeed, there were so few plays out of the routine that any which drew any note are unusual.

60. "I could have put a cup of coffee": *Sports Illustrated,* June 1, 2009.

60. Description of Logan's liner to Schofield in the third as "perhaps the hardest hit" is per the *Milwaukee Journal*, May 27, 1959. Said liner was also described as "[t]he only ball that looked like a hit before Joe Adcock's smash in the 13th inning" in *Pittsburgh Press*, May 27, 1959.

60. Account of Logan's grounder in sixth per *Pittsburgh Press*, May 27, 1959.

61. "The remarkable feature": *The Sporting News*, June 3, 1959.

61. "It was the only inning": Langford interview.

61–62. Haddix's smoking and dugout ritual from *Sports Illustrated*, June 1, 2009.

62. "just good enough to hit": Langford interview.

62. Virdon leaping to catch the ball is per his comments in *Pittsburgh Press*, May 27, 1959. Freedman 140 says Joe Christopher leapt to try to catch the ball.

63. "A pitcher does this": *The Sporting News*, June 3, 1959.

63. The fraternity letter is per *Sports Illustrated*, June 1, 2009.

63. "The way he saw it": Ibid.

64. "That was the only time": Langford interview.

64. "With the crack of the bat": Ibid.

66. Marcia's recollections of the change in statistics from 1991 is per *Sports Illustrated*, June 1, 2009.

67. "That game probably gets more attention": Freedman, 170.

67. "I polished that silverware": *Pittsburgh Post-Gazette*, November 9, 2010.

CHAPTER 6: "YOU'VE GOT TO BE KIDDING ME"

69. "Here I was": Author's interview, July 31, 2015.

70. "He followed me": Ibid.

70. "practically lived with the Pappas family": *The Sporting News*, January 11, 1961.

70. "[h]e paid particular attention": Ibid.

70. "got along fine talking": Ibid.

70. Account of signing and "We got him": Ibid.

70. Account of first game, and quotes including "I figured when it's time": Author's interview, July 31, 2015.

70. Pappas definitely pitched first in Baltimore and then was sent to Knoxville, although it is often reported the other way around. One source within Pappas's file at the Baseball Hall of Fame Library indicates that Pappas was sent down because he returned to the team hotel at 2:30 in the morning and had to awaken the hotel's assistant manager to get into his room.

71. "With a lively fastball": Gentile, 577.

71. "Any player rep": Unknown source, July 1970, located within Baseball Hall of Fame Library player file.

72. Pappas's health issues are per the *Chicago Daily Tribune*, September 3, 1972.

72. Pappas considering retirement is per the *Chicago Daily Tribune*, September 22, 1972.

72. "My dad was dying": Author's interview, July 31, 2015.

74. "When I felt strong": Ibid.
75. "was at least five feet deep": *The Sporting News*, September 16, 1972.
75. Kessinger's thoughts and quote per Ibid.
75–76. "A little tapper": Author's interview, July 31, 2015.
76. "You could hear a pin drop": Ibid.
76. "Rookie center fielder": *The Sporting News*, September 16, 1972.
76. "I could only think one thing": Pappas, 256.
76. "My heart was really pounding now": Ibid.
77. "Bruce Froemming, in his infinite wisdom": Author's interview, July 31, 2015.
77. Pappas's thoughts on Mitchell/Larsen and the pitch that "almost hit him in the chin" per Ibid.
77. "I said to him": Ibid.
77. "The pitches were balls": Pappas, 258.
77. "never entered my mind": Pappas, 259.
78. "I said a lot of things": Pappas, 258.
78. "has a smirk on his face": *Chicago Tribune*, June 7, 2006. Pappas made similar comments in author's interview, July 31, 2015.
78. "I saw [Froemming]": Ibid.
78. "Pappas goes around telling": Weinbaum, http://sports.espn.go.com/mlb/news/story?id=3019597 (9/20/07).
78. "As an umpire": Ibid.
78. Hundley's quotes are from Ibid. His initial recollections from Pappas, 258.
78. "Bruce Froemming robbed me": Pappas, 259.
78. "I have to admire the guy": Weinbaum.
79. "The only other thing": Author's interview, July 31, 2015.
79. "Oh God, yeah": Ibid.
79. "No, not any more": Ibid.
79. Pappas's thoughts on the Hall of Fame and his comparison with Drysdale per Ibid.
80. "[W]hen he makes a call" and Froemming voted as best NL home plate umpire in Nash and Zullo (*Baseball Confidential*), 27.
80. Information on Carole Pappas's disappearance per *Chicago Sun-Times*, May 18, 1983.
80. Information on finding Carole Pappas's body per *Chicago Tribune*, August 8, 1987.
80. "I'm totally speechless": Ibid.
81. "So many questions, no answers": Author's interview, July 31, 2015.
81. "To this day": Ibid.
81. "Oh God, yeah": Ibid.
82. "Hey everybody, greatest fans": Remarks transcribed from telecast of the events.

CHAPTER 7: FROM THE TIGERS TO THE DOGS

83–84. "I've been in front": *Sports Illustrated*, July 2, 2007.
84. "I didn't throw the hardest": Ibid.

84. "Wilcox's ability to throw": 1971 Cleveland Indians press release, from the Baseball Hall of Fame's clippings file on Milt Wilcox.

84. "I tried to pitch too soon": Kates at 420.

85. "I told my wife": *The Sporting News*, August 6, 1977.

85. "I couldn't throw real hard": Ibid.

85. "I feel stronger": *The Sporting News*, November 12, 1977.

86. Information on Tommy John from Thorn and Holway, 85–86.

86. Pittsburgh drug trial information per *New York Times*, March 1, 1986.

87. Wilcox's minor injury and his move in the rotation per *Chicago Tribune*, April 16, 1983.

87. Wilcox's repertoire per James and Neyer, 425, and unnamed and undated article within newspaper clippings file on Milt Wilcox at Baseball Hall of Fame.

88. "pitched the best ballgame": unnamed, undated newspaper article within newspaper clippings file on Milt Wilcox at Baseball Hall of Fame.

89. "[A]s the night grew chillier": *Cincinnati Enquirer*, April 16, 1983.

89. "You know you have a no-hitter": unnamed, undated newspaper article within newspaper clippings file on Milt Wilcox at Baseball Hall of Fame.

90. Ovation from road crowd per *Chicago Tribune*, April 16, 1983.

90. "In the ninth": unnamed, undated newspaper article within newspaper clippings file on Milt Wilcox at Baseball Hall of Fame.

90. Anderson's comments on Craig shaking per *Washington Post*, April 16, 1983.

91. "Our pride was at stake": *Washington Post*, April 16, 1983.

91. Hairston's intent to jump on first pitch from unknown newspaper clipping within Milt Wilcox's newspaper clipping file at Baseball Hall of Fame, dated April 17, 1983.

91. "I knew he'd be swinging": Ibid.

91. "It was the worst pitch": unnamed, undated clip from Wilcox's clipping file at Baseball Hall of Fame.

91. "If you pitch a perfect game": *Washington Post*, April 16, 1983.

92. "We'd inject the joint": Kates at 423.

92. Information on injections and dimethyl sulfoxide per Ibid. at 423–24.

92. "I stayed healthy enough": Ibid. at 423.

93. "I make money by playing again": Prewitt, http://espn.go.com/espn/page2/index?id=5714622 (10/22/10).

93. Wilcox meeting Cathi at dog jumping event is per Horn, http://patch.com/michigan/royaloak/from-world-champion-to-royal-oak-icon (9/15/11).

94. Workers' compensation claim reported within *Battle Creek* (MI) *Enquirer*, July 7, 2015.

94. "[The Tigers] are not real happy with me": Ibid.

94. "If any of those players": Ibid.

94. "I'm still going to stay young": Prewitt.

CHAPTER 8: THE TRUE CREATURE AND CHARLIE HUSTLE

95. "I had been called up": Author's interview, August 1, 2015.

96. "I was around sports all my life": Ibid.

97. "Robinson's job": *The Sporting News*, July 28, 1986.

97. "kind of thought": Ibid.

97. "In the meanwhile": *The Sporting News*, August 24, 1987.

97. "It complicated the rest": Author's interview, August 1, 2015.

98. Pallone's history with the Reds as well as "tried to pick up" and "gone out of his way" per Reston, 229.

98–99. Description of Pallone/Rose confrontation based on review of video, and Reston, 230–33.

100. "Warming up that night": Author's interview, August 1, 2015.

100. "Robby had arm troubles all year": Browning and Stupp, 82.

100. "They were hitting the first pitch, they were hitting the second pitch": Author's interview, August 1, 2015.

101. Robinson's repertoire per James and Neyer, 361.

101. "I remember Bo Diaz": Author's interview, August 1, 2015.

101. "There's not enough mustard": Nash and Zullo (*Baseball Confidential*), 82.

101–2. Pérez's beanball history per *New York Times*, November 2, 2012.

102. Robinson entering the fray and being coached back down by Breeden per *The Sporting News*, May 16, 1988.

102. "after the top of the seventh": Author's interview, August 1, 2015.

102. "It was business as usual": Ibid.

102. "I got a standing ovation": Ibid.

103. "really good": Ibid.

103. "I thought it was": Ibid.

103. "If I tried to pull that pitch": *Los Angeles Times*, May 3, 1988.

103. "a little bit better defensively": Author's interview, August 1, 2015.

103–4. "You threw that pitch": *The Sporting News*, May 16, 1988.

104. "I'm sorry as hell": Ibid.

104. "I'm just glad a guy": *USA Today*, May 5, 1988.

105. "He totally deserves": Author's interview, August 1, 2015.

105. Story of Rose weeping and admitting to "disrespecting baseball" from *Sports Illustrated*, March 10, 2014.

105. "I was healthy, but I wasn't pitching": *New York Times*, March 11, 1991.

106. "The best thing that happened": Author's interview, August 1, 2015.

107. "chasing my grandkids around": Ibid.

107. "That anybody could do it": Ibid.

CHAPTER 9: TOMORROW I'LL BE PERFECT

110. "So far as I can tell": Stieb and Boland, 22.

110. "Steve was the one": Ibid., 11.

110. "decent power and an exceptional arm": Ibid., 14.

110. Encounter with LaMacchia and "The Blue Jays drafted me": *New York Times*, June 3, 1982.

111. "[not] just the worst stadium": *Globe and Mail* (Toronto), September 25, 2015.

111. "It was a learning experience": Author's interview with Dave Stieb, January 23, 2016.

111. "They finally caught on": Ibid.

112. "I can't imagine anyone": *Inside Sports*, August 1985.

113. "That particular day": Author's interview, January 23, 2016.

114. "I went out there": Ibid.

114–15. "There were never any great": Ibid.

115. "I just kept going": Ibid.

116. "[H]e threw me mostly sliders": *New York Times*, August 5, 1989.

116. "I threw that sidearm-curveball thing": Author's interview, January 23, 2016.

116. "I surely don't want": Ibid.

116. "He threw me a slider": *Chicago Tribune*, August 5, 1989.

117. "It was probably a mistake": Author's interview, January 23, 2016.

117. "If I haven't gotten a no-hitter": *New York Times*, August 5, 1989.

117. "I got so close so many times": Author's interview, January 23, 2016.

118. "I had much better stuff the other times": *Lexington* (KY) *Herald-Leader*, September 3, 1990.

118. "The biggest thing about it": Author's interview, January 23, 2016.

118. The details of Stieb's injury travails are all reported in *The Sporting News*. Stieb's shoulder injury reported in June 10, 1991 issue. Herniated disc reported in July 29, 1991 issue, and surgery for same in December 16, 1991 issue. Finally, Stieb's elbow tendinitis is documented in the August 17, 1992 issue.

118–19. "It was very bittersweet": Author's interview, January 23, 2016.

119. "Obviously, I was one of the biggest fans": Ibid.

119. Information regarding Stieb's comeback, including quote from Clemens and Stieb's own thoughts are per Ibid.

120. The contractual situation regarding Stieb is referenced in *Chicago Tribune*, June 21, 1998, which also mentions the Rangers' attempt to sign him.

120. "I realize I've come full circle": Author's interview, January 23, 2016.

120. "It was an awesome thing": Ibid.

121. "I want to be remembered": Ibid.

CHAPTER 10: "IT'S JUST BASEBALL"

123. Labor background and Curt Flood story from *Sports Illustrated*, September 11, 2006.

124. Collusion information from Neyer (*Neyer's Big Book*), 221–25.

125. Information regarding Holman and Dick LeMay from author interview, June 16, 2015.

126. "When Dave Dombrowski called me in": Ibid.

126. "What was great": Ibid.

126. "I remember in 1990 sitting on my ranch": Ibid.

128. Meeting with La Russa per Ibid.

128. "I didn't have it": Ibid.

129. "I talked to him early on": Undated and unsourced newspaper article from Holman's file in the Baseball Hall of Fame Library.

129–30. "As I come off the field": Author's interview, June 16, 2015.

130. "The crazy thing": Ibid.

130. "Henry Cotto went up": Ibid.

131. "I think the most special thing": Ibid.

131. "I'm literally thinking": Ibid.

131. "I was looking for something": *Seattle Times*, April 21, 1990.

131. "I'd been getting ahead": Ibid.

131. "At the moment": Author's interview, June 16, 2015.

131–32. "We needed something spectacular": *Spokane Spokesman-Review*, April 21, 1990.

132. "Give him credit": Ibid.

132. "I was glad I broke I up": Ibid.

132. "About 4:40 in my hotel room": Author's interview, June 16, 2015.

132. Story about Jennifer Holman and her fellow student per Ibid.

132. "Of all the crazy things": Ibid.

132. "No matter what happens": Ibid.

134. "My baseball people": *Seinfeld* dialogue recounted in *Seattle Times*, April 15, 2010.

134. "Nothing in the negotiations": *Chicago Tribune*, March 25, 1990.

135. "A perfect game is a great thing": *Seattle Times*, April 15, 2010.

135. "You can't describe": Ibid.

135. "We had three kids": *Seattle Times*, December 19, 2004.

135. "It took her about fifteen minutes": Ibid.

135. "a very special kid": Author's interview, June 16, 2015.

135–36. "When Kassidy got sick": Ibid.

136. "I'm extremely proud of David": Ibid.

136. "He never complained": Ibid.

136. "To be so high one moment": *Seattle Times*, December 19, 2004.

CHAPTER 11: LITTLE BROTHER NO MORE

139. "This is Ramon's little brother": Martinez and Silverman, 35.

140. Pedro's homesickness and the "f—ing dirty bastards" quote are from Ibid., 43–46.

140–41. Martinez's sad memories from Manoguayabo are from Gammons, http://m .mlb.com/news/article/17115606 (3/25/11).

141. "When Pedro was very little": *Boston Globe Magazine*, April 2, 2000.

141. "It was time": Ibid.

141. "I can't describe": Ibid.

142. "I didn't know any French": Martinez and Silverman, 85.

142. "a minor league facility": Keri, 62.

142. Issues with MLB and the failure to complete Olympic Stadium per Luchuk, 25.

143. Beaning of Sanders and headhunting reputation per Martinez and Silverman, 96–111, as well as *Washington Post*, June 20, 1997.

143. Incident with warning and Froemming per Martinez and Silverman, 106–7.

146. "big league pitching at its best": *New York Times*, June 5, 1995.

146. "When I heard the crowd": *Los Angeles Times*, June 4, 1995.

147. "I saw that": Ibid.

148. "I don't regret throwing": Ibid.

148. "It was a lucky hit": Ibid.

148. "Oh, that's tough": *New York Times*, June 5, 1995.

148. "one of the best": *Los Angeles Times*, June 4, 1995.

150. Martinez's charitable work from many sources, including Gammons, http://m.mlb .com/news/article/17115606 (3/25/11) and *New York Daily News*, March 9, 2008.

150. "I want children": Gammons, http://m.mlb.com/news/article/17115606 (3/25/11).

150. Martinez's Hall of Fame remarks are from a transcript run in the *Eagle-Tribune* (North Andover, MA), July 27, 2015.

CHAPTER 12: MR. ALMOST AND AMERICA'S TRAGEDY

154. "not large by any means": *Baltimore Sun*, April 28, 1996.

154. Information on Mussina's childhood from Ibid. and from the *Augusta Chronicle*, October 27, 2001.

154. Valedictorian story is from the *Wall Street Journal*, November 25, 2008.

154. Information on collegiate academics is from Ibid.

154. "the most dominant pitching performance": *Baseball Weekly*, June 4–10, 1997.

155. Mussina coaching info from several sources, including *The Sporting News*, August 29, 1994.

155. Information on Mussina's wife from the *Baltimore Sun*, April 28, 1996 (although she was then his girlfriend).

155. Information on Cellini's from *The Sporting News*, March 3, 1997.

155. "I'm comfortable": Ibid.

155–56. Information on crash and Mussina's reaction to same is per Ibid.

155. "It's not going to be easy": *USA Today*, July 19, 1996.

156. Mussina's contract information from *The Sporting News*, September 25, 2000 and February 26, 2001.

156. "everybody assumes": *The Sporting News*, February 26, 2001.

157. Mel Stottlemyre's thoughts on the warmup from the *New York Times*, September 3, 2001.

157. Mussina's repertoire is per James and Neyer, 320.

157. "You never got a good pitch": *New York Daily News*, September 3, 2001.

157. "I never said a word to him": Ibid.

158. Bernie Williams's thoughts from the *New York Times*, September 3, 2001.

159. "It actually flashed": *New York Daily News*, September 3, 2001.

159. "Part of me": *New York Times*, September 3, 2001.

160. "I thought, 'Maybe'": Ibid.

161. "I thought it was a hit": Frommer and Frommer, 202.

161. "I've never been part": Ibid., 203.

161. "It was supposed to happen": *New York Times*, September 3, 2001.

161. Mussina being informed of 9/11 by his wife is from Heist, www.pressboxonline
.com/story/751/orioles-and-yankees-remember-9-11(9/12/06).

161. "It was like I was watching": Feisand, http://m.mlb.com/news/article/1651279
(9/8/06).

161. "I just stayed at the house": Ibid.

162. "Getting back on the field": Ibid.

162. "Baseball was the furthest": Ibid.

163."I tell him": *New York Times*, October 4, 2004.

164. "I don't think": Ibid.

164. There is, if you can believe such a thing, YouTube footage of Mussina and his sons.

CHAPTER 13: PERFECTLY IMPERFECT

169. Account of Armbrister bunt in 1975 Series from Frost, 173–76.

169. The Denkinger call and "Jesse James" nickname are from Nash and Zullo (*Baseball Hall*), 88.

169–70. Other missed calls and information on same from *USA Today*, August 15, 2013.

170. The story of baseball's first instant replay use by Frank Pulli is per Pulli's obituary, *New York Times*, August 29, 2013.

170. Story of baseball's first instant replay official reversal is from *Seattle Times*, September 20, 2008.

171. "Anyplace you go": Author's interview, November 15, 2015.

171. Pitchers Galarraga followed per Ibid.

171. Galarraga's school arrangement and "It was a tiring routine": Galarraga and Joyce with Paisner, 31–32.

171. Signing story and "No, Dad, I think they're going to pay": Author's interview, November 15, 2015.

171. Galarraga's arm troubles and surgery, Galarraga and Joyce with Paisner, 99–102.

172. Galarraga's 2009 struggles: Galarraga and Joyce with Paisner, 71–73.

173. "In the bullpen": Author's interview, November 15, 2015.

173. "I was a pitcher who didn't throw that hard": Ibid.

174. "I am feeling very strong": Galarraga and Joyce with Paisner, 133.

174. "The first [few] innings": Author's interview, November 15, 2015.

174. "It is very lucky": Galarraga and Joyce with Paisner, 138.

175. "To get twenty-seven outs in a row": Ibid., 141.

175. "The fans . . . start to go crazy": Ibid., 141–42.

175. "I am relaxed": Ibid., 142.

175–76. "Now I leave the field": Ibid., 143.

176. "I thought it was a home run": Author's interview, November 15, 2015.

176. "As soon as Austin Jackson": Ibid., 148.

177. "It was not an easy groundball": Author's interview, November 15, 2015.

177. "Man, you were running fast on that play": Ibid.

177. "At that time, when I catch the ball": Ibid.

177. ESPN poll information is from "Jim Joyce Named Best Umpire, CB Bucknor Worst in ESPN The Magazine 'Baseball Confidential' Players Poll", http://espnmediazone.com/us/press-releases/2010/06/jim-joyce-named-best-umpire-cb-bucknor-worst-in-espn-the-magazine-%E2%80%9Cbaseball-confidential%E2%80%9D-players-poll (6/13/10).

177. "My eyes tell me": Galarraga and Joyce with Paisner, 210.

178. Galarraga's memory of Cabrera yelling is per author's interview, November 15, 2015.

178. "[T]hen everything kicks up": Ibid., 213.

178. "This is a history call": From audio of Joyce's press conference, available from multiple sources on YouTube.

178. "He probably feels": *USA Today*, June 3, 2010.

178. "I was in shock": Author's interview, November 15, 2015.

178. "It's a crying shame": Ibid.

178. "It happened to the best umpire": *Sports Illustrated*, June 14, 2010.

179. Account of Joyce's long night per Ibid.

179. The story of Nick Hamel is from Galarraga and Joyce with Paisner, 238–39, and *Sports Illustrated*, June 14, 2010.

179. Videos of the Joyce/Galarraga meeting from June 3, 2010, circulate widely on the Internet.

179. Galarraga's memories of chocolates and flowers at his house per author's interview, November 15, 2015.

179–80. "I am happy with this decision": Galarraga and Joyce with Paisner, 232.

180. Joyce's thoughts on overturning the call per Ibid., 234.

180. "If I was [Commissioner] Selig": "Selig Won't Reverse Call," http://sports.espn.go.com/espn/print?id=5248118&type=story (6/3/10).

180. Pappas's thoughts per Ibid.

180. Galarraga's recollection of the call from MLBPA from author's interview, November 15, 2015.

181. Replay expansion and Scherzer's comment per *New York Daily News*, January 17, 2014.

181. Midseason 2014 replay information from *USA Today*, July 20, 2014.

182. "I want people to know me": Author's interview, November 15, 2015.

182. Account of Joyce saving Jayne Powers and quote from *New York Daily News*, August 22, 2012.

CHAPTER 14: NEAR PERFECTION FROM THE LAND OF THE RISING SUN

185. The story of Japanese soldiers yelling "TO HELL WITH BABE RUTH!" is infamous, but it is actually documented at Whiting, 46.

185–86. Roots of Japanese baseball discussed at Whiting, 27–40, and Rains, 11–13.

186. Information on Tobita and "until they were half dead": Whiting, 38.

186. Tobita's motto: Ibid.

186. Information on Sawamura and his game from Whiting, 42–43, and Rains, 14 (although Rains erroneously credits Ruth with the winning home run).

186. "My problem is": Rains, 14.

186. Change in baseball terminology per Whiting, 46 and Rains, 15.

186–87. Information on Murakami from Rains, 21–24.

187. Information on other Japanese stars from Rains, 24–25.

187. Nomo "retirement" story from *Chicago Tribune*, June 18, 1995.

188. Information on Darvish's parents from Passan, "Iconic Ace Darvish Pushes Japan's Boundaries," http://sports.yahoo.com/news/iconic-ace-darvish-pushes-japans -062000885--mlb.html (3/24/08).

188. "Japan prides itself": Ibid.

188–89. Information on Darvish's development in baseball from Ibid.

189. Darvish negotiation information from Durrett, "Rangers Introduce Yu Darvish," http://espn.go.com/espn/print?id=7485609&type=story (1/20/12).

189. "Baseball is universal": Ibid.

189. "I want to become": "Yu Darvish's Goal: World's Best Pitcher," http://espn.go .com/espn/print?id=7496355&type=story (1/24/12).

191–92. Description of game and broadcasters' comments from the Fox Sports telecast of the game, as preserved on YouTube at https://www.youtube.com/ watch?v=ZjRrUeXcl6g.

192. "a nice catch": *New York Daily News*, April 3, 2013.

193. Darvish's pitch count info, and Washington's comments per Fraley, "Rangers' Ron Washington Says He Was Ready to Yank Yu Darvish with No-Hitter Intact," http:// rangersblog.dallasnews.com/2013/04/rangers-ron-washington-says-he-was-ready-to -yank-yu-darvish-with-no-hitter-intact.html (4/3/13).

194. "I didn't want to be the last out": *Dallas Morning News*, April 3, 2013.

194. "That was impossible to catch": *New York Daily News*, April 3, 2013.

194. "I can now go back to the dugout": *New York Daily News*, April 3, 2013.

194. "I went that far": Ibid.

194. "I think my teammates were more disappointed": *Dallas Morning News*, April 3, 2013.

195. Darvish's injury history per "Yu Darvish to Miss 2015 Season," http://espn.go .com/espn/print?id=12475357&type=story (3/13/15).

195. "I didn't think this was going to happen": Ibid.

196. Rehab information from *Ft. Worth Star-Telegram*, November 9, 2015.

196. Museum information from *Japan Times*, November 12, 2013.

CHAPTER 15: DOWN TO A DREAM

199. Petit's status for 2011 and his residence in Oaxaca are from *San Francisco Chronicle*, October 18, 2014.

200. "I didn't have an answer for anybody": Author's interview, August 19, 2015.

200. "I had to make an adjustment": Ibid.

200. "It's hard.": Ibid.

200. "There are challenges": *2015 San Francisco Giants Media Guide*, 208.

200–201. Petit's childhood and background info from *2015 San Francisco Giants*, 208 and author's interview.

201. "When I was 16": Author's interview, August 19, 2015.

201. "My dad gave me a chance": Ibid.

201. Information on Mexican League and connection with Giants from *San Francisco Chronicle*, October 18, 2014.

202. "He never thought": Ibid.

203–8. Recounting of near perfect game based on review of video of CSN broadcast of game, https://www.youtube.com/watch?v=ZykFWOouSS4.

204. "I had good stuff": Author's interview, August 19, 2015.

204. "He is throwing darts" is from CSN broadcast of game.

206. "I realized what was going on": *New York Daily News*, September 7, 2013.

206. "It pumped me up": Author's interview, August 19, 2015.

208. "When I got to 3-2": Ibid.

208. "I didn't throw a bad pitch": Ibid.

208. "It felt like": *San Jose Mercury News*, September 7, 2013.

208. "Wow! That's too close!": Author's interview, August 19, 2015.

208. "He's kind of sent": *San Jose Mercury News*, September 7, 2013.

210. Petit's admission of becoming aware of the record from the media is from author's interview, August 19, 2015.

210. "It was hard!" Ibid.

210. "It's pretty cool": Ibid.

211. "That's my dream": Ibid.

211. Petit salary information from baseball-reference.com.

CHAPTER 16: THE ILLUSION OF CONTROL

214. Information on Scherzer's childhood from Sanchez, "Max Scherzer: A Brother's Passage," http://espn.go.com/mlb/story/_/id/9130536/detroit-tigers-max-scherzer-pitches (4/8/13).

214. "classic, All-American kids": Ibid.

215. Stories of Max and Alex and the statistical debates are per *Arizona Republic*, August 6, 2009.

215. "It took about a year": Ibid.

215. "I'm well aware": Ibid.

215–16. The relationship between Max and Alex from numerous sources, including Sanchez, "Max Scherzer: A Brother's Passage," http://espn.go.com/mlb/story/_/id/9130536/detroit-tigers-max-scherzer-pitches (4/8/13), which provided information regarding Alex's depression.

216. "If there's anything I've taught you": Sanchez, "Max Scherzer: A Brother's Passage," http://espn.go.com/mlb/story/_/id/9130536/detroit-tigers-max-scherzer-pitches (4/8/13).

216. Information on Alex's promotion and subsequent suicide per Ibid., among other sources.

216. Account of game against Pirates is per Ibid.

216. "It's a situation where": *Detroit Free Press*, June 26, 2012.

216. Scherzer's statement to press is per Beck, "Heavy-Hearted Scherzer Discusses Brother's Death," http://m.mlb.com/news/article/33973770 (6/26/12).

216. Scherzer keeping texts is from Sanchez, "Max Scherzer: A Brother's Passage," http://espn.go.com/mlb/story/_/id/9130536/detroit-tigers-max-scherzer-pitches (4/8/13).

216. Scherzer's letter to McGwire is per *USA Today*, July 15, 2013.

216–17. "A happy amnesia": Sanchez, "Max Scherzer: A Brother's Passage," http://espn.go.com/mlb/story/_/id/9130536/detroit-tigers-max-scherzer-pitches (4/8/13).

217. Scherzer's contract info from multiple sources, including "Nationals Land RHP Max Scherzer," http://espn.go.com/espn/print?id=12190547&type=story (1/20/15).

217–23. Game information is derived from viewing MASN broadcast of the game on YouTube, viewed at https://www.youtube.com/watch?v=6o94p7SYo8M.

219. "They were a very aggressive team": Taken from video of Scherzer postgame press conference at MASN Nationals, https://www.youtube.com/watch?v=DDUctVEp92w.

219. "I almost gave up a home run": Ibid.

219. "Once I got through the lineup": Ibid.

220–21. "It was pretty exhausting out there": Ibid.

221. "Once I got rest": Ibid.

221. "I'm not even watching": from the MASN broadcast, viewed at https://www.youtube.com/watch?v=6o94p7SYo8M.

221–22. "When it was off the bat": Taken from video of Scherzer postgame press conference at MASN Nationals, https://www.youtube.com/watch?v=DDUctVEp92w.

222. "I felt great": Ibid.

223. "He was really battling me": Ibid.

223. "I know the slider": Ibid.

223. "He tried to throw me a slider": *Boston Herald*, June 21, 2015.

223. "That's just the worst way": from the MASN broadcast, viewed at https://www.youtube.com/watch?v=6o94p7SYo8M.

223. "Did he make an effort": Ibid.

223. "It's a call they never make": Ibid.

223. Account of Drysdale's experience with 6.08(b)(2) from *Los Angeles Times*, June 30, 2005 (batter Dick Dietz's obituary).

223. "That's my job": *Boston Herald*, June 21, 2005.

223. "[R]eally, it wasn't my intention": *Washington Post*, June 22, 2005.

224. "You focus on what you can do" and other comments per video of Scherzer postgame press conference at MASN Nationals, https://www.youtube.com/watch?v=DDUctVEp92w.

224. "What else can you give us": from the MASN broadcast, viewed at https://www.youtube.com/watch?v=6o94p7SYo8M.

224. "My last two starts": per video of Scherzer postgame press conference at MASN Nationals, https://www.youtube.com/watch?v=DDUctVEp92w.

BIBLIOGRAPHY

Hall of Fame Library Archive Collection
- Tommy Bridges file
- Tommy Bridges photo file
- Yu Darvish file
- Armando Galarraga file
- Harvey Haddix file
- Harvey Haddix photo files
- Harvey Haddix oral history interview (7/3/1987, by Walter Langford)
- Brian Holman file
- Pedro Martinez file
- Mike Mussina file
- Mike Mussina photo file
- Milt Pappas file
- Yusmeiro Petit file
- Billy Pierce file
- Billy Pierce oral history interview (2/24/1992, by Thomas Liley)
- Ron Robinson file
- Max Scherzer file
- Ernie Shore file
- Dave Stieb file
- Milt Wilcox file
- George Wiltse file
- George Wiltse photo file

NEWSPAPERS AND MAGAZINES

The Arizona Republic
Augusta (GA) *Chronicle*
Baltimore Sun
Baseball Magazine
Baseball Weekly
Battle Creek (MI) *Enquirer*
Boston Globe
Boston Globe Magazine
Boston Herald
Brooklyn Daily Eagle
Chicago Daily Tribune
Chicago Sun-Times
Chicago Tribune
Cincinnati Enquirer
Dallas Morning News
Detroit Free Press
The Detroit News
The Eagle-Tribune (North Andover, MA)
Ft. Worth Star-Telegam
The Globe and Mail (Toronto)

Inside Sports

The Japan Times

Kansas City Star

Lexington (KY) *Herald-Leader*

Los Angeles Times

Mid York Weekly (Utica, NY)

Milwaukee Journal

New York American

New York Daily News

New York Evening Telegraph

New York Herald

New York Herald Tribune

New York Times

New York World Telegram & Sun

Pittsburgh Post-Gazette

Pittsburgh Press

San Francisco Chronicle

San Jose (CA) *Mercury News*

Seattle Times

Spokane Spokesman-Review

Sporting Life

The Sporting News

Sports Illustrated

The *State* (NC)

Sunday Eagle-Tribune (Lawrence, MA)

USA Today

Wall Street Journal

Washington Evening Star

The *Washington Post*

The *Wilson* (TN) *Post*

Winston-Salem (NC) *Journal*

BOOKS AND ARTICLES

2015 San Francisco Giants Media Guide.

Anderson, William Mark. *The Glory Years of the Detroit Tigers: 1920–1950.* Detroit: Wayne State University Press, 2012.

Auker, Elden. *Sleeper Cars and Flannel Uniforms: A Lifetime of Memories from Striking Out with the Babe to Teeing It Up with the President.* Chicago: Triumph Books, 2006.

Browning, Tom, and Dan Stupp. *Tales from the Cincinnati Reds' Dugout: A Collection of the Greatest Reds Stories Ever Told.* New York: Sports Publishing, 2012.

Bryson, Bill. *One Summer: America, 1927.* New York: Doubleday, 2013.

Cicotello, David. "Cy Rigler," *Deadball Stars of the National League.* Dulles, VA: Brassey's, Inc., 2004.

Creamer, Robert W. *Babe: The Legend Comes to Life.* New York: Simon and Schuster, 2005.

Deford, Frank. *The Old Ball Game.* New York: Atlantic Monthly Press, 2005.

Dickson, Paul. *The Dickson Baseball Dictionary.* New York, W.W. Norton & Company, 2009.

Enders, Eric. "George McQuillan," *Deadball Stars of the National League.* Dulles, VA: Brassey's, Inc., 2004.

Freedman, Lew. *Hard-Luck Harvey Haddix and the Greatest Game Ever Lost.* Jefferson, NC: McFarland & Company, 2009.

Frierson, Eddie. "Christy Mathewson," *Deadball Stars of the National League.* Dulles, VA: Brassey's, Inc., 2004.

Frommer, Harvey, and Frederic J. Frommer. *Red Sox v. Yankees: The Great Rivalry.* Champaign, IL: Sports Publishing, 2005.

Frost, Mark. *Game Six.* New York: Hyperion, 2009.

Galarraga, Armando, and Jim Joyce with Daniel Paisner. *Nobody's Perfect: Two Men, One Call, and a Game for Baseball History.* New York: Atlantic Monthly Press, 2011.

Gentile, Derek. *The Complete Chicago Cubs: The Total Encyclopedia of the Team.* New York: Black Dog & Leventhal Publishers, 2004.

James, Bill. *The New Bill James Historical Baseball Abstract.* New York: Free Press, 2001.

James, Bill, and Rob Neyer. *The Neyer/James Guide to Pitchers: An Historical Compendium of Pitching, Pitchers, and Pitches.* New York: Fireside, 2004.

Jensen, Don. "John McGraw," *Deadball Stars of the National League.* Dulles, VA: Brassey's, Inc., 2004.

Kates, Maxwell. "Milt Wilcox," *Detroit Tigers 1984: What a Start! What a Finish!* Phoenix, AZ: Society for American Baseball Research, 2012.

Keri, Jonah. *Up, Up, and Away: the Kid, the Hawk, Rock, Vladi, Pedro, le Grande Orange, Youppi!, the Crazy Business of Baseball, and the Ill-Fated but Unforgettable Montreal Expos.* Toronto: Random House Canada, 2014.

Lindberg, Richard C. *Total White Sox: The Definitive Encyclopedia of the Chicago White Sox.* Chicago: Triumph Books, 2011.

Luchuk, David. *Blue Jays 1, Expos 0: The Urban Rivalry That Killed Major League Baseball in Montreal.* Jefferson, NC: McFarland & Company, 2007.

Martinez, Pedro, and Michael Silverman. *Pedro.* Boston: Houghton Mifflin Harcourt, 2015.

Miller, Mark. "Harvey Haddix," *Sweet '60: The 1960 Pittsburgh Pirates.* Phoenix, AZ: Society for American Baseball Research, 2013.

Montville, Leigh. *The Big Bam: The Life and Times of Babe Ruth.* New York: Anchor Books, 2006.

Murphy, Kait. *Crazy '08: How a Cast of Cranks, Rogues, Boneheads, and Magnates Created the Greatest Year in Baseball History.* New York: Smithsonian Books, 2007.

Nash, Bruce, and Allan Zullo. *Baseball Confidential.* New York: Pocket Books, 1988.

———. *The Baseball Hall of Shame 3.* New York: Pocket Books, 1987.

Neyer, Rob. "Billy Pierce," *The Neyer/James Guide to Pitchers: An Historical Compendium of Pitching, Pitchers, and Pitches.* New York: Fireside, 2004.

———. *Rob Neyer's Big Book of Baseball Blunders: A Complete Guide to the Worst Decisions and Stupidest Moments in Baseball History.* New York: Fireside, 2006.

———. "Tommy Bridges," *Detroit the Unconquerable: The 1935 World Series Champion Tigers.* Phoenix, AZ: Society for American Baseball Research, 2014.

———. "Tommy Bridges," *The Neyer/James Guide to Pitchers: An Historical Compendium of Pitching, Pitchers, and Pitches.* New York: Fireside, 2004.

Pappas, Milt, with Wayne Mausser and Larry Names. *Out at Home: Triumph and Tragedy in the Life of a Major Leaguer.* Oshkosh, WI: LKP Group, 2000.

Pomrenke, Jacob, ed. *Scandal on the South Side: The 1919 Chicago White Sox.* Phoenix, AZ: Society for American Baseball Research, 2015.

Rains, Rob. *Baseball Samurais: Ichiro Suzuki and the Asian Invasion.* New York: St. Martin's, 2001.

Reston, James Jr. *Collision at Home Plate: The Lives of Pete Rose and Bart Giamatti*. New York: Harper Collins, 1991.

Ruth, Babe, and Bob Considine. *The Babe Ruth Story*. Wilkinsburg, PA: Scholastic Books, 1964.

Schecter, Gabriel. "George Wiltse," *Deadball Stars of the National League*. Dulles, VA: Brassey's, Inc., 2004.

Stieb, Dave, and Kevin Boland. *Tomorrow I'll Be Perfect*. Garden City, NY: Doubleday & Company, Inc., 1986.

Thorn, John, and John Holway. *The Pitcher*. New York: Prentice-Hall Trade, 1987.

Vanderberg, Bob. *Sox: From Lane and Fain to Zisk and Fisk*. Chicago: Independent Publisher's Group, 1984.

Whiting, Robert. *You Gotta Have Wa*. New York: McMillan, 1989.

Wood, Allan. "George Herman Ruth," *Deadball Stars of the American League*. Dulles, VA: Potomac Books, 2006.

INTERNET

Various articles from www.baseball-reference.com and various video clips from YouTube were utilized to confirm information. I have tried to cite links to the videos in the Sources section and below in instances where they are "official."

Beck, Jason. "Heavy-Hearted Scherzer Discusses Brother's Death." http://m.mlb.com/news/article/33973770 (6/26/12).

Bigham, Jim. "July 27, 1958: Billy Pierce's Near-Perfect Game." *Society for American Baseball Research Games Project*. http://sabr.org/gamesproj/game/june-27-1958-billy-pierces-near-perfect-game.

Durrett, Richard. "Rangers Introduce Yu Darvish." http://espn.go.com/espn/print?id=7485609&type=story (1/20/12).

Feisand, Mark. "Yanks Learned Their Importance on 9/11." http://m.mlb.com/news/article/1651279 (9/8/06).

Fraley, Gerry. "Rangers' Ron Washington Says He Was Ready to Yank Yu Darvish with No-Hitter Intact." http://rangersblog.dallasnews.com/2013/04/rangers-ron-washington-says-he-was-ready-to-yank-yu-darvish-with-no-hitter-intact.html (4/3/13).

Francis, Bill. "Billy Pierce Debuts on Hall of Fame Golden Era Committee Ballot." http://baseballhall.org/hall-of-fame/golden-era/pierce-billy.

Gammons, Peter. "Pedro a Portrait of Wisdom, Emotion, Goodwill." http://m.mlb.com/news/article/17115606 (3/25/11).

Heist, Craig. "Orioles and Yankees Remember 9/11." www.pressboxonline.com/story/751/orioles-and-yankees-remember-9-11 (9/12/06).

Horn, John. "Milt Wilcox: From World Champion to Royal Oak Icon." http://patch.com/michigan/royaloak/from-world-champion-to-royal-oak-icon (9/15/11).

"Jim Joyce Named Best Umpire, CB Bucknor Worst in ESPN The Magazine 'Baseball Confidential' Players Poll." http://espnmediazone.com/us/press-releases/2010/06/jim-joyce-named-best-umpire-cb-bucknor-worst-in-espn-the-magazine-%E2%80%9Cbaseball-confidential%E2%80%9D-players-poll (6/13/10).

Leeke, Jim. "Ernie Shore." *Society for American Baseball Research Bioproject.* http://sabr.org/bioproj/person/6073c617.

Liptak, Mark. "Billy Pierce Interview" (July 2005). www.baseball-almanac.com/players/billy_pierce_interview.shtml.

MASN Nationals. "Max Scherzer Meets with the Media after Throwing a No-Hitter." Filmed June 20, 2015. YouTube video. Posted June 20, 2015 at https://www.youtube.com/watch?v=DDUctVEp92w.

"Nationals Land RHP Max Scherzer." http://espn.go.com/espn/print?id=12190547&type=story (1/20/15).

Passan, Jeff. "Iconic Ace Darvish Pushes Japan's Boundaries." http://sports.yahoo.com/news/iconic-ace-darvish-pushes-japans-062000885--mlb.html (3/24/08).

Prewitt, Alex. "Ex Detroit Tiger Milt Wilcox Has Gone to the Dogs." http://espn.go.com/espn/page2/index?id=5714622 (10/22/10).

Sanchez, Robert. "Max Scherzer: A Brother's Passage." http://espn.go.com/mlb/story/_/id/9130536/detroit-tigers-max-scherzer-pitches (4/8/13).

"Selig Won't Reverse Call." http://sports.espn.go.com/espn/print?id=5248118&type=story (6/3/10).

Weinbaum, William. "Froemming Draws Pappas' Ire, 35 Years Later." http://sports.espn.go.com/mlb/news/story?id=3019597 (9/20/07).

"Yu Darvish's Goal: World's Best Pitcher." http://espn.go.com/espn/print?id=7496355&type=story (1/24/12).

"Yu Darvish to Miss 2015 Season." http://espn.go.com/espn/print?id=12475357&type=story (3/13/15).

INTERVIEWS

Armando Galarraga, November 15, 2015
Brian Holman, June 16, 2015
Milt Pappas, July 31, 2015
Yusmeiro Petit, August 19, 2015
Ron Robinson, August 1, 2015
Dave Stieb, January 23, 2016

INDEX

ABOUT THE AUTHOR

Joe Cox is a member of the Society for American Baseball Research (SABR) and is the coauthor of multiple sports books, including *Fightin' Words: Kentucky vs. Louisville* and *Voice of the Wildcats: Claude Sullivan and the Rise of Modern Sportscasting.* He lives with his wife and children near Bowling Green, Kentucky.